Praise for *The Leadership Lab*

'*The Leadership Lab* rightly shines a white-hot spotlight on the need for 21st-century leaders to be thinking about gender and provides a valuable snapshot on how to get started.'
JULIA GILLARD, 27TH PRIME MINISTER OF AUSTRALIA, CHAIR OF THE GLOBAL INSTITUTE FOR WOMEN'S LEADERSHIP, KING'S COLLEGE LONDON

'It's time to recognize that the orthodoxy of leadership has done terrible damage to the fabric of society. This book lays out clearly what we can do to change the way leadership operates to the benefit of all of us.' LORD MAWSON, OBE, SOCIAL ENTREPRENEUR

'Wise words on leadership to steer you through perilous waters.'
SIR ANTHONY SELDON, MA, PHD, FRSA, MBA, FRHISS, VICE-CHANCELLOR OF THE UNIVERSITY OF BUCKINGHAM, CONTEMPORARY HISTORIAN, EDUCATIONALIST, COMMENTATOR AND POLITICAL AUTHOR

'The forward thinking in *The Leadership Lab* forces us to revisit how we frame our judgements and how we put teams together. This new thinking is so important when the pace of change is so high. Adopting empathetic leadership and diverse thinking will create *the* critical competitive advantage.' JACQUELINE DE ROJAS, CBE, PRESIDENT OF TECHUK, CHAIR OF DIGITAL LEADERS, NON-EXECUTIVE DIRECTOR AND ADVISER

'*The Leadership Lab* comes at an important moment when we're moving from traditional management approaches to an enabling leadership philosophy. The authors identify the new expectations required of leaders "to do the right things and not just to do things right". This message is critical at a time when uncertainty is the new norm.' CHARLOTTE LINDSEY-CURTET, DIRECTOR OF DIGITAL TRANSFORMATION, INTERNATIONAL COMMITTEE OF THE RED CROSS

'*The Leadership Lab* is *The Art of War* and *The Prince* for the 21st century.' GREG WILLIAMSON, HEAD OF STRATEGY, PLURIBUS LABS

'I've made *The Leadership Lab* required reading for my entire team. Chris Lewis and Pippa Malmgren have done a masterful job summarizing global trends and the tools every 21st-century leader requires to not only succeed but to thrive. Anyone interested in making sense of the forces that shape our ever-more complex world needs to read this book!' KENNETH TODOROV, BRIGADIER GENERAL, USAAF (RET) AND VICE PRESIDENT, NORTHROP GRUMMAN MISSION SYSTEMS

'This book will make you think afresh about leadership. Chris Lewis and Pippa Malmgren challenge the narrative and perspective on leadership, from a hierarchical, experience-led, "show of authority", to a flatter, experience-shared, "show of responsibility". What a ride! Read on.' SIR GEORGE ZAMBELLAS, FORMER FIRST SEA LORD AND TECHNOLOGY ADVOCATE

'In this robustly researched and powerfully articulated book, Chris Lewis and Pippa Malmgren explore the contemporary geopolitical and economic challenges facing today's leaders. They cut through the prevailing confusion to provide an invaluable world-view and perspectives on new social, cultural, technological, behavioural, political and economic realities.' AMIR HUSSAIN, COE (CHIEF OF EVERYTHING), YEME ARCHITECTS

'*The Leadership Lab* provides leaders with great insight and will help them make the right decisions. With this breadth of vision, readers can follow the Nelson Mandela leadership mantra: "Lead from the back – and let others believe they are in front." A must-read for all who lead or aspire to lead.' EDMUND V KING, OBE, AA PRESIDENT, VISITING PROFESSOR OF TRANSPORT, NEWCASTLE UNIVERSITY

'In a world that seems to be changing faster than ever before, one constant remains – the need for inspirational and effective leaders. With disruptive forces showing no sign of slowing, this is a vital contribution at a timely moment.' ANDY SILVESTER, *THE SUN*

'This is a unique book, summarizing today's realities and the trends that will dictate the future. It is the voice of today's leaders, obtained by the authors visiting numerous cities around the globe, holding open-ended sessions with key individuals from a variety of walks of life. I highly recommend it.' ROBERT J HERBOLD, CHIEF OPERATING OFFICER (RET), MICROSOFT CORPORATION

'Interesting, insightful, innovative. A must-read if you choose to lead.' LORD HOLMES OF RICHMOND, PARALYMPIAN

'Like other all-pervading technologies, the internet has brought both wonders and terrors. To cope in this world, leaders will need new ways of thinking, and this book promises them just that.' MATT RIDLEY, *THE TIMES*

'How do you lead in a world of constant confusing change? Not in the same way you did 20 years ago. That's a lesson too many leaders have failed to learn – and why *The Leadership Lab* has to be a must-read for all of them.' MERRYN SOMERSET WEBB, EDITOR-IN-CHIEF, *MONEYWEEK*

'The book that proves the reign of the "hero CEO" is over. Chris Lewis and Pippa Malmgren make a compelling case for the philosophy that many of us have already bought into – successful modern leadership is about how you interact with the people around you and the information at your fingertips.' MELANIE RICHARDS, VICE CHAIR, KPMG

'*The Leadership Lab* is essential reading for aspiring civilian and military leaders alike.' KARIN VON HIPPEL, DIRECTOR-GENERAL, ROYAL UNITED SERVICES INSTITUTE

'Reading *The Leadership Lab* is an eye-opening experience. It gives much-needed context to a world with changing cultures and a new expectation of leaders. The writing affirms the advantages of diversity whether it be in geography, culture or gender. I recommend it to all leaders who are open to new ideas.' TOM HOENIG, FORMER PRESIDENT OF THE FEDERAL RESERVE BANK OF KANSAS CITY AND VICE CHAIRMAN OF THE FEDERAL DEPOSIT INSURANCE CORPORATION

'Society is changing at an exponential rate. To thrive, our thinking also has to change at an exponential rate. *The Leadership Lab* provides a much-needed road map for that change.' HAP KLOPP, FOUNDER OF THE NORTH FACE AND PROFESSOR OF ENTREPRENEURSHIP AND INNOVATION AT HULT UNIVERSITY

'I'm proud to say that many of the ideas in *The Leadership Lab* were developed in San Diego. This is no accident: our city is home to world-class global companies and leadership thinking, where inspiration springs from inclusivity and innovation.' REP SCOTT H PETERS, MEMBER, US HOUSE OF REPRESENTATIVES

'Everywhere you look, someone has a tale of uncertainty to tell, but how many of us are really preparing for the future? *The Leadership Lab* prepares us to turn uncertainty into transformative opportunity.' TOM SAVIGAR, SENIOR PARTNER, THE FUTURE LABORATORY

'The insights, observations and recommendations in *The Leadership Lab* are incredibly relevant to the myriad of challenges facing leaders today. This must-read book turns the traditional model of leadership on its head and proposes a more inclusive one that takes into account the increasingly fast-paced and interconnected world in which we operate.' BRENDA TRENOWDEN, CBE, GLOBAL CHAIR OF THE 30% CLUB AND HEAD OF FINANCIAL INSTITUTIONS, EUROPE, AT ANZ

'*The Leadership Lab* is a must-read for anyone in a leadership role in either the private or public sector. Global political leadership is embarrassingly poor or non-existent, whilst corporate leaders seem more concerned about their careers than the sustainability of their business. This book is a call to arms about real leadership.'
PROFESSOR SIR CARY COOPER, ALLIANCE MANCHESTER BUSINESS SCHOOL

'Leaders are struggling to adapt to change and it is clear that the education system is also struggling with the demands of the new world. Experienced leaders are realizing that what worked in the past is no longer viable in the multigenerational, agile and non-hierarchical organizations of tomorrow. This book provides essential guidance on how best to operate in the disruptive Now Economy.' MARK BORKOWSKI, FOUNDER, BORKOWSKI PR

'Globalized capital benefits everyone most when it is driven by enlightened, forward-thinking, innovative visionaries. As Chris Lewis and Pippa Malmgren point out, the pace of change has a dark side and this is a warning to follow the light.'
BILL THORNHILL, GLOBALCAPITAL

'The ideas in this book show how global leadership is responding to change. It comes not only from decades of experience but from those who have the appetite, the ambition and the attitude to see the future as an opportunity.' GREG CLARK MP, SECRETARY OF STATE FOR BUSINESS, ENERGY AND INDUSTRIAL STRATEGY

'A concisely written, meticulously researched and intellectually challenging treatise. Importantly, it will challenge our young leaders to ask: "What kind of a person do I need to be – or become – if I am to take up any leadership role and be really effective in this new world?"' PETER GUMMER, BARON CHADLINGTON, ENTREPRENEUR

'*The Leadership Lab* points out the truth of the gender debate – that inequality works to the detriment of both genders. It is the authentic sound of the trumpets of Jericho, but this time from within the citadel.' BARONESS ANNE JENKIN

'There is a crisis in leadership across all sectors of society, from government, business, healthcare and academia. Those who attempt to lead often lack the skills and those who should lead don't know how. *The Leadership Lab* provides all of us with the tools to understand the nature of good leadership, the knowledge to reject those who lead poorly and the confidence to embark upon a leadership role.' PROFESSOR RUSSELL FOSTER, CBE, FRSB, FMEDSCI, FRS, NEUROSCIENTIST, UNIVERSITY OF OXFORD

'*The Leadership Lab* is for leaders who are ready to embrace the bold transformation needed to lead in a time of exponential change. It points us in a clear direction – leverage what it means to be human and lead with dignity.' GARY KRAHN, BRIGADIER GENERAL, US (RET) AND HEAD OF LA JOLLA COUNTRY DAY SCHOOL

'This book should be gifted to politicians the day after they are elected and used as a career bible for all those who aspire to lead. Now, more than ever, they need to be armed with skills which embrace a new way of thinking focused on how we lead in an era where there is an extensive lack of faith in what has gone before.' KATIE PERRIOR, FORMER DIRECTOR OF COMMUNICATIONS AT NO 10 DOWNING ST, *TIMES* WRITER, BROADCASTER AND CHAIR OF INHOUSE COMMUNICATIONS

'*The Leadership Lab* is an excellent and thought-provoking analysis of today's leaders and a unique look at the skills of tomorrow. It shows the factors influencing executives and how they make their decisions and their mistakes. It is indispensable reading for all current and aspiring leaders.' MARC-OLIVER VOIGT, *COMMUNICATION DIRECTOR* MAGAZINE AND FOUNDING CHAIRMAN OF THE EUROPEAN EXCELLENCE AWARDS

'All leaders and the next generation should have a good read of this thought-provoking book. It is written as Chris speaks, a million ideas a minute, so perfect aeroplane and toilet reading. Take time out in order to do something positive for the society and environment that we live in.'
PETER DE HAAN, SOCIAL ENTREPRENEUR

'A fascinating and thought-provoking read – once again, Chris Lewis and Pippa Malmgren have perfectly gauged the political and corporate temperature of our times.'
ALISON CORK, ENTREPRENEUR AND BROADCASTER

'Fascinating and insightful, this book analyses the key elements of future leadership in a rapidly changing world.'
DR JULIE MAXTON, CBE, THE ROYAL SOCIETY

'*The Leadership Lab* represents a tour de force in the topic of change and the challenges facing the modern leader. Justifiably critical of the status quo, it challenges us to think in the modern multiplicity of change to improve leadership competencies for a 21st century. Full of tips, it doesn't pull punches, yet is optimistic and inspiring, and should be mandatory reading for the aspiring leader. Read it. Our world needs you to.' PETER PEREIRA GRAY, THE WELLCOME TRUST

'*The Leadership Lab* is ambitious in scope and utterly original in its approach to the leadership task in the 21st century. It recognizes and embraces the challenges of complexity. Rather than simplify by omission – our traditional reductionist and largely quantitative approach – Chris Lewis and Pippa Malmgren identify the origins of this complexity and suggest how, as leaders, we can begin to make sense of it and act. Nicely combining abstract concepts with deep experience, this is a well-argued and essential read!' PROFESSOR DAVID BROWN, LANCASTER UNIVERSITY MANAGEMENT SCHOOL

'Chris Lewis and Pippa Malmgren lay out a compelling case for the richer outcomes derived from a more holistic style of leadership. In *The Leadership Lab*, we find the left brain and right brain need not be mutually exclusive. Successful leaders integrate their creative and analytical assets to lead diverse groups to achieve higher levels of organizational success.'
LANCE NAIL, DEAN, SAN DIEGO STATE UNIVERSITY

The Leadership Lab

*Understanding Leadership
in the 21st Century*

Chris Lewis and Pippa Malmgren

Kogan Page
INSPIRE

First published in Great Britain and the United States in 2019 by Kogan Page Limited

2nd Floor, 45 Gee Street
London EC1V 3RS
United Kingdom
www.koganpage.com

c/o Martin P Hill Consulting
122 W 27th St, 10th Floor
New York, NY 10001
USA

4737/23 Ansari Road
Daryaganj
New Delhi 110002
India

ISBN   978 0 7494 8343 2
E-ISBN   978 0 7494 8344 9

British Library Cataloguing-in-Publication Data

A CIP record for this book is available from the British Library.

Library of Congress Cataloging-in-Publication Data

Names: Lewis, Chris, 1961- author. | Malmgren, Philippa, author.
Title: The leadership lab : understanding leadership in the 21st century / Chris Lewis and Pippa Malmgren.
Description: London ; New York : Kogan Page, 2019. | Includes index.
Identifiers: LCCN 2018023838 (print) | LCCN 2018025651 (ebook) | ISBN 9780749483449 (ebook) | ISBN 9780749483432 (pbk.)
Subjects: LCSH: Leadership.
Classification: LCC HD57.7 (ebook) | LCC HD57.7 .L4758 2019 (print) | DDC 658.4/092–dc23
LC record available at https://lccn.loc.gov/2018023838

Typeset by Integra Software Services, Pondicherry
Print production managed by Jellyfish
Printed and bound by CPI Group (UK) Ltd, Croydon, CR0 4YY

'Only it is so *very* lonely here!' Alice said in a melancholy voice; and at the thought of her loneliness two large tears came rolling down her cheeks.

'Oh, don't go on like that!' cried the poor Queen, wringing her hands in despair. 'Consider what a great girl you are. Consider what a long way you've come to-day. Consider what o'clock it is. Consider anything, only don't cry!'

Alice could not help laughing at this, even in the midst of her tears. 'Can *you* keep from crying by considering things?' she asked.

'That's the way it's done,' the Queen said with great decision: 'nobody can do two things at once, you know. Let's consider your age to begin with – how old are you?'

'I'm seven and a half exactly.'

'You needn't say "exactly,"' the Queen remarked: 'I can believe it without that. Now I'll give *you* something to believe. I'm just one hundred and one, five months and a day.'

'I can't believe *that*!' said Alice.

'Can't you?' the Queen said in a pitying tone. 'Try again: draw a long breath, and shut your eyes.'

Alice laughed. 'There's no use trying,' she said: 'one *can't* believe impossible things.'

'I daresay you haven't had much practice,' said the Queen. 'When I was your age, I always did it for half-an-hour a day. Why, sometimes I've believed as many as six impossible things before breakfast.'

Lewis Carroll, *Through the Looking Glass*

Contents

About the Authors

The authors of this book advise the world's leaders. These include: heads of state, entrepreneurs, key investors, CEOs, senior politicians, humanitarian organizations, military leaders, household consumer brands, educationalists and scientists all over the world.

Chris Lewis is an entrepreneur and author of the bestselling book on ideas and creativity *Too Fast to Think*. He is a former journalist and founder of LEWIS, one of the largest creative agencies in the world. Founded in 1995, his practice now encompasses 25 offices and 500 staff. He is British but splits his time between the United Kingdom and the United States.

Dr Pippa Malmgren is an economist and an entrepreneur. A former White House presidential adviser, she now advises the British government and the world's largest financial and military organizations. She is the author of the bestselling economics book *Signals*. She correctly forecasted the financial crisis, the slowdown in China, Brexit and the rise of American nationalism. She is American but splits her time between the United States and the United Kingdom.

Foreword

This is an important book. It is highly engaging, clearly written and practical. The chapters you are about to read provide the foundation for re-evaluation of modern leadership. With each turn of the page, you'll explore the new skills required for today's leaders. This includes situational fluency – the most important skill of all for those who wish to narrate and navigate the evolving social, behavioural and economic realities.

The reason I'm so confident this book will be read by leaders is because they wrote it. The research was compiled through the LEWIS Advisory Boards which were held in various cities all over the world. The leaders came from governments, corporate boardrooms, military command HQs, international NGOs, newsrooms, charities, religious bodies, grassroots organizations, law firms, investment banks, art colleges and especially business schools around the world.

I had the pleasure of experiencing this at first hand. The discussion and engagement with leaders from such a broad spectrum of industries, disciplines and styles led to the richness of Lewis and Malmgren's model. This is embodied and summarized in the Kythera – the perfect model to explain the multiple paradoxes of the new world.

Leadership is the backbone of every society. History has taught us that courageous and thoughtful leadership can guide a society through its most difficult times. Ignorant and authoritarian leadership, however, leaves an indelible black mark on a country's legacy.

Superb leadership inspires, empowers and guides. It uses its influence constructively and positively, for the benefit of many. As we've seen on a global scale, however, some leaders have used their skills in previously unimagined ways that have caused terrible harm to their constituents. Therefore, thoughtful exploration of leadership is a critical part of the advancement of our societies.

My own leadership journey has included collaboration with Members of Congress, elected officials and corporate executives. I am motivated by a desire to create environments that eliminate antiquated thinking around male–female roles, corporate culture and the associated emphasis on the short-term, the tactical and the egotistical.

Modern developments and technology have enhanced the potential of leaders to advance their ideas and causes. If leaders want to thrive in a fast-changing world of evolving attitudes, diverse cultures and technology, they must adapt. In other words, the old corporate leadership style of structured and predictable outcomes will not survive in the technological world.

Pippa Malmgren and Chris Lewis truly get it. From the moment I met them, I knew their vision and approach would lead to a unique and precious understanding of leadership in the 21st century. Their years of extensive and painstaking research have culminated in this fascinating book.

Enjoy the Ride!

Cherylyn Harley LeBon
Lawyer, Strategist, Adviser
2018 LEWIS Advisory Board (LAB) Participant
harleylebon.com

Foreword

There are a number of things that I like about this book. First, it is the original thinking. The authors address complex issues and provide fresh perspectives. Second, they provide a genuinely global perspective. We cannot allow ourselves to be divided by nationalism and populism. Leaders seek unity and common purpose. This is vital for all those who would occupy high office. Most importantly, this book addresses the problem of equality from multiple perspectives and across genders. It is not difficult to convince women of the need for female equality. So we must go further. We need men to understand and make the argument, too. In this respect, Chris Lewis has been at the forefront of the argument for over a decade, both in politics and business. The point he makes with Pippa Malmgren is clear – equality is not just a matter of justice. It is a matter of efficiency. Although that is a good start, true equality will not be addressed just by gender representation alone. It would be a missed opportunity if in filling boardrooms with women, they all behave like men. We need more balanced thinking, irrespective of the gender. This means acting long-term, towards qualitative, strategic goals. It means generosity and inclusive thinking. This might look short-term inefficient, but as the authors point out, it is quite the opposite.

This then, is the reason we fight for equality. It is to allow not just women to reach their potential, but all of us. If we, each of us, cannot reach our potential, then what hope does humanity have?

The Rt Hon Penny Mordaunt MP
Minister for Women and Equalities
Secretary of State for International Development

Acknowledgements

Thanks to:

Sarah Aitchison, Sarah Aitchison and Sarah Aitchison, Kris Balderston, Sinclair Beecham, George Blacklock, Robin Boon, Myriam Boublil, Dr Nikolaus Braun, Dr Günther Burkhard, Michael A Cappello, Carolyn Cawley, Nikia Clarke, Géraldine Collard, Catherine Connolly, David Cook, (the brilliant) Sir Cary Cooper, Miles Daniels, Sir Kim Darroch, Carolyn Davis, Hans de Gier, Paul de Lara, Wiebe de Vries, Bas Dekker, Thomas Deutschmann, Umang Dokey, Stephan Dörrschuck, Amanda Downes, Emma Draude, Ad Eijkemans, Mike Ettling, Ken Ford, (the amazing) Professor Russell Foster, Derrick and Hillary Fox, Steve Frampton, James Freddo, Allison Fried, David Friedman, Frédéric Gillant, Steve Glickman, Julia Gorham, Sanjeev Gupta, Bob Herbold, Fred Hermans, Peter Heule, Jeremy Hillman, André Hoekzema, Thomas M Hoenig, Klaus Hommer, Dan Horowitz, Rob Jessel, Luke Johnson, Greta H Joynes, Madelon Kaspers, Ronald Knoop, Melissa Koskovich, Andreas Kraut, Vivek Kumar, Erik Lamers, Harold Langenberg, Cherylyn Harley LeBon, Sir Geoffrey Leigh (for the 'J' word), Jeanne Leong, Richard Levick, Georgia Lewis, Jo Lewis, Pip Lewis, Charlotte Lindsey-Curtet, Professor Bruce Lloyd, Hans Martens, Meredith McPhillips, Dr Rainer Mehl, Mike M Möhlheinrich, Audrey Mok, Martin Moran, The Rt Hon Penny Mordaunt MP, Ken Muché, Teymoor Nabili, David Nicholl, Frank Niemann, Penny O'Donnell, James Oehlcke, Pierre-Michel Passy, Peter Pereira Gray, Andrew Pickup, Venka Purushothaman, Kelly Redding, Andie Rees, Sir Ken Robinson, Emma Rogers, Martijn Roordink, Christine Schaefer, Daniel Scheijen, Dr Manfred Schlett, Helmut Schmid, Peter Shaw, Dr Kirpal Singh, Sir Martin Sorrell, John Stewart, Jürgen Sturm, Pieter Swinkels, May Lin Tan, Caleb

Tiller, Kenn Todorov, Kathy Townend, Sebastian Ulbert, Yvonne van Bokhoven, Jeroen van Glabbeek, Patrick Van de Wille, Pieter Van den Broecke, Femke van der Hoeven, Scott Wightman, Greg Williamson, Sarah Wincott, Chetan Yardi, Admiral Sir George Zambellas and Jeffrey Zubricki.

Prologue

The defining characteristics of the 21st century did not reveal themselves at midnight on 31 December 1999. Like any other year, the new year was welcomed with refreshed intent, expectation and hope.

Just under two years later at 08.45 am Eastern Standard Time on a clear blue morning in downtown New York, the 21st century finally arrived. The United States was suddenly and dramatically attacked by religious fundamentalists. The human cost was immediate: 2,996 people were killed with more than 6,000 injured. More were killed in the attack on the Twin Towers than at the attack on Pearl Harbour almost 60 years earlier.

It was played out live on TV with all its visual and graphic horrors. It shocked us because we saw in real-time not just an act of violence and hatred but an attack on a city and a country that so many admire. We just couldn't understand why anyone would want to do this. Besides, airline hijackings normally start with guns or bombs. This one was started with box-cutters. Like so many other events, we just researched the past and extrapolated our linear thinking. We didn't link laterally. We didn't use our imagination. We just didn't see it coming.

The immediate priority was the US economy, which was already reeling from the millennium boom and dotcom crash. After the Twin Towers attack, it threatened to collapse. The White House was already dealing with the Enron scandal and some of the largest bankruptcies in US history. The fear was that the US economy might be mortally wounded, so emergency measures were needed. Interest rates were slashed and Americans were told it was their patriotic duty to spend and keep the economy moving.

The attack catalysed the invasion of Iraq in pursuit of the 'War on terror'. It also accelerated and deepened the crash. In so doing, it inadvertently sowed the seeds for the next credit boom, which rolled on until 2008 when the economic bubble burst again. Shortly before it did, another great defining moment of the 21st century occurred.

At 10 o'clock on Tuesday 9 January 2007, a man walked into a spotlight on the stage of the Moscone Convention Center in downtown San Francisco. He wore his trademark black sweater and jeans and the audience greeted him like a hero. They'd been told to expect something big. Steve Jobs announced the iPhone as, 'An iPod, a phone, an internet mobile communicator. An iPod, a phone, an internet mobile communicator... these are *not* three separate devices!'[1] The information acceleration had begun.

Meanwhile, the damage being done to the global banking system was also under way. Mortgage companies and insurance firms, having been told it was their duty to encourage spending, started to notice some investments failing. The momentum gathered until the US government stepped in to save all the essential financial players, such as the banks and mortgage providers, to preserve some sort of economic infrastructure. Billions of dollars changed hands and there was a massive transfer of debt from the private to the public sector, as governments were forced to buy distressed financial assets that were just too big to fail. Even by 2017, many global economies had still not returned to pre-crash levels of wealth and many of the banks had still not been returned to the private sector. Some countries lost not one decade of economic growth, but two.

The question that continues to haunt us is simple – did the medicine make it better or make it worse? Governments almost everywhere flooded the world economy with record amounts of cash ('quantitative easing' as it is awkwardly known), throwing money at the problem. They slashed interest rates to the lowest levels ever. Those who owned stocks, bonds, homes and property all watched the value of their assets rise dramatically as the money supply expanded. The Dow Jones Industrial Average, property prices, the prices paid for art and other hard assets all ran away to all-time record highs. Meanwhile, those who did not own assets watched their dreams of home ownership disappear. They felt the pain of inflation that their political leaders had told them didn't exist.

The measures designed to boost confidence inadvertently undermined it as savers were punished with all-time low and even negative interest rates. This created both income inequality and inherent uncertainty about the true condition of the economy. As ever, those at the bottom of the economic ladder – the blue collars – thought it was terrible. Those at the top were 'intensely relaxed about people getting filthy rich', as Lord Mandelson, an architect of Britain's New Labour, put it.[2]

The greatest stimulus programme ever resulted in the most nervous recovery in history. Naturally, so much economic hardship and uncertainty has led the public everywhere to question their leaders. As pointed out in Pippa Malmgren's book *Signals*,[3] the ever-increasing debt burden bears down on society and stresses the social fabric. Its weight breaks the promises that hold societies together and begs the simple question: 'Why are you in charge?' We mixed together record debt, short-termism, deep uncertainty and income inequality. In this way, the conditions for an anti-establishment movement were brewed.

The first sign of this came on Thursday 23 June 2016,[4] when against all opinion polls, Britain voted to leave the European Union. In the United Kingdom and Europe, the result was disbelief. The media hadn't seen it coming. Nor had the pollsters or the rest of the British establishment; 2016 would turn out to be an eventful year.

In the evening of Tuesday 8 November 2016, another defining event occurred. Republican supporters were packed into the Ballroom of New York's Hilton Midtown. Punctuated by occasional shouts of triumph, it became clear that the voters' contempt for the orthodoxy was about to surprise the pollsters again. At 10.20 pm EST a double shock was delivered to the United States. The first report was Ohio, a swing state, which finally swung for Trump. The state had always voted with the eventual president since Lyndon B Johnson in 1964. The cheering grew to a sustained roar shortly before 11.00 pm when the Associated Press called Florida for Trump. The United States had put a businessman and reality TV show host into the White House for the first time since its foundation. He had never held any sort of political office. He had no experience in politics. His campaign had caused controversy. A great American revolt had begun.

As if any further indication of unpredictability were required, six months later British Prime Minister Theresa May opted to call a General Election on Thursday 8 June 2017. The polls had predicted a landslide for her party.[5] The result – a hung parliament – left everyone shocked. They just didn't see it coming. Eleven days later, Emmanuel Macron was elected President of France. He'd started his own political party only 18 months earlier. France turned its back on all previous politicians and political parties.

Was an overconfident leadership responsible for this? Or was it economic policy? There's no doubt that the encouragement and later chastisement of 'animal spirits' in capital markets led to quantitative rather than qualitative criteria. When the cost of money is reduced to zero and it can be had with less consideration and care, risk-taking bordering on recklessness is the result.

The animal spirits fed overconfident 'Alphazilla' male role models and 'greed is good' cultures. These are muscular and not always aesthetic or even ethical. They are not geared to liberate potential in the many. They foster a model based on taking rather than giving. This ultimately slows things, destroys value and alienates people. Those who stand in the way are called resistant to change, but it's not change that people resist, it's change they can't control or be included in.

Why did this style become so encouraged? The popular media played a role. TV shows like *The Apprentice* emphasize the top-down patriarchal, short-term judgemental nature of leadership. We also have *Shark Tank* in the United States and *Dragon's Den* in the United Kingdom where privileged wealthy people sit in judgement of hopeful entrepreneurs. Both shows are built on this hierarchical nature where the people at the top are encouraged to be rude, condescending and outright cruel. This is not leadership. It's a perversion of it manufactured by the times we live in. Leaders are water carriers, not water boarders. They're there to quench thirst and put out fires. It might make great TV, but it's a bad image of leadership.

This could be one reason why American entrepreneurship is in decline and has been so for 40 years. *Inc Magazine*[6] certainly thinks so, saying that 'Fear of Failure' is holding people back. In fact, the fastest-growing group of entrepreneurs in the United States is black females[7] (incidentally it is also the group that finds access to capital hardest[8]).

Why this intense focus on short-term success? New York Stock Exchange companies need to report to shareholders every 90 days. Why would they want to do that? Fear, greed and lack of trust are the usual suspects – fear that you can't trust the leaders of the company, greed in that you want maximum returns and a lack of trust driven by multiple leadership failures. It's a vicious circle. This ever more reductive short-term view of the world represents a dangerous narrowing of the field of vision.

It's why leadership thinking needs to evolve and be balanced between long- and short-term, between quantitative and qualitative, between forward- and backward-looking, between male and female, between artistic and scientific.

Successful leadership needs a diverse and inclusive view because it's now much more visible. It cannot now be solely about narrow interests. A wider parenthesis of what constitutes successful leadership needs to be considered.

Success and failure are both imposters as far as balance is concerned. Success has been termed as the ability to go from failure to failure without losing enthusiasm. Leadership thinker Arie de Geus pointed this out in *The Living Company*: 'The only enduring market advantage of any organisation is its ability to learn.'[9] This is another perfectly legitimate purpose of an organization. Learning organizations do tend to maximize profits in the long term.

This is why thinking needs to be more inclusive. Currently, qualitative and quantitative are like oil and water. Left without dynamic leadership, they separate. The truly efficient leadership team is an emulsion of thinking. This is not about tokenism. It's because leaders need to harness all the potential available to them.

We can't see these recent changes in leadership in isolation. Technology, in particular, has transformed the landscape. The advent of the iPhone in 2007 was putting more computing power in our pockets than was needed to send a man to the moon in 1969. This underpinned the explosion of internet services that changed the way we communicate, entertain, work and understand the world. It dramatically transformed information cultures. We now speak of the 4th Industrial Revolution, which is bringing an unprecedented wave of innovation and invention. Yet the same technology is also being used to promote and further the rise of extremism, nationalism and terrorism. To these horrors we have added technical, geopolitical, economic and philosophical changes to create the greatest leadership challenge ever.

These events are not the cause of great behavioural and cultural change. They are the effect of it. If we didn't already realize it, our behaviour, economics, politics and the technology just ahead are fuelling *both* the solutions and the problems.

There will be no return to normal. We cannot go back to an era before 9/11, to some haven with no political shocks. Even if there were such a place, easy conditions never made for better leaders. On the contrary, we should reach out in anticipation of the changes ahead of us. By doing so, we are fundamentally em-powered and energized. We may have no choice but to embrace the future, but we have every choice over how we deal with the unparalleled opportunities and threats of the 21st century.

Endnotes

1   https://www.engadget.com/2007/01/09/live-from-macworld-2007-steve-jobs-keynote

2   http://www.telegraph.co.uk/news/politics/labour/8963450/Lord-Mandelson-secrets-of-a-filthy-rich-fortune.html

3   Malmgren, P (2015) *Signals: The breakdown of the social contract and the rise of geopolitics*, Grosvenor House Publishing, Surbiton

4   http://www.telegraph.co.uk/news/2016/06/24/eu-referendum-how-right-or-wrong-were-the-polls

5   https://www.newstatesman.com/politics/june2017/2017/05/should-we-trust-general-election-2017-polls

6   https://www.inc.com/steve-blakeman/us-entrepreneurship-is-at-a-40-year-low-heres-why-now-is-perfect-time-to-launch-your-start-up.html

7   http://fortune.com/2015/06/29/black-women-entrepreneurs

8   https://www.inc.com/kimberly-weisul/why-its-so-hard-for-black-women-entrepreneurs-to-get-funded.html

9   de Geus, A (2002) *The Living Company: Habits for survival in a turbulent business environment*, Harvard Business School Press, Boston, MA

Introduction

The LEWIS Advisory Board (or LAB) has consulted with many global leaders from all walks of life since its foundation. This book aggregates and paraphrases their feedback on how the world is changing and how leadership, in all its forms, is evolving.

In the past 25 years, the world's leadership culture has shifted on its axis. It used to be an overwhelmingly male, heterosexual, patient, predictable, factual, planned, white, long-term, Western-orientated, technology-leveraged, deflationary, structured, left-brained rational, broadcast, top-down, militarily symmetric world.

Now, leadership is operating in an inverted, unreal, amoral, impatient, inflationary, selfish, spiritual, irrational, gender-fluid, polysexual, asymmetric, strategically multipolar, everywhere-facing, bottom-up, information-soaked, multi-racial, androgynous, fluid, opinionated, rapidly moving, asymmetric world.

The rapid change has exposed real leadership failure. Since the turn of the century, we have learnt that around the world, our corporate leaders have illegally avoided taxes,[1] lied about emissions in the car industry,[2] rigged interest rates,[3] sheltered customers from taxes,[4] laundered Mexican drug money,[5] presided over an offshore banking system that was larger than anyone ever thought,[6] forced good companies into closure[7] and destroyed pension funds as they themselves grew wealthier.[8] Collectively, they oversaw unprecedented destruction of wealth and the collapse of the financial system,[9] and watched as life savings placed into investment funds set up by leaders of unimpeachable integrity turned out to be Ponzi schemes.[10] Our spiritual leaders have covered up sex abuse in the Church.[11] Our charity leaders have sexually abused the vulnerable.[12] Our child welfare leaders have permitted child abuse.[13] Our political leaders have allowed an epidemic of gun crime.[14] They have cheated on their expenses,[15] admitted sexually inappropriate behaviour,[16] started ruinously expensive unpopular wars[17] on the basis of false information[18] and were taken completely by surprise by the Brexit vote.[19] Our education leaders have presided over exam cheating[20] and sexual harassment.[21] Our defence industry leaders have settled claims relating to the bribery of government officials.[22] Our leaders of public utilities have poisoned customers.[23] Our entertainment leaders are facing multiple allegations of sexual harassment and abuse.[24] Our leading broadcasters have falsely accused political figures of being child abusers,[25] while allowing actual abusers to commit crimes on their premises.[26] Meanwhile, our sporting leaders have been caught cheating and doping.[27] Our medical leaders have chronically mistreated patients.[28] Our human rights lawyers have been struck off for misconduct and dishonesty,[29] while our military leaders have admitted using torture[30] and our service personnel have died through their negligence.[31]

These events sound unlikely, unbelievable, even impossible, but they all happened. Outside of the cataclysmic events of the world wars, it is difficult to remember a time when leadership has appeared more thoroughly and completely discredited. If you are starting to feel as if this is a knife to the throat, then you might like this book. It is not anti-leadership. Quite the contrary. It is against bad leadership. It's not interested in blame or retribution. It searches for the truth.

What do these events have in common? Did they lack professionally qualified university-educated leaders? If not, why didn't they notice what was happening? Were they distracted by too much or too little information? Did they know they were doing wrong? Did they lack the imagination to see the effects of this? Did they feel they couldn't speak out? Did they think they would just get away with it? Did their size play a part? Did it matter that they were led mainly by middle-aged men? What role did technology play? Finally, is there a pattern here? We know good leaders, great leaders, are out there. Leaders with integrity, courage, wisdom. Inclusive leaders. Leaders who change the lives of the many. Leaders who think. Thinking is an underrated activity. So, we need to find the best modern leaders by studying the worst. By studying failure. So, in summary, this book:

- Concludes that the skills and qualities of a leader in the 20th century are very different from the ones needed in the 21st century.
- Recommends that 'leadership' become more of a focus than 'leaders' themselves. A team defrays risk and shares burden. A single leader increases vulnerability and risk.
- Points out that leadership is distracted by an overload of insistent, disruptive and attention-getting communications. This diverts thinking to the short-term, the quantitative and tactical and has a negative effect on creativity, imagination, community values and even mental health.
- Notes that leadership is subject to impatience from electors, staff, shareholders and other stakeholder groups. There is no patience to take in complexity or even to read and understand. Attention spans are falling.
- Suggests that leaders often cling to comfortable but inaccurate and outdated models of a macroeconomic environment that no longer exists.

- Offers thoughts to allow leaders to orient themselves more firmly in the new social, cultural, technological, behavioural, political and economic realities.
- Proposes 'situational fluency' as a new area of study – the ability to understand and move between multi-dimensional spheres and silos of expertise. This will allow leaders to join the dots across the landscape of reality to create a new global narrative on which a fresh leadership approach can be based.
- Proposes that this new cross-connectivity requires a shift in thinking. Current leadership understands depth of analysis. Leadership in the future will need both 'drill-down' analysis *and* 'look-across' parenthesis.
- Identifies eight areas of paradoxical change that have both good and bad effects simultaneously. These 'quantum super-positions' are at the heart of the problem leaders face. These spokes are part of a device called the Kythera, which leaders can use to navigate in this new world.
- Points out the dangers of over-reliance on analysis and extrapolation based on historic data. It proposes a cyclical rather than linear model. It calls for less prediction of one outcome and greater preparation for many outcomes. It highlights the importance of imagination to plan for contingencies and crises.
- Suggests that leadership needs a better understanding of long-term qualitative as well as short-term quantitative values. Twenty-first-century leaders need to develop 'to be' as well 'to do' lists.
- Concludes that the economic response to change and uncertainty has been short-termism. This has created a new macroeconomic landscape which is very different from that which prevailed. For the longest period in history, governments have lowered interest rates and printed money to encourage long-term growth. This is creating record debt and stimulating inflation that contributes to inequality and instability.

- Shows that contrary to the commonly held view that the internet is deflationary, the internet is having an inflationary effect. It forecasts that new internet currencies will add to the problem.
- Reviews the nature of geopolitical change at the points of the compass in China, the United States, Russia, Europe and the Middle East. It also shows how global infrastructure is being built outwards from China towards the source of many of the planet's resources.
- Suggests that those either in show business or currently leading businesses (especially in tech) may become the provenance of a new age of political leadership. This leadership has created and understands many of the trends and may be better at implementing them in government. It further suggests that political leaders can learn from the show-business style.
- Discusses how short-termism, impatience and economic pressure challenge leadership and may even disrupt diplomacy and contribute to conflict. This has significant implications for global leadership in terms of transparency, information flows, secrecy and trade relations with some of the fastest-growing economies in the world.
- Explains that a new technological, virtual world is emerging, which is atomizing behaviour, disintermediating human relationships and diminishing productivity.
- Shows why we are ever more connected yet communicating ever less. It also explains why technology causes people to feel more impatient, angry and atomized.
- Forecasts that the turmoil can be defended by a return to enduring values. This will mean longer-term, more qualitative metrics that seek to understand the diverse needs of leaders' communities. It predicts that all organizations will need to demonstrate the way in which they add value to their local communities.
- Provides 'Quick tips' for those without the patience to read a book that promotes the virtues of calm contemplation.

When change isn't allowed to be a process, it becomes an event

In our daily work over the past 20 years, we the authors have witnessed a growing confusion in the leadership forums of the world. This is true whether they be boardrooms, governing councils, committees or government cabinets. A failure to understand the polarities caused by technological change has resulted in a toxic brew of conflict. This is creating an almost revolutionary atmosphere that threatens to overwhelm leaders. Leadership frequently appears to be in crisis as a seemingly endless sequence of revelations undermines respect for leaders.

There has thus never been a greater need for leadership to evolve. This book asserts that there is an imbalance in leadership thinking. It is too steeped in Western Reductionist thinking.

In the context of *The Leadership Lab*, we define Western Reductionist thinking as the tendency to apply narrow logic, data, key performance indicators (KPIs) and quantitative thinking. There are reasons for this, such as the constant overload of data, the interruptions, causing rising impatience and ever-greater leadership expectations.

The rationalism of Western Reductionism has been a great servant for scientific progress. The ability to compare, contrast and analyse has often been associated with so-called left-brain thinking. It allows us to drill down into data, which, by its very nature, is historic. This tends to be more short-term, quantitative and tactical. It also tends to be more often associated with a 'masculine' way of thinking.

There's nothing wrong with this of itself, except that it's not enough. It can miss the insights that come from parenthetic or more inclusive so-called right-brain thinking. This focuses on the irrational – belief, faith or trust. It encompasses more long-term strategic values such as community, spirit and purpose. It encompasses looking forward and using imagination rather than facts.

Scientists have, of course, shown that the left and the right sides of the brain are not the exclusive provenance of these processes. They work in tandem more than previously thought. Similarly, a masculine way of thinking and a feminine way of thinking are complementary and perhaps overlap. What is clear is that using only one part of the brain or one type of thinking leads to less than optimal results.

There is a powerful movement to balance gender in leadership and we applaud it, but only as a first step. What is the point, however, of having equal representation if all genders are encouraged to think in the same drill-down analytical way? We should be looking for balance. A parenthetical complements the deep-dive view. Leadership should be capable of all types of thinking, regardless of its gender.

The pressure on leaders to perform commercially and operationally has never been greater. They are held to higher expectations and subject to almost permanent comment through social media. Their organizations have never been more transparent. Almost every aspect of their personal and professional lives is visible.

On top of this, their vision is often obscured by either too much or too little information. Consequently, we've seen them blindsided by events, where drill-down data research has strongly indicated one outcome only for another to happen.

One reason this happens is because behaviour is not always logical. We also follow values. It's no use, for instance, arguing that Brexit will force the rest of Europe to reform in the British style. That might be logical to some, but the values of Europe encompass more than just logic. Continental Europeans were far more affected by the catastrophe of war and are more motivated to seek unity and commonality.

We suggest that too many leaders don't get out and talk to people enough. Leaders travel constantly and easily, but going somewhere is not the same as truly understanding it. People can't easily follow someone who lacks a broad-based understanding.

What's required is something the military calls situational aware-ness or fluency. In other words, they need to understand that how people feel *is* also what is actually happening. It doesn't just depend on data. Real leadership combines both logic and emotion, both short- and long-term thinking.

Joining the dots

Leaders often struggle to knit these capabilities together. Their background usually is degree educated – steeped in the Western Reductionist tradition. This does not recognize softer skills as important in reaching their full potential. This also means they cannot draw out the potential in others either. If a leader wants success, it requires the building of trust that entices others to follow. Currently, only 18 per cent of people believe business leaders are truthful.[32]

Change happens whether people are aware of it or not. Taken individually, the changes we've seen since the turn of the century would be a challenge for leadership. When taken all together, it is bewildering. It's becoming hard for leaders to make sense of what appears to be an increasingly disorderly world. This is par-ticularly the case with their current skills of logic, analysis and comparison. There is, however, a clear pattern to change and we can no longer lead by analysing the dots separately; we must learn to join them up.

One of the tasks that humans will always be better at than computers is imagination. We can blend temperature, sound, emotions and aromas to interpret atmosphere. We can link be-haviours and situations to create understanding. We can dream. We can empathize. We have curiosity.

Leadership has become increasingly 'professionalized' and classically educated, with more formal qualifications, aca-demically and technically. Of course, this helps, but we must guard against a belief that this type of education is all that is needed. Leaders may be unnecessarily excluding those who come from different educational backgrounds. Education is changing fast, too.

Mediocrity is the provenance of certainty

All leadership improvement, especially post qualification, starts with the humility to admit ignorance. This is a powerful indicator of real leadership. Curiosity matters; in fact, it's a key leadership resource. Asking questions such as: 'Why did that happen?', 'Why do we do it that way?' and 'What if we did it a different way?' is not a sign of weakness.

On the contrary, the ignorance of potential failure through overconfidence has led directly to the collapse of many organizations. We will explore this in detail in Chapter 7. Failure is always the parent to success. How many tasks or skills have we all tried and failed? Toddlers taking their first few steps before falling may get up again by instinct, but later failure is overcome by determination, encouragement, even a sense of fun. Success owes more to determination and attitude than to skill alone.

This is not a call for soft, woolly thinking. Drilling down into quantitative detail is part of where the answer lies. The reverse is also true. Joining the dots is hard. It requires going against familiar analytical processes. There is, however, little point to arriving at the top of the mountain if all you can see is the detail of the square foot of ground under your feet. The view is the whole point. Leaders need this to show the vision and not just give direction. This can only be achieved if all faculties are devoted to the task, for instance analytical thinking, yes, but imagination, curiosity and emotion as well.

Our own methods, prejudices and biases determine our view of the landscape and our view of others. The solution is a different way of thinking that includes more of the insights available to us in the 21st century. You might be an expert in any field of endeavour, but this is a profundity, not a parenthesis. What do we mean by this? The Western Reductionist model becomes more and more efficient until it reaches its ultimate incarnation – the algorithm. This serves only the most relevant information based on what you have already consumed. This means that our knowledge becomes deepened and exaggerated. At face value, this appears to be a great strength, but the opposite is true. By excluding all but the most obviously relevant information we exclude the ostensibly irrelevant. It is this that is most often the source of leadership vulnerability – the thing that no-one sees coming, because no-one imagined it.

Multiples causes of leadership failure

The causes of leadership failure are usually the issues no-one planned for, because no-one foresaw them. No-one thought the systemic failure of the entire banking system was possible, for instance. In November 2008, HM The Queen asked some British economists why it had happened. Six months later they provided a three-page document, signed by some of the country's top thinkers, blaming 'a failure of the collective imagination of many bright people'.[33] They just didn't see it coming and they failed to imagine it was possible. How many leaders are at risk of a similar situation today?

The leader is responsible for the thinking culture of the entire organization. In this way, they can liberate the latent human talent and engender the trust that is essential for success. This is especially important because the 21st century poses complex and multi-dimensional problems. It demands creativity and imagination, but this can't thrive if we don't respect its origins or pre-conditions.

Why do leaders leave aside so many useful techniques? The short-term values of efficiency and performance are highly prized. It's impossible to get these without long-term qualities such as passion, joy, forgiveness, empathy, courage (above all), compassion, belief and humour. These are long-term goals that never seem to be credibly addressed. This is the hallmark of Western Reductionist thinking. The quantitative is revered while the qualitative is belittled because it can't be measured. Our job is to show leaders how and why they should engage in this inclusive thinking – to access all the tools, people and forces at their disposal.

By doing this, they will learn how to knit together both the left and right processes of the brain and marry the quantitative to the qualitative and the short- to the long-term. They should develop binocular vision: instead of a quantitative, mathematical lens, they should open the other eye to the qualitative evidence as well. Yes, we want the microscope that drills down into data but we also need a telescope that gives a view of the landscape and even of the stars.

We need to cast our view internally as well as externally. Achieving true awareness of the situation involves us looking at our own motives for action. Are we leading teams with our values? What are our values? Does it matter that we behave morally? This is not to exclude quantitative analysis, but we believe we can create a more emulsive approach where the dynamism of leadership combines the oil and water of logic and emotion. The purpose is permanent learning, not snapshot by snapshot.

Leaders need to check their vectors. Is the organization excessively 'male' and patriarchal in its thinking? It's not just women who think feminism is a good idea. You might prefer hard thinking, muscular ideas, rigid targets, cold calculations, but what room does this leave for values that drive others – passion, joy and love? This is not just about having women on leadership boards, especially if they only replicate masculine thinking. Ask yourself what range of subjects your leadership board could discuss. Numbers? Research? What would happen if you wanted to discuss passion and purpose? Would you be shown the door? Can't compassion and care be a corporate value, too? Or does that need to be coldly referred to as corporate social responsibility (CSR)? When we refer to people as human resources (HR) or corporate responsibility (CR), a little piece of the personal and human element disappears.

Harnessing potential also requires an understanding that all competence follows preference – people get good at what they like doing. This means that the process in business is supposed to be fun. Is your leadership fun? Is it fun following you?

This is not inconsistent with vaulting ambition and growth. We must be careful to ensure that the traditional 'Alpha male' approach creates the actuality of speed and progress, rather than just the mere illusion of it. Bigger does not create better, but better can create bigger. We have seen countless incidences of leaders travelling so fast they can taste nothing and where everything is measured by size, volume, scale: how many clicks, sales, news stories, shareholders. It leads to recklessness.

Top-down, Alpha-male leadership often asks the wrong question and gets the wrong answer. It's important, however, to allow bottom-up access to the success. This is not just in monetary terms. Everyone wants to share success and to own it. Part of the reason is that we confuse confidence with competence. We revere and reward the overconfident and dismiss those who carefully double check everything. Leaders need to ask: Is someone who double checks things in your organization an asset or a neurotic?

We must also have a process for adapting to change. If there is no evolution, then the stage is set for revolution. With a process, change can be an ally. Without it, change creates 'events' that drain time and trust. Events then become like architecture. First we shape them, then they shape us. Leaders shape events and then are subsequently shaped by them.

What we're talking about here is intellectual and emotional suppleness. We should be able to switch between the two. It's a quality that young people have in abundance. They ask: What is the purpose of this organization or community? What is its story? Profitability is not enough. An organization's success may be measured in how influential, trusted and followed it is and whether it serves a relevant purpose. Leaders must understand the values their teams follow. They have to follow the followers.

This is as true in politics as in other areas of leadership. As a leader, what is your purpose? Leadership is nothing if not a moral crusade. Good leaders must have spiritual virtues – not just commercial, not just technical, not just transactional. This speaks to the Harvard Business School definition of business – 'the management of social relationships for profit where profit may be financial'. It's about social relationships.

All leaders say they want more intelligent people, but how many recognize the different types of intelligence?[34] The more skills or experiences leaders have, the greater the level of connection they will display to their team.

We also need to ask: What's the price of a mistake under your leadership? Victory and defeat are just learning signs. They're not the 'be all and end all'. If failure is not acceptable, how do we spur imagination and vision?

Our goals here are to replace the analytically, economically efficient with a more balanced approach. We aim to point out that capital excess with a deficit of purpose will ultimately lead to failure. This book is a gesticulating arm that points to the hidden inefficiencies and growing disillusionment with leadership. We've been shaken to our foundations over the past decade: the financial crisis, Brexit, numerous terrorist events and the results of the 2016 US presidential election. The landscape today is different from what many expected and predicted. So, how did the experts miss it every time? We think there is another way of seeing the landscape more clearly so we are not blindsided again.

Acquiring situational fluency

Sometimes we see what looks like chaos, but what is chaos except a pattern we have yet to understand? Now is the time to ask, because a new world with new leaders is emerging. It will have different forces, different infrastructures, different centres, different priorities and different objectives. Now is the time to develop a better understanding of the world, to know what is actually happening instead of assuming we already know.

It is the moment to acquire situational fluency to see the facts in a wider perspective. Then we may have some hope of what is required for success in this new fluid environment. This is the ability to respond to, and anticipate, events because we are fluent with the global trends and drivers.

To help leaders achieve this greater fluency, we held a series of conversations throughout 2017 and 2018 called the LEWIS Advisory Board (LAB). The purpose of the LAB was to convey a sharper, more accurate image of reality, even if it is not what we'd like it to be. It was also to listen to successful leaders explain how they see the world and make business decisions. We held these meetings around the world. We were privileged to hear many opinions and witness great ingenuity and determination. While not all leaders agreed on every one of the points raised here, there was great consensus about the problems.

What we found were brave leaders prepared to throw themselves back into situations time and time again. They were often coping with extreme pressure and risk. Some had a narrow view of the world on some issues and yet were ahead of the curve on others. They could, for instance, still believe that 'all the jobs are moving to China' even as the Chinese begin to invest in manufacturing facilities in places such as the United States and Mexico. They can have extraordinary insight into the behaviour of their clients and broader customer trends, but be blindsided by more macro forces and trends. A macro view in itself isn't very helpful for a CEO who is running a specific business with a narrow focus. The question is how to bring the two together in a way that will help others improve their ability to navigate the fast-changing global landscape.

This book therefore seeks to provide leaders with the additional insight and understanding that come from joining things up, for instance between the corporation and the rest of humanity. We wanted to review countries with a joint narrative rather than looking at them in isolation. We want to understand the future as a function of the past. We want the generations to understand each other better.

For this reason, we've taken soundings from many perspectives. We asked many leaders from both the LAB and others all over the world to help. We've sought views and opinions from politicians and business people on our changing world. We've talked to artists and admirals, to strategic consultants and scientists. We've spoken with politicians and entrepreneurs. These have been from all industries, nationalities, genders and age groups.

We've referenced these people at the back of the book, but the terms under which they were interviewed were 'Chatham House' so there have been no attributions. The idea was quite simple. What if we created a top-down, bottom-up snapshot of what was happening that would be diverse, wide-ranging and interesting? This would especially be geared towards leaders of all types so that they could build situational fluency with the technical, cultural, economic and geopolitical world in which they work. We also wanted to make the book accessible for lay people. Many of the changes occurring go much wider in society and affect all aspects of life and its many relationships.

An obstacle to writing a book with ambitious goals is what structure to use. So many of the problems we describe are interconnected and 'join the dots'. Many of the changes also have paradoxical effects depending on who you are, what your situation is and where on the planet you are. These effects are sometimes good and bad at the same time. A physicist might say they were quantum super-positioned.

Should we organize the analysis by country, by trend, by problem or by leadership lesson? Our hypothesis is that our over-reliance on analytical, reductive thinking *is* part of the problem. This is because the changes we're seeing are often paradoxical. So, we've tried to avoid an overly structured analysis. We are, after all, trying to show the bigger picture. Once we have this, the leadership response is obvious.

The LAB Kythera is our response to this challenge (Figure 0.1). It is a thinking tool that was inspired by the Greek Antikythera.[35] This highly complex device was discovered on a shipwreck in the Peloponnese in 1900 and is now considered to be the very first computer in history. It was used to calculate the exact position of the stars, the moon and other celestial bodies. It is a calendar,

FIGURE 0.1 The eight 'I's model or 'Kythera'

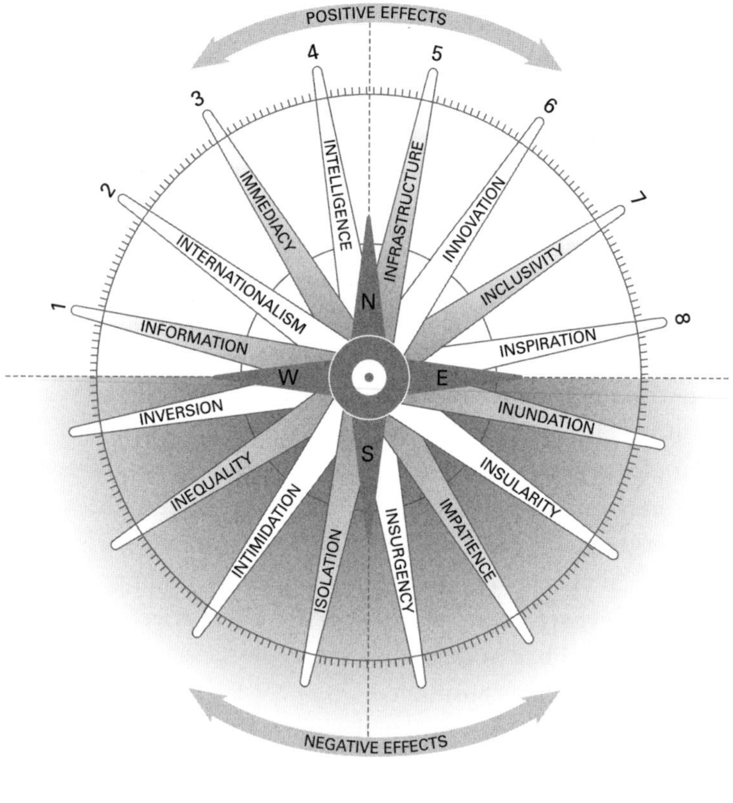

a predictor of eclipses, a foreteller of moon phases. It even indicated the timing of Hellenic athletic games. It is remarkable because it was unimaginable that it could possibly date to somewhere between 205 BC and 87 BC. Astronomical clocks did not appear in Western Europe until the 14th century. Mechanical calculators like this did not arrive in Europe until the 16th century. The Kythera, therefore, captures the notion that unimaginable, and even impossible, things are indeed possible.

On a compass, there are four cardinal points: North, South, East and West. We've used these in conjunction with inter-cardinal points which provide the qualitative overlay. These explain the bipolar paradoxes that we're seeing.

This is to be imagined in four dimensions as a 360-degree sphere spinning. The objective is to keep the sphere upright on its axis and balanced. The faster the technology changes the faster the sphere spins. The axes are therefore subject to centrifugal force making them more and more polarized.

The first obvious element of the Eight 'I's model or Kythera is that it is divided into a light and a dark side. This shows both the progressive and the reciprocal negative effects being created by change.

Next, you will notice the eight 'I's. Working clockwise, these are Information, Internationalism, Immediacy, Intelligence, Infrastructure, Innovation, Inclusivity and Inspiration. Their opposite counterparts are Inundation, Insularity, Impatience, Insurgency, Isolation, Intimidation, Inequality and Inversion.

These correspond to the first eight chapters of this book. The ninth chapter is a summary.

Many of the issues are inter-related. So, our chapters start in one area, then we analyse and parenthesize to come to different conclusions. In Chapter 1, we start off by talking about the change in behaviour caused by the overload of data. We end by talking about how left-brain driven and androcentric this might be making our thinking. This links parenthetically with Chapter 7 on inclusivity.

Similarly, in Chapter 2, we reveal the world economy as it is, rather than as it was. Many commonly held views about it are now hopelessly out of date. The consequences of the emergency economic measures from the financial crisis are still unfolding. Global debt, whether public or private, is now three times the level of global GDP. The fast-moving fluid nature of the world economy keeps blindsiding leaders and leaving them exposed to mistakes and misinterpretation. The chapter reviews the landscape and cautions about the rise of unexpected outcomes such as the return of inflation and the unprecedented defence spending. Again, we make the link parenthetically.

In Chapter 3, we look at the effects the internet is having on behaviour and make the link to the rising tide of impatience. We see how the rise of this behaviour seriously affects qualitative aspects of our lives. The immediacy of the internet is creating great flexibility and efficiency. It's also creating impatience, uncertainty and inequality.

In Chapter 4, we look more closely at philosophical change. Of course, the enormous benefits of shared intelligence and understanding can lead to optimism. At the same time, despite the abundance of information, some are choosing to ignore it, which leads to fear, anger and cynicism. This is a good example of the 'super-positioning' effect. This can lead to both a dystopian *and* a utopian view of the world ahead.

In Chapter 5, we look at the infrastructures and the geopolitics of the world and how the East and West are converging in their goals. We look at the rise of nations such as Mexico and how the great Chinese undertaking of One Belt, One Road, One Circle will change everything. We look specifically at the United States, China, Europe, Russia and the Middle East. Such is their interconnectedness that no global leader can make sense of daily changes without building a situationally fluent view of the world.

In Chapter 6, we see how the inception of technologies yet to come will change things further. We review the leadership opportunities offered by the radical new technologies and how the world is likely to change further. We join the dots still further to look at where the technology is taking us.

In Chapter 7 we explore one of the trends from Chapter 6, namely, how technology is disintermediating relationships at every level. Leadership is profoundly threatened in this sphere because its primary goal is unity of purpose. This chapter primarily analyses the gender effects of multiple trends.

In Chapter 8, we parenthesize all aspects to date to look at how the 21st-century world has profoundly inverted the previous century's values. This looks at how the 'looking glass' environment fundamentally challenges all aspects of leadership.

Finally, in Chapter 9, we look at what the world's leaders need now to make sense of the future. We analyse the fundamentally paradoxical nature of the change. Leaders cannot manage just for the positive outcomes of change; they must also mitigate the loss from the change ahead. It may be the latter – with all the greater scrutiny that the new environment brings – that decides their fate.

This is a book that analyses leadership through both the quantitative and qualitative lens. It builds a bigger perspective on global leadership because it needs to understand both tactics and strategy. It also points out that its greatest challenge is going to be liberating the potential of the change ahead without destroying those who are unwilling or unable to participate.

This is a book about not just what has happened, or what is going to happen, but what is happening *to the way leaders think and perceive the world around them*. By allowing leaders to take time to think and equipping them with a telescope as well as a magnifying glass, we hope to encourage better outcomes and less blindsidedness.

As entrepreneur Peter Thiel put it, the challenge is to integrate the small and the big such that all things make sense. He said that arts and humanities students may well learn a great deal about the world, but they don't learn career skills through their studies. Engineering majors learn great technical detail, but not how they might apply their skills in the workforce. 'The best students, workers, and thinkers will integrate these questions into a cohesive narrative.'[36]

The biggest challenge we've ever faced lies just ahead. The crisis in leadership is clear for everyone to see. In the past, our predecessors found the creativity, generosity and common humanity to meet great crises with great people and ideas.

Their eyes are upon us now. Will we rise above the pettiness and merely tactical and draw upon all our faculties? They call upon us to look back through the centuries and through the geographies, through the periods of blind faith and compelling logic. We don't need a left wing or a right wing. We don't need a male approach or an exclusively female one. We need unity. We need a common sense of purpose. We need leadership. Our challenges demand that we combine our skills to reach both our individual and collective potential because, self-evidently, we cannot achieve the latter without the former. Our planet is just too small and precious a place not to have leadership equipped with the highest-value endeavour and insight.

During the writing of this book, we have been blessed to hear many voices, to experience many minds and hear many opinions. It has been our honour to structure and present them here. It's also been tremendous fun. We hope you think so, too.

Endnotes

1 http://fortune.com/2017/11/06/apple-tax-avoidance-jersey/

2 https://www.theguardian.com/environment/2015/oct/09/mercedes-honda-mazda-mitsubishi-diesel-emissions-row

3 https://www.reuters.com/article/us-deutschebank-libor-settlement/deutsche-bank-fined-record-2-5-billion-over-rate-rigging-idUSKBN0NE12U20150423

4 http://www.bbc.com/news/business-31248913

5 https://www.theguardian.com/business/2012/jul/17/hsbc-executive-resigns-senate

6 https://www.forbes.com/forbes/welcome/?toURL=https://www.forbes.com/
   sites/kenrapoza/2017/09/15/tax-haven-cash-rising-now-equal-to-at-least-10-of-
   world-gdp/&refURL=https://www.google.co.uk/&referrer=https://www.google.
   co.uk/
7 https://www.theguardian.com/business/2016/nov/08/rbs-facing-400m-bill-to-
   compensate-small-business-customers
8 https://www.ft.com/content/87f72e9e-bafb-11e7-9bfb-4a9c83ffa852
9 https://www.theguardian.com/business/2008/dec/28/markets-credit-crunch-
   banking-2008
10 http://www.businessinsider.com/how-bernie-madoffs-ponzi-scheme-
   worked-2014-7
11 https://www.cnn.com/2017/06/29/world/timeline-catholic-church-sexual-abuse-
   scandals/index.html
12 http://www.bbc.co.uk/news/uk-43121833
13 http://www.bbc.com/news/education-11621391
14 https://www.livescience.com/59528-shootings-are-3rd-leading-cause-of-kids-
   deaths.html
15 https://www.telegraph.co.uk/news/newstopics/mps-expenses/5357568/MPs-
   expenses-Sir-Peter-Viggers-claimed-for-1600-floating-duck-island.html
16 http://www.foxnews.com/politics/2017/12/25/7-biggest-political-scandals-2017.
   html
17 https://www.militarytimes.com/news/your-military/2016/09/12/report-wars-in-
   iraq-afghanistan-cost-almost-5-trillion-so-far
18 http://www.nbcnews.com/id/22794451/ns/world_news-mideast_n_africa/t/
   study-bush-led-us-war-false-pretenses
19 https://www.standard.co.uk/news/politics/damn-eu-referendum-result-shocks-
   world-leaders-as-britain-backs-brexit-a3280031.html
20 https://www.theguardian.com/education/2018/feb/11/thousands-of-teachers-
   caught-cheating-to-boost-exam-results
21 https://www.huffingtonpost.com/topic/teacher-sex-scandal
22 http://www.independent.co.uk/news/business/news/bae-systems-pays-400m-to-
   settle-bribery-charges-1891027.html
23 http://www.latimes.com/local/california/la-me-hinkley-20150413-story.html
24 http://www.bbc.co.uk/news/entertainment-arts-41594672
25 https://www.theguardian.com/media/greenslade/2014/feb/19/newsnight-lord-
   mcalpine
26 https://www.telegraph.co.uk/news/uknews/crime/jimmy-savile/12172773/
   Jimmy-Savile-sex-abuse-report-to-be-published-live.html
27 http://www.bbc.co.uk/sport/athletics/43301116
28 https://www.theguardian.com/society/2013/feb/06/mid-staffs-hospital-scandal-
   guide

29 https://www.theguardian.com/law/2017/feb/02/iraq-human-rights-lawyer-phil-shiner-disqualified-for-professional-misconduct

30 http://www.bbc.com/news/world-us-canada-33739480

31 https://www.cnn.com/2017/08/21/politics/navy-ships-accidents/index.html

32 https://hbr.org/video/5760615517001/the-authenticity-paradox

33 http://voxeu.org/article/invisible-hand-meets-invisible-gorilla-economics-meets-psychology

34 http://www.tecweb.org/styles/gardner.html

35 https://www.smithsonianmag.com/history/decoding-antikythera-mechanism-first-computer-180953979

36 http://www.businessinsider.com/peter-thiels-stanford-class-2012-5

CHAPTER ONE

Understanding the Effects of Overload

Information and Inundation

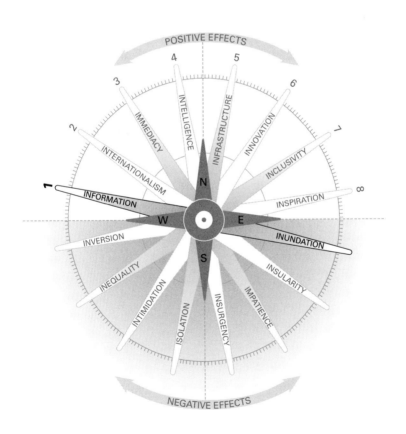

There's more information around us than ever before. E-mail, 24-hour news and social media are an almost constant source of distraction. We know more about our world than any previous generation. We also measure everything. We measure our weight, steps, heart rate, the time we take for activities, our sleep, our calorie intake – and that's just the personal information. In the workplace, the compulsion to measure and analyse is even greater. But what if all this information that we rely upon so much for our logical, analytical approach had become so abundant that it was inundating us and our understanding?

In this chapter, we look at how the volume and type of information are changing leadership culture. We'll see how it is undermining our ability to make sense of the world by constantly interrupting and changing our thought processes. We'll also see how our own filtering and that of others can narrow our field of vision. We'll look at the technological changes of the past decade and show how, in many instances, they have created paradoxical effects. This is creating polarities that demand a new type of thinking away from just analysis towards parenthesis. Analysis focuses leadership goals on the short-term, quantitative (often financial), tangible goals. It marginalizes those of little economic value and ignores wider community goals such as caring and compassion. Leaders need more balance between the two kinds of thinking and more fluidity to shift between them.

In this chapter, this is what we will cover:

- Left-brain process
- Right-brain process
- The overload
- How it changes us
- The algorithms make this worse
- News is about profits, too
- Is the overload hurting our creativity?

- The sort of people we're becoming
- The siren call of the numbers
- Analysis versus parenthesis
- Our socio-economic perspective also dictates our understanding
- A mixed reality environment
- How this changes the leader's mandate
- Spotting the signs of a waterboarded leader
- Conclusions

Before we explore this further, we must review how we process information using the two main techniques that we have at our disposal.

Left-brain process

These are the logical, rational processes at the core of Western Reductionism. Although it has its roots in antiquity, in the work of Aristotle and Plato, its modern application really dates from the age of Enlightenment. This was an intellectual and philosophical movement of the 18th century that saw the flourishing of science and the pushing back of theology in Europe.

At its core, reductionism or the left-brain process allows us to compare, contrast, analyse and measure. It provides us with our convergent or analytic capability. By its nature, this process separates and atomizes because it focuses attention on that which is different. Computers are excellent assistants when it comes to processing and breaking down data because they are founded on logic. They allow us to calculate answers and build complex models which can be run and re-run to test hypotheses and assumptions.

Analysis allows us to reach the correct answer with certainty. It allows us to develop scientific thinking and has been the single most productive philosophy mankind has embraced. This is why it has been adopted by all of the most industrially advanced nations, in schools, universities, government, the military and commerce. The most skilled intellects (as defined by their ability to use logic and rational thinking) are the most highly prized and sought after in all walks of life.

When first meeting someone or when we're interrupted, alerted or distracted, it is to the left-brain process that we turn. The process helps us assess a situation, tells us what the information is, what we need to do with it and how and when to respond. This analytic, logical and reductionist ability is so powerful and all-encompassing as to almost completely eclipse the other major process which we know is there, but is harder to spot.

Right-brain process

These processes don't just deal with the opposite of reductionism, they also deal with synthesizing, contextualization and broader vision. These are termed divergent processes, because they seek to join things up rather than separate them. They are slower and rely heavily on what we might call offline processing. How do we know this? Well, it's difficult to prove scientifically. In *Too Fast to Think*[1] a survey of leaders from many different backgrounds was undertaken. All the leaders were experts in the Western Reductionist tradition. They all had one degree, some even had two, with further professional qualifications on top of that. They were asked where they were when got their epiphanies or best ideas.

The results were fascinating. More often than not, they reported their best ideas came when they were away from their workplace, not doing something work related and, most importantly, not trying. These leaders all reported their greatest ideas when they were in the shower, the gym, driving, walking the dog, about to fall asleep, listening to music, in conversation, sitting on a train or plane, in fact almost everywhere except the office. Can this be mere coincidence?

It was Einstein who said: 'Creativity is the residue of time wasted.' The implication here is quite clear. When we're doing nothing, we're really doing quite a bit. Einstein also added: 'If I had an hour to solve a problem, I'd spend 55 minutes thinking about the problem and 5 minutes thinking about solutions.'[2] It's unlikely he would have made much progress on his problem had he been constantly interrupted by e-mail and social media notifications.

This points to the power of the right-brain process, which is slower and constantly churning whether we're aware of it or not. It comes forward when the left-brain process recedes for whatever reason. By its very nature, it is difficult to prove logically, but we know it's happening because so many report it. We don't just use this process for painting or writing; our right-brain creative ability is an important part of how we solve problems and reach potential. Right-brain process accounts for beliefs such as faith, trust and hope, which are all as important as logic, if not as ostensibly credible.

Creativity is the residue of time wasted.

The overload

We see our world from under an ocean of information and interruption. The scale of the information overload and disruption is enormous. If we just take e-mail, for instance, according to Radicati Group the average business user sent and received 121 e-mails a day in 2014, and this is expected to grow to 140 e-mails a day by 2018.[3] If we assume a 10-hour day at work, even at today's levels, that's twelve an hour or one every six minutes, often with an alert attached to it.

The number of worldwide e-mail accounts is expected to grow from over 4.1 billion in 2014 to over 5.2 billion by the end of 2018. The total number of worldwide e-mail users, including both business and consumer users, will increase from over 2.5 billion in 2014 to over 2.8 billion in 2018.[4]

So, on average, we check our e-mails at least 20 times a day.[5] In a normal working day, that's an interruption at least every 20 minutes. Once you add social media notifications from Facebook, LinkedIn, Twitter, WhatsApp, Instagram and so on, we're being interrupted every few minutes. This makes us the most distracted audience ever. We've stopped paying attention to anything other than basic headlines and what's front and centre. One survey showed that millennials were checking their phone 150 times a day.[6]

> QUICK TIP Leaders should use aggregators like Hootsuite to ensure they can see all social media in one place. This also allows multiple channels, eg Facebook, LinkedIn, Twitter, to be updated simultaneously.

It's hard enough just to keep up with the information we're being given. Worse still, the information is in many formats and locations, so we can't escape it. People send us messages on so many different platforms that we can't remember where to find it – WhatsApp, Facebook Messenger, LinkedIn, WeChat, Instagram messaging – the list goes on. The current affairs news media are the same – too many channels with too much stuff. Social media have become like drinking from a fire hose.

Users of the top messaging apps have now accelerated past those on the social networks. Monthly active users on the big four messaging apps, WhatsApp, Messenger, WeChat and Viber, outnumber those on Facebook, Instagram, Twitter and LinkedIn.[7] People already use these channels to interact with each other and expect brands to do the same. Brands are now struggling to answer all those messages because of the sheer volume. Sixty-six per cent of consumers prefer to interact with brands through messaging apps.[8] This is where so-called chatbots can add value to close that gap (more on this in Chapter 6).

How it changes us

In responding to overload, our behaviour changes in many ways. Some people are overwhelmed by the relentlessness of it and opt out. Some create windows of time when they can deal with it. Most of us just start to filter:

- We filter in news about the family. We now know more than ever about what our cousin is doing than we did before. People we only ever heard about previously once every few years are now updating in real-time.
- We filter in news about friends. Now we don't wait for a postcard or until they return from holiday, we get the detail in real-time.
- We filter in stories about violence. We hear about shootings, murders, sexual violence, thefts and muggings. We hear about events that people think were acts of terrorism but turn out not to be. We hear about terror unfolding in real-time. We even hear victims' last words.

> **QUICK TIP** Leaders need to actively pull in good stories and avoid being sucked in to negative stories and thinking. They need to remind their teams that the world is not always as terrifying as it's reported to be.

- We filter in news from sources that agree with us. This has always been the case. Most consumers of media have always subscribed to channels that support and reflect their views.

- We filter in stories about celebrities. According to London's *Daily Mail* it is now the largest online site in the world having overtaken *The New York Times*.[9] This is largely down to its coverage of celebrity gossip.
- We filter in stories about cats that look like Hitler ('Kitlers', if you're wondering).

Our information is also layered as if to create multiple realities. Take a tennis match for instance. We can see it first hand in immediacy. We can see it shortly after on social media. We can then view it on TV a little bit later. Then we can read about it in the press even later and maybe in history books long after the match.

For business performance, it's very similar. We can produce a set of business results, then wait for social media, read the minutes, see mainstream media, with accountants and then lawyers commenting. At every stage, we understand more about the truth, but frequently we don't have time for anything other than the headlines. This is because everyone can see everything as it happens all the time, in real-time. At each stage, though, different detail is released. This is because speed is inverse to truth (Figure 1.1).

So, we can see an event that contains all the same basic facts but reported in very different ways. This gives us multiple versions of reality, depending on where the process is joined. We give priority to the first version of the truth we heard.

FIGURE 1.1 Speed against truth

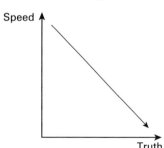

Source: LEWIS Rise Academy

The algorithms make this worse

To make the provision of news more efficient, internet algorithms recognize what news we have consumed, then we're automatically served more information about what we already have shown interest in. We end up unconsciously drilling down into a subject area because an algorithm has decided that's what we want. Algorithms focus our vision on what we've already consumed. This denies us the capacity to look across the landscape. That means we are often protected from information that for whatever reason we don't normally hear. It's difficult to be tolerant of other opinions if you never hear them. Social media similarly create an echo chamber or a silo where the capacity to drill down is not matched by the ability to look across. Not only do we not hear about other opinions, but we don't care or we discount them.

The constant interruptions also have another effect. They make us stressed. We feel constantly short of time. We are unable to complete tasks. We lose the thread of our thoughts. Every time we try to concentrate we get interrupted, which further undermines our ability to cope. It undermines our confidence in decision-making because there is always someone who is better informed.

News is about profits, too

Why do we want the news anyway? Is it because we want important facts? Well, without doubt transport, weather and local news can be helpful. Being informed in general can be useful to our careers. News providers know, however, that they can gain more attention if the news is entertaining. But let's be clear: the purpose of news media is not to inform. It is to make a profit. That too influences what we get to see and how we see it.

Scandal, sensationalism and threat to the community have long provided a source of stories. A good story is never just a true story, it's an entertaining one. Never let the facts get in the way of a good story. Why does this matter to leaders? Because leaders will always have stories told about them. Leaders should decide who tells that story and what it should be. If they don't, then the story could be very different. What is beyond doubt, though, is that there will be one.

Of course, people want entertainment but they also want validation. They want to agree with opinions they hear. That's why traditional outlets have been split along political, regional or gender lines. Now information is so intricate that, in theory, we need never listen to disagreeable or boring information again. We consume according to our tastes, but then wonder why the world makes no sense.

The implications of the above for all types of leadership are profound. Messages that are subtle, slow, dull, complex and sensitive are filtered out. So, if you're in any type of leadership role, it's difficult to get people's attention unless you speak with passion, emotion and you use the primary colours.

Is the overload hurting our creativity?

In short, yes. The interruptions are having obvious effects on us. What about the not so obvious effects? Short-term distractions are without doubt a hindrance to our long-term, sustained creative thinking. The brain has inherent deep processing capability which continues even when we are unaware of it. Only when we stop do these thoughts have the chance to surface and come to the attention of the conscious mind. It is our innate ability to solve problems that dictates how much of our potential we're able to attain.

It's not that the smartphone isn't a great utility for mankind. It makes us more connected, more productive and more aware.

However, there is a cost of accessing these benefits. Despite its simplicity, the most difficult feature to use on the smartphone remains the off switch.

The sort of people we're becoming

The filtering we talked about above is just like a sedimentary process: it gradually builds, layer upon layer, into a view of the world. We have become more:

- Frightened
- Angry
- Distracted
- Bored
- Intolerant
- Impatient
- Cynical
- Opinionated
- Informed (but not always helpfully).

Being constantly fed with news and information also creates a false sense of security that we know what's happening. The problem is that we think we're choosing the information we want without realizing that, in so many instances, it's already been chosen for us.

To some extent, this is happening to all of us and narrowing our field of vision. Over this must be overlaid an increasing tendency to analyse.

In this increasingly complex and specialist world, we have experts everywhere. We have more graduates than ever before. People who like to analyse things. Analysis has become our default method of examining the world. As explored in *Too Fast to Think*, analysis is part of the left-brain process. It loves to compare, contrast and analyse. Most criticism comes from this source. Of course, we also have another – the right-brain process – which takes us in an opposite direction towards trust, purpose and belief. These are the irrational, but nonetheless vital, elements.

The siren call of the numbers

It is nigh on impossible to gain entry into the world of leadership unless one is comfortable conversing in numbers. Maths, models and algorithms are the language of a financial priesthood that values and measures everything numerically. Spreadsheets and balance sheets are the foundations of this religion.

As a result, boards the world over spend ever more time and money sharpening these analytical tools so that they can crunch more numbers and process data at an ever-faster pace. Fiduciaries have been seduced by the deeply alluring promise that technology will help them perform better. Anyone who suggests that the answer might not lie in the numbers risks being excommunicated, even though they know financial accounts are only as good as the numbers they are given. This applies across all industries and leadership teams. The phrase is that decision-making must be 'data driven', as if somehow qualitative data were inadmissible or that numbers were not nuanced.

Numeric skills alone do not automatically equate to better performance – witness what investors missed in the past decade alone despite their mathematical tools: the 2007 financial crisis, the Arab Spring, the US economic recovery, Brexit and the migrant crisis.

Why did they miss all this? It seems that the most important forces in the world economy today are not the ones that can be quantified or predicted. Leaders shy away from these areas for the very reason that they involve subjective data. If they need to enter these areas, they like to equate polls with facts. They like to believe that human inclinations can be systematically measured and valued. The real drivers in these areas have to do with the level of anger in society, the loss of community and the destruction of hope. The perception that wealth and power are distributed unfairly and the collective failure of leadership are some of the most powerful forces that leaders face.

How else do we explain the anger that has resulted in the anti-establishment movement which gave rise to nationalist movements such as the 2016 US presidential election result and Brexit? How do we put a number on the sense of loss that drives immigrants everywhere to endure deep physical and emotional trauma in their search for a better life somewhere else? How do we assign a number or measure the anti-immigration mentality that is gaining ground everywhere today?

Consider what the father of public opinion polls had to say about all this. Daniel Yankelovich founded the original New York Times/CBS poll. He said:

> The first step is to measure what can be easily measured. This is okay as far as it goes. The second step is to disregard that which cannot be measured, or give it an arbitrary quantitative value. This is artificial and misleading. The third step is to presume that what cannot be measured is not very important. This is blindness. The fourth step is to say that what cannot be measured does not exist. This is suicide.

Perhaps leadership should spend more of its time looking at new methods to measure that which cannot be measured?

> **QUICK TIP** Leaders should seek to assess data by value as well as volume. For instance, knowledge of a competitor's move may mean more than spotting a trend in their own organization.

So, perhaps we need to add something new to the existing armoury of tools – things that precede movements in data, including stories, anecdotes, narratives and early signals. We need to suss the Zeitgeist/situational fluency and capture the mood before the data catch up. Leaders will recoil in horror at this suggestion. After all, these are all unreliable because they are subject to human judgement. They cannot be scientifically proved. They are not systematically observable because human opinions vary so much. But perhaps the industry will indulge in this notion given that performance has been so poor for so long.

The great problem with analysis is that, by its very nature, it focuses on historical data and logic. This means it concentrates on the past. It might provide insight for management, but it won't help leadership.

Let's take a simple example. If we analyse a car, we can conclude it is made up of systems such as steering, transmission, an engine and instrumentation. They work together to create a beneficial transportation device for humans. If we use parenthesis, we look at how the car's systems interact with other systems. For instance, it takes unsustainable fossil fuels and turns them into carbon dioxide. It takes well human beings and injures them. It takes quiet countryside and turns it into noisy congestion. If we apply two similar intellectual processes, we arrive at two paradoxical conclusions. At once, the car is both a help and a hindrance.

QUICK TIP Leaders should use the telescope as well as the microscope. By all means analyse, but remember to parenthesize.

Leaders may be inclined to fall back on number-based tools but they are, by definition, backward-looking – they rely on historic information. Data, maths, models and even algorithms are all backward-looking. They rely on events and information accumulated in the past. We like to think we can extrapolate this into the future. This seems especially odd and even ironic given that everyone in the fiduciary world knows that past returns are no guarantee of future performance.

As if it needed restating, leadership is not just a science; it's an art, too.

There's another problem here. Data and events, when analysed, tell you 'what' something did, but it doesn't explain 'why' it did it.

We need business to start looking into the future and joining things up instead of rooting everything in the recent past. Of course, prediction is impossible, but a greater degree of 'preparedness' is possible. What is required to be better prepared for an uncertain future?

The facts do not always speak for themselves because imagination is more powerful than knowledge.[10] There are many ways to be more imaginative, but business must engage in practices that it may find uncomfortable, such as case scenarios. No leader is inclined to use imagination when they could be using cold hard logic. Scenarios drive fund managers insane because they have less time to waste on speculation. The simple approach is therefore to take the opposite side of any sure bet. If the market consensus is that Clinton wins the Presidency, Britain stays in the EU, NATO and Russia never engage in military confrontation, then it's always worth simply asking the opposite.

It's been said before, but the difference between management and leadership is that the former learns how to *do things right*. The latter learns how to *do the right things*. They sound and look very similar words, but in fact they are very different. The latter tends to concentrate on the past, the former on the future.

In his book *The Metaphoric Mind: A Celebration of Creative Consciousness*,[11] Bob Samples said:

> The metaphoric mind is a maverick. It is as wild and unruly as a child. It follows us doggedly and plagues us with its presence as we wander the contrived corridors of rationality. It is a metaphoric link with the unknown called religion that causes us to build

cathedrals – and the very cathedrals are built with rational, logical plans. When some personal crisis or the bewildering chaos of everyday life closes in on us, we often rush to worship the rationally planned cathedral and ignore the religion.

This was summarized later and often falsely attributed to Einstein as: 'The intuitive mind is a sacred gift and the rational mind is a faithful servant. We have created a society that honours the servant and has forgotten the gift.'

Analysis versus parenthesis

What if we have become too dependent on our Western Reductionist left-brain process? Has it spawned knowledge acquisition that simply feeds us more about what we already know? How could this have happened when the internet has given us so many great things? Like all great advances of mankind, it's not about what it does. It's about how it's used. The atom bomb may have been the most destructive weapon ever invented, but maybe that's why the peace has been kept so long? The truth, as ever, is more complex. The internet has created equal and opposite effects. It is both good and bad. Its effects are paradoxical.

Let's look more closely at the positive, as well as negative, effects of information. If we care to use it that way, information gives us visibility and then transparency. The more information we have, the more we can understand. This is a well-trodden path and perhaps the genius of the internet as a knowledge- and experience-sharing device.

The opposite effect, though, comes when we allow the internet to be our main source of communications and server of news. It interrupts us, narrows our parentheses and then causes us to shorten the time we spend speaking face-to-face.

Well, so what? Who cares if conversation dies? Well, when you lose the ability to converse, you also lose negotiating skills, the ability to solve emotional problems and the ability to listen to ordinary people. A factor in leadership popularity and respect is the time taken by leaders to say hello and chat to even the most junior people in an organization.

Worse still, when taken at the global level, the narrowed outlook then leads to gross levels of ignorance and, as we'll see later, impatience and bigotry. The net result of this cocktail is a revolutionary fervour driven by half-digested news and a narrowing parenthesis caused by short-termism, ignorance and intolerance.

We have been here before several times in history. The Bourbon monarchy in France lasted for hundreds of years but was in part helped on its way by the social media equivalent of its day – pamphlets. These were scurrilous, cheap to produce, opinionated and widely circulated. When combined with the agrarian food crisis of 1789 and an ineffective monarch, the conditions for an uprising coalesced.

The difference between management and leadership is that the former learns how to do things right; the latter learns how to do the right things.

This is similar to the social media of today, but this alone is not enough to trigger a revolution. This requires a catalyst of a more existential nature. In 18th-century France, it was the failure of the agriculture that drove food prices up at a time of discontent. The social media of the time, though, made sure people were aware of the event by feeding them short, scurrilous material, sometimes in pictorial form.

We're seeing the same phenomena today. People may be unable to read detail in depth, but it seems they're also becoming more unwilling. Newspaper readership is in decline. Television consumption is becoming on demand and personal. The patterns are becoming harder to spot.

This should be no surprise. If we were analysing climate change, we would not look at the weather for data. The view is too close. The same is true of news. To understand it, we must ask through what lens we see it. If it's through the daily deluge of news stories, it's likely to make no sense at all. To make sense of it, we need to zoom out to a higher level so that we can look across to take into account everything that is happening in the world, from geopolitics to economics to sociological analysis and key cultural changes. Sometimes, the more we analyse a subject, the less sense it makes. This is why an opposite logic needs to be applied. This involves zooming out or reframing to a higher context. This way, we can join the dots to get a clearer view of the issues in context.

We need a new framework for understanding that permits us to see patterns, which in turn improves our ability to anticipate. Perhaps the one thing that machines will never be able to replicate is the subtle nuanced pattern recognition that humans are capable of. A human might be able to view *Le Déjeuner sur l'Herbe*, listen to Beethoven's Symphony No. 6 (the 'Pastoral'), smell new-mown grass and think of ice cream and a happy time spent with friends. Computers cannot do this yet and if they ever could, it would be the last area they would conquer.

Humans are also good at contextualizing knowledge, particularly if they have a wide generalized knowledge. If knowledge begets knowledge, then we can say that what makes people understand is the ability to add more to an existing knowledge structure. To do this necessarily involves the perspective to see where the new knowledge fits. Different people will file different subjects into different parts of their structure. The earlier this starts, the easier the knowledge acquisition process becomes.

Our socio-economic perspective also dictates our understanding

The extent to which people understand depends heavily on what questions they ask. In Ian Leslie's book *Curious: The Desire to*

Know and *Why Your Future Depends on It*, he points out that children from lower socio-economic groups are far less likely to question authority than those from higher ones. This is not just about the extent to which the child is encouraged. It's also about the child's attitude towards authority figures.[12] Middle-class kids begin life with more sense of entitlement and with that a willingness to challenge authority, ask questions and persist until they get answers. Adults who don't ask questions to challenge authority learn this behaviour at an early stage.

Another key factor that inhibits questions is fear. This could be fear of criticism, not wanting to look stupid or being thought to be dissenting. This is important for leaders to understand. Dissent is not a sign of weakness. On the contrary, we need to encourage it to maximize the resources of the organization. The more lookouts the ship has, the less likely it is to collide with the iceberg. This means we need to listen to opinions even when we don't like their provenance.

Invariably, the process of questioning is about how things join up at the bigger level. The questioning process starts with the silent dialogue that comes in contemplation. It is not easy to do this when faced with the cacophony of the overload. Yes, paradoxically, withdrawing from all the noise actually helps us achieve a greater understanding of it by contextualizing. The torrent of new information washes around our knowledge structures and many report the phenomenon of having learnt one thing only to have forgotten another. Our understanding of the world is limited if we try to make sense of it day by day. The overload thus has profound effects on our thinking. By swamping us with information, it's removing the time and opportunity for asking questions, and this is the leader's most important job.[13]

It's difficult to escape an unpleasant conclusion here. Information may at once be enhancing our understanding while diminishing our presence and capabilities. It can help leaders understand, but it can also undermine their curiosity and prevent them from being effective leaders.

How this changes the leader's mandate

Leaders have got to their position by making data their friend. In the same way, golfers get to a basic level of proficiency by trying hard. There comes a point, though, in all golfers' path of progression when they need to stop trying and relax. They need to use another approach.

The same is true of leaders. Yes, data are important to get you to a certain level, but after that, there's no point waterboarding yourself with data. You need to work out whom to talk to and whom to listen to. Yes, leadership is about conversation, not just communication. The former allows you to negotiate and resolve problems. The latter is just data.

What is true for the individual is also true of organizations that exist at a nexus of information. Managing communications has not only become a profession with many people who are responsible within an organization, it's also become a large part of the leader's role. Even at the very basic level, the increased transparency challenges the leader's mandate and responsibility. The wider access to information encourages participation and democracy from shareholders, community members and voters. No wonder business leaders are behaving more like politicians. Like politicians, however, no business leader can provide a running commentary or consultation on every decision to everyone all the time.

So how much do they tell you and when? This is a constant problem of judgement of which issues to engage with and when. Sometimes, leaders choose to hide behind the waterfall of news, with the most dangerous times being when the flow dries up during holiday periods.

Never was this truer than in the world of politics, where some leaders have become so frustrated by threading their messages through the media that they decide to go direct. The best example of this is President Trump. In this case, Twitter has created an unfiltered and direct channel where everyone can hear the President talking in his own words – for good and bad.

Speaking with immediacy subjects the source to the inverse relationship between speed and truth (see Figure 1.1). If the input source of the data is faulty, then so will the output be, too.

Social media can also be dangerous in this respect when giving access to leadership. Let's call this the 'Wizard of Oz' syndrome where the perception of the leader varies inversely with the access granted. Familiarity can breed contempt.

Spotting the signs of a waterboarded leader

The physical effects of overload are easy to spot. Leaders find it hard to concentrate. They're easily distracted. They answer all e-mails all the time and pride themselves on fast turnaround. They vacillate and often request yet more information. They come to conclusions astonishingly quickly. They fail to converse and pick up anecdotes. Sometimes, this is accompanied by a display of supreme self-confidence. Ignorance can be very reassuring.

> **QUICK TIP** Leaders should create 'no zones' of up to 45 minutes where they cannot be interrupted. This requires discipline, but it also pays dividends.

What are the leadership safeguards against a narrowing parenthesis brought about by overconfidence or over-reliance on analysis? First is to be able to recognize that logic and plans are very convincing, but as Marshal Suvarov said: 'No plan survives contact with the enemy.' Perhaps Professor Ian McGilchrist best sums up the power of the analytical mind[14] this way: 'the left hemisphere's talk is very convincing because it shaved off everything that it doesn't find fits with its model and cut it out. This model is entirely self-consistent largely because it's made itself so. The right hemisphere (the imagination) doesn't have a voice and it can't make these arguments.'

In other words, we need to keep imagination and doubt alive in the boardroom. Most leaders do not attain office by displaying doubt. It's usually the opposite. The doubting Thomas tends not to thrive. This is why the role of non-executive directors, even in privately held companies, is essential. Their job is to ask questions, not confirm assumptions. This ability to question constructively is an important and subtle skill.

College-educated people are taught to question and critique often in a direct, sometimes brutal way. But questions needn't be so. Questions are a way of transmitting a concern or raising an issue without making a statement. 'Are you concerned about?' is not the same as 'You should be concerned about'. The implication, though, is subtly different.

In Ian Leslie's book, he points out that 'The future belongs to people who are curious'.[15] This is an important point. Questions such as 'Why are we doing this in such a conventional way?' or 'What happens if this doesn't go according to plan?' need to be asked. Perhaps the biggest point he makes is that the smarter the internet gets, the dumber we become. We don't need to know how to add up when we have a calculator. We don't need to know facts when we have the internet. The smarter the search engine, the dumber the questions are allowed to be. Leaders need to ask intelligent questions.

Leslie describes this time as: 'Rather than a great dumbing-down, it's likely we are at the beginning of a cognitive polarization – a division into the curious and the incurious. People who are inclined to set off on intellectual adventures will have more opportunities to do so than ever before in human history; people who merely seek quick answers to someone else's questions will fall out of the habit of asking their own or never ask them in the first place.'

There's an important point here. The presence in volume of a commodity, eg data, is in no way a reflection of its likelihood to be used. Anything present in abundance is likely to have diminished values. This applies as much to data as it does to opinions.

So, at once, information can provide greater visibility and hence caution, but also the complete opposite. The more dependent on analytical data we become, the more convinced we are that the numbers alone are enough. Doubt is banished and we become 'data driven'.

Conclusions

Since the turn of the century, we've seen a massive increase in information overload. This is having both good and bad effects, some of which are unforeseen and some are paradoxical. The data overload forces us to filter towards information we see as important or relevant. This means we hear a lot more about bad things and less about good. It also creates a binary approach as we summarize at speed to decide whether something is good or bad, relevant or not. This is changing behaviour, not always in a good way. The longer-term, more qualitative information is often missed, for two main reasons. The interruptions force us to move faster, thus prioritizing only what we need right now. It also forces us to an analytical mind set because when we are constantly interrupted we operate in 'compare, contrast, analyse' mode. This is the left-brain process which focuses on the short-term, quantitative and narrow goals. This narrowed focus means we can miss vital information which may be at the parenthesis of the framework. This can lead to overconfidence in the numbers and logic alone and an unshakeable belief in 'rightness' or a complete absence of doubt. This increases risk and marginalizes long-term qualitative thinking and ultimately diversity in leadership. This is because leadership becomes less qualitative and less focused on intangibles such as long-term community interests, gender, ethnicity and so on.

The implication is that of course information can be useful and a great boon for efficiency. Unfortunately, it also comes with side effects which have a negative impact on behaviour.

The overwhelming amount of information leads to overload which narrows our attention into more analytical, short-term, tangible thinking at the expense of longer-term, softer, less measurable qualities. We may not be immediately aware of this, but over time the change is becoming clear.

Endnotes

1 Lewis, C (2016) *Too Fast to Think: How to reclaim your creativity in a hyper-connected work culture*, Kogan Page, London

2 https://quoteinvestigator.com/2014/05/22/solve

3 http://www.radicati.com/wp/wp-content/uploads/2014/01/Email-Statistics-Report-2014-2018-Executive-Summary.pdf

4 http://www.radicati.com/wp/wp-content/uploads/2014/01/Email-Statistics-Report-2014-2018-Executive-Summary.pdf

5 http://fortune.com/2012/10/08/stop-checking-your-email-now

6 https://www.inc.com/john-brandon/science-says-this-is-the-reason-millennials-check-their-phones-150-times-per-day.html

7 http://www.businessinsider.com/the-messaging-app-report-2015-11

8 https://www.twilio.com/learn/commerce-communications/how-consumers-use-messaging

9 http://www.dailymail.co.uk/news/article-2092432/MailOnline-worlds-number-Daily-Mail-biggest-newspaper-website-45-348-million-unique-users.html

10 https://manyworldstheory.com/2012/11/26/einsteins-imagination-is-more-important-than-knowledge

11 Samples, B (1976) *The Metaphoric Mind: A celebration of creative consciousness*, Addison Wesley Longman, Reading, MA

12 Leslie, I (2015) *Curious: The desire to know and why your future depends on it*, Basic Books, New York

13 https://hbr.org/2017/01/being-a-strategic-leader-is-about-asking-the-right-questions

14 https://www.ted.com/talks/iain_mcgilchrist_the_divided_brain

15 Leslie, I (2015) *Curious: The desire to know and why your future depends on it*, Basic Books, New York

CHAPTER TWO

Understanding a New Type of Economics

Internationalism and Insularity

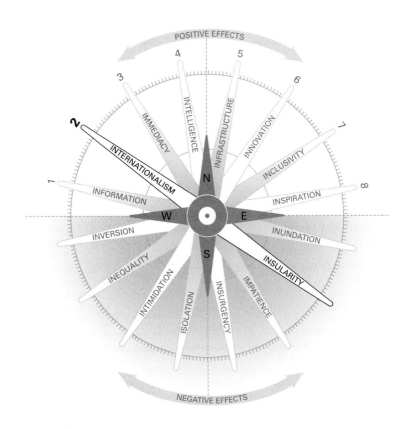

This chapter will help leaders strengthen their awareness of the world economy as it *actually* is, not as it was, or as one hopes it might be. This is vital if employees, customers and even regulators are to trust them. Leaders who rely on out-of-date notions about the world economy are not only unlikely to inspire confidence, they're also a danger to investors and employees alike.

The barrier to situational fluency is the ephemeral distraction. Often, we're too busy dealing with the waves to see the tide, which is why we must find time for situational fluency – it's the leader's job to know where they are and where they're going. Leaders are often too busy with their everyday business to notice the changes on the macroeconomic horizon. They may fall back on commonly accepted fallacies such as 'all the manufacturing jobs are moving to China' or 'interest rate hikes cause stock markets to fall'. Like all of us, leaders are products of their past and under pressure revert to past behaviours.

This 'avoidance of regression' also applies to leaders' thinking. They achieve success on their logic and drill-down ability. After that, they need a wider view to get the full context. For example, in theory, more connected global markets can make economies more efficient. In actuality, the increased trade links may create internationalism, which itself is the provenance of insularity as a backlash.

Too many leaders missed the so-called unpredictable events driven by populism such as the election of Donald Trump, the decision to Brexit, the result of the last General Election and so on. They missed the rise of social media and still hesitate to empower their teams to manoeuvre freely in that space.

> **QUICK TIP** Data are not the only truth. Leaders need to walk the floor and talk to as many sources as possible. Communication and data are not enough. Conversations and opinions matter. Trust the mood, not just the maths. Leaders can pick this up by using social media as a listening tool.

The macroeconomic landscape is especially important for leaders because they need to understand into the future. They may work in organizations that are insular, but without an understanding of the world economy they will make mistakes, which are remembered, amplified and scrutinized more than ever. It's OK to make mistakes. Everyone does, but too many mistakes create doubt, delay and damage.

Leaders trade on experience. They should also deal in hope.[1] It's what defines them. The past, though, is not a comprehensive guide to the future. For instance, many leaders grew up in a post-Berlin Wall world. That brings certain assumptions that may not still be valid. It's always hard for any leader to recognize that much of what they know may no longer apply. The first task of enlightened leadership is, therefore, cultivated doubt. Opinionated certainty is the hallmark of mediocrity.

Of course, data still matter, but increasingly so does imagination, too. We live in a world economy where the data and the facts seem increasingly to contradict each other. For instance, we may think people are broadly better off after years of income growth. These data, viewed in isolation, don't tell us the whole story if, for instance, inflation is running above income growth. People may believe the world economy is not serving them even as it has lifted more people out of poverty than at any other time in history. Leaders need to constantly re-examine assumptions and distinguish between what the data indicate and how people actually feel. In a similar way, government says there is no inflation but people see rents, healthcare costs and the general cost of living all rising. This creates suspicion and cynicism. It undermines confidence.

Stop trying to predict the future and start preparing for it instead.

The nature of data is also changing. Countries, companies and communities currently rely on paper forms to find out how the economy is doing. That will increasingly be replaced by automated data collected from sensors. In the future, it will be uploaded into blockchain structures that are both immutable and independently verified, giving a high degree of confidence about the authenticity and reliability of the data. More about this later. Real-time sensors may reveal what the public already know – that governments and companies have not always been as honest or transparent as had been assumed. In other words, the freshness and accuracy of data will bring more questions about conduct.

How can leaders better manage a fast-changing macro-economic environment? The LAB's answer is that they should stop trying to predict the future and start preparing for it instead. There's a difference between predicting and preparing. The former anticipates one outcome. The latter, however, plans for a range of outcomes. The traditional rational left-brain approach encourages leaders (and commentators) to engage in linear thinking and in predictions. The world, however, isn't linear; it's more likely to be cyclical, as William Strauss and Neil Howe pointed out in *The Fourth Turning*.[2] This summer is more similar to last summer, as a season, than it is to spring, the season that preceded it.

In this chapter then, we'll analyse data but also look at perceptions and feelings. We'll discuss new ideas and destroy a few myths. This is what we will cover:

- Fear stalks the economic landscape
- Fear has no respect for data
- Offshore revelations
- Avoiders and evaders
- The wrong sort of data
- So don't tell me there's no inflation
- How inflation is hidden
- Hedonics
- The topography of inflation
- Meet the cause of inflation – debt, debt and more debt
- Bad leadership hides bad news
- Nothing new under the sun
- In office, but not in power

- Is the internet deflationary or inflationary?
- Time to get nerdy
- The ultimate solution to Inflation – smash it up
- Cryptocurrencies
- A booming stock market
- It's the same the whole world over/It's the poor what gets the blame/It's the rich what gets the pleasure/Ain't it all a bloomin' shame?[3]
- Living in the present, but destroying the future
- Leadership implications of these economic changes
- Conclusions

Fear stalks the economic landscape

The persistent feature of the economic landscape is that it keeps changing. It is the one thing leaders can count on, but some leaders don't see change because they don't look for it. Perhaps there are good reasons. As the US writer of social protest novels, Upton Sinclair, pointed out, the problem with change is that: 'It is difficult to get a man to understand something, when his salary depends on his not understanding it.'[4] Schumpeter called the process of economic change 'creative destruction'.[5] He assumed change would destroy some businesses and some jobs but it would also create new ones. Today, people are not so sure. Now we fear robotics, automation, new start-up competitors and more. We fear because the old ways are not working well, but the new ways are hard to understand. People wonder why everyone is so angry. It's partly because everyone is so frightened.

When confronted by unexpected change, fear drives people towards one side of the Kythera – the side that involves insularity, nationalism and protectionism. Leaders have other options, though. They can, instead, understand the fear, face it down and inspire people towards the more positive side where we find internationalism, greater communication and trade. This is how they deal in hope. It's hard, though, for leaders to inspire or guide if their understanding of the economic landscape is out of date. They may end up as surprised as everyone else.

Fear has no respect for data

So, what is the truth about the world economy? There is a palpable sense that some people feel the world economy is not delivering the desired outcome. Income inequality has been rising and the middle classes everywhere are squeezed by rising costs. Many no longer believe that they will become rich before they get old. In the industrialized world, the record levels of debt contribute to a sense of foreboding, guilt and fear, as everyone waits for a reckoning. It was said the debt would kill growth.[6] The projections, however, have been proved consistently wrong. Yet we find that almost the entire world is growing better now than it has in years. The world economy has lifted more people out of poverty during the past 30 years than at any time in human history. That's true globally, but not in the West, where people remain afraid that automation, robotics and artificial intelligence will leave them unemployed and unemployable. The culmination of 100 years of relentless automation, however, is near-record high levels employment. Interest hikes have made stock markets rise, not fall, so far. The paradoxes of heart and head contribute to uncertainty. This weakens confidence and trust in the global economic system and in the leaders who are running it. Irrational fear and fact live comfortably side by side.

Offshore revelations

For this reason, leaders must not only understand the economy better, they also need to understand how people feel. For instance, in the aftermath of the financial crisis, the public and leaders alike were shocked to discover the size of the offshore financial market. Prior to this, people had not even registered that there was a shadow banking system. Then, later, with the release of the Panama Papers and revelations about The Appleby Affair,[7] experts and the public alike began to realize that the onshore financial system was a fraction of the size of the offshore system (which is $21–32 trillion).

The public don't understand the banking system, but it's become clear to them that neither do the regulators and experts. Either they don't know it as well as they should or, more likely, they just turn a blind eye. Writing in the *Financial Times*, Gillian Tett explained the rationale in 'The Copernican Revolution'.[8] She described the sudden realization that the financial universe is not as aligned as the public had thought: 'They no longer know their bank manager personally. An algorithm decides everything now. They feel the financial system is unfairly rigged against them globally and locally, too.'

Avoiders and evaders

This is exacerbated by the realization that tax policy does not treat all participants equally. They see public services cut, while, somehow, big firms and wealthy people take advantage of loopholes in the tax system. The wealthy deposit their monies abroad while small businesses and the poor bear the brunt of higher taxation and compliance costs. Of course, it's all perfectly legal. It's a grand joke in taxation circles that tax avoidance is legal, whereas tax evasion isn't. Such is the depth of accounting humour. Gaming the tax laws and the regulations may be perfectly legal, but it is resented because taxes, regulations and the law always weigh most heavily on those who are least capable of carrying them. Such policies feel unfair and untrustworthy. Even so, big businesses and the wealthy feel unfairly persecuted, while small businesses and the poor feel unfairly burdened.

The offshore community complains that it's too expensive to build the economy of tomorrow if they come back onshore. Onshore resents offshore and vice versa.

> **QUICK TIP** The higher leaders rise, the more they need to understand the perception that somehow the system is rigged. Transparency does not, of itself, ensure trust, but it at least lessens the perception of unfairness.

The wrong sort of data

The revelations about the offshore economy illustrate an obvious truth. Governments are insular and national. The economy is international and global. Data about the economy are domestic but transaction flows are international. Policies in one country can affect economies abroad. International trends may overwhelm national policy. Surely, we have enough data to know what's what? We are getting better at gathering data and analysing them every day, as we will see in Chapter 6 on technology, yet there remains a problem. Turning to nationalism as a credible response to these sorts of international problems illustrates perfectly that political leadership is seldom, if ever, about logic.

Twentieth-century leaders think in terms of data points. A modern leader needs to appreciate that data are more like a wave. The level of inflation, for example, might be described as, say, 2.3 per cent, but that's an average across the entire economy. The wealthy may not feel any inflation at all. The poor may feel a very small amount of inflation because it hits them disproportionately hard. The Consumer Price Index (CPI) can be, say, below 2 per cent, but people may be finding it impossible to cover their rent. In other words, it is not as useful anymore to describe the economy with static data points. It is more useful to think about the waves rolling through it. These hit some harder and sooner and others less or later. Economists are happy to drill down into prices, but not to consider the wave of pain that price changes cause.

Consider the price of prescription drugs. The overall inflation rate in the United States in 2017 was 2.2 per cent[9] yet the price of a 100 mg tablet of Viagra jumped by 39 per cent. The price of morphine rose by 93 per cent in 2017, when the cost went from $30 for a 25-pack of vials to $58. Another pain killer, Chantix, jumped by 29 per cent in 2017.[10] Telling people that their inflation rate is only 2.2 per cent insults their intelligence and undermines their trust. The overall cost of healthcare is also rising. Evercore ISI estimates that the average US family spends some $4,000 per year on healthcare.[11] This is expected to rise by 25 per cent in 2018 to $5,000. The problem is so severe that both President Obama and President Trump have made it a central political campaign issue, albeit from opposite perspectives. Three of the United States' most respected business leaders, Warren Buffet, Jeff Bezos of Amazon and Jamie Dimon of JP Morgan, have jointly announced their intention to introduce a new healthcare system to lower the cost for their collective 500,000 employees.[12] This is not a purely US phenomenon. The National Health Service in the United Kingdom is under constant price pressure. Increasingly, citizens are being asked to pay a bigger portion of the public budget on healthcare costs or to pay more for specific treatments.

So don't tell me there's no inflation

Housing costs are also rising. Rents across the United States are at a historic high of almost 29.1 per cent of income.[13] In New York City, rents have risen 75 per cent since 2000.[14] Nationwide, rents have risen by 2.4 per cent in 2017. But hikes in some cities are much greater. In 2017, rent in Portland, Oregon was up by 4.6 per cent, in San Diego 5.5 per cent, in Las Vegas 6.3 per cent and even in Odessa, Texas by 33 per cent.[15] The Pew Research Center reported in July 2017 that more US households are renting than at any time in the past 50 years.[16] In addition, 79 million US adults are sharing their living space to save on costs because millennial children cannot afford to rent or buy.[17]

Rents and property prices have been rising all over the world. In Beijing, one study estimated that property prices rose by 1,538 per cent from 2004 to 2016. Housing costs across China, but especially in the big cities, have risen enough to compel Xi Jinping, China's leader, to take on the problem at the highest level: 'Houses are built to be inhabited, not for speculation. China will accelerate establishing a system with supply from multiple parties, affordability from different channels and make rental housing as important as home purchasing',[18] he said. Elsewhere in the world, it is hard to name a city that has not experienced significant rent increases in recent years. Rent in Sydney was up by 6.5 per cent in 2017. London may be falling slightly but it was still the most expensive city for rent in Europe for three years.[19]

Groceries and food prices are also important. The UN Food and Agriculture Organization says that food prices rose by 8.2 per cent in 2017.[20] The price of every kind of food but sugar went up. Taken together, one can see why people are suspicious of the traditional data. Leaders must be suspicious too, for many reasons.

QUICK TIP Leaders should develop tools that measure the economic impacts on their teams, clients and constituents and not simply rely on or parrot government statistics. Confidence matters more than calculation.

How inflation is hidden

An open-eyed, open-minded leader looks for qualitative insights as well as quantitative data. Qualitative changes are perceptible but too often dismissed. For example, we have seen a clear rise in something called 'shrinkflation'. A basket of products is measured for inflation by price, not by volume or weight. If the products shrink in size but the price stays the same, technically no price hike has occurred. But people aren't stupid, they know what that means. You can see this in everything from the reduced amount of cereal in a box to smaller-sized chocolate bars. You can see it in the form of ever-larger apertures in toothpaste tubes[21] and powders of various sorts. The purpose of these changes is to make the consumer use up the product faster and to pay more per weight. Toilet paper and paper towel rolls have ever-larger tube centres and ever-fewer sheets,[22] while the price remains the same.

There are fewer potato crisps in the bag and cookies in the box. Bottles of liquids such as perfumes have ever-larger dimples on the bottom that displace the product and create the illusion of more inside than there is. Shrinkflation is not restricted to retail products. Apartments are shrinking, too. Micro apartments are smaller than anything we lived in before but cost more per square foot.

An open-eyed, open-minded leader looks for qualitative insights as well as quantitative data.

Shrinkflation is a signal that tells us that companies are facing higher costs. It is a signal that price pressures are starting to build. Attentive leaders cannot ignore these trends because they affect their followers. They must show they care about the quality of life. The data may say there is no inflation but your followers may be having a terrible time paying their rent.

Hedonics

Leaders should be aware of the methods used to calculate prices because the quantity of inflation is not the same as the quality. Central banks are the most trusted sources of information on inflation and deflation. They have long used hedonic methodology to adjust prices for quality changes. In practice, this means they tend to show that prices are falling. Each year the new Apple computer typically has vastly more computing power than before. This means that the quality has increased even though the price has not risen. Central bankers count this as a price decline. Car prices are similar. You get many more features in your car now for the same old price. Some people might prefer an Apple computer with less power at a lower price, but that is not on offer. They might prefer a car that has fewer features and a lower sticker price, but that is not on offer either. In these ways, inflation is hidden and built in. The buyers know this but are helpless to change it. Hedonics creates the image of a deflationary world while consumers still experience inflationary forces.

The topography of inflation

Inflation and deflation are unevenly distributed in the world economy. The rich don't feel inflation because their wealth protects them from it. Economists (often not quite living in the real world) say that people can buy cheaper food if prices rise. If steak goes up, they can swap it for, say, tofu. The problem arises when the price of protein rises so much that the poor are forced into cheaper calories. This almost always means emptier calories. Inflation can push the poor into malnutrition or no nutrition at a time when the price pressure itself is not universally acknowledged. The economy touches a leader's followers in many ways. Junior staff may be feeling inflation due to their rising rentals in big cities at the moment that senior staff are enjoying the mortgage relief from record low interest rates. One employee is working hard just to stay in the city and in the job despite having lost all hope of ever owning a home. Another employee in the same firm now owns a home outright and uses the proceeds from the rising stock market to decrease mortgage costs and to take more expensive vacations. Astute, alert leaders will not care just about the data points the economy sends them. They will also care about the quality of life they are providing. Good leaders feel for the ways in which the economy impacts their followers.

Meet the cause of inflation – debt, debt and more debt

There's no two ways around it – debt destroys the social fabric and breaks the promises that hold us together. Debt is what causes governments to institute lower levels of social services and higher levels of tax. Debt burdens typically force governments to raise the retirement age and the cost of transportation, and to reduce public services in healthcare and schools. In this way, debt breaks the promises leaders make.

Global debt is now three times the level of global GDP. The debt stood at 318 per cent of global GDP or some $233 trillion as of the third quarter of 2017.[23] The horrifying facts are constantly repeated in the press and by international organizations. The IMF says that China's debt levels ballooned to 234 per cent of GDP in 2016.[24] Local government debt continues to expand at what appears to be an unsustainable pace. In 2017, the increase doubled on the previous year.[25] Forty-six per cent of US workers are so indebted that they don't have $500 in savings to cover an emergency.[26] A study by the Royal Society of Arts echoed this and showed that around 70 per cent of British workers are chronically broke, with some 32 per cent having less than £500 in savings.[27] Being in debt and being broke give rise to anger. More and more the public turn this anger on leaders in the form of populism.

Forty-six per cent of US workers are so indebted that they don't have $500 in savings to cover an emergency.

The debt problem is overwhelming most major economies in the world, from Japan to almost all European nations. The debt burden encompasses both public and private sectors, although

FIGURE 2.1 General government debt (2015) – total debt as a percentage of GDP

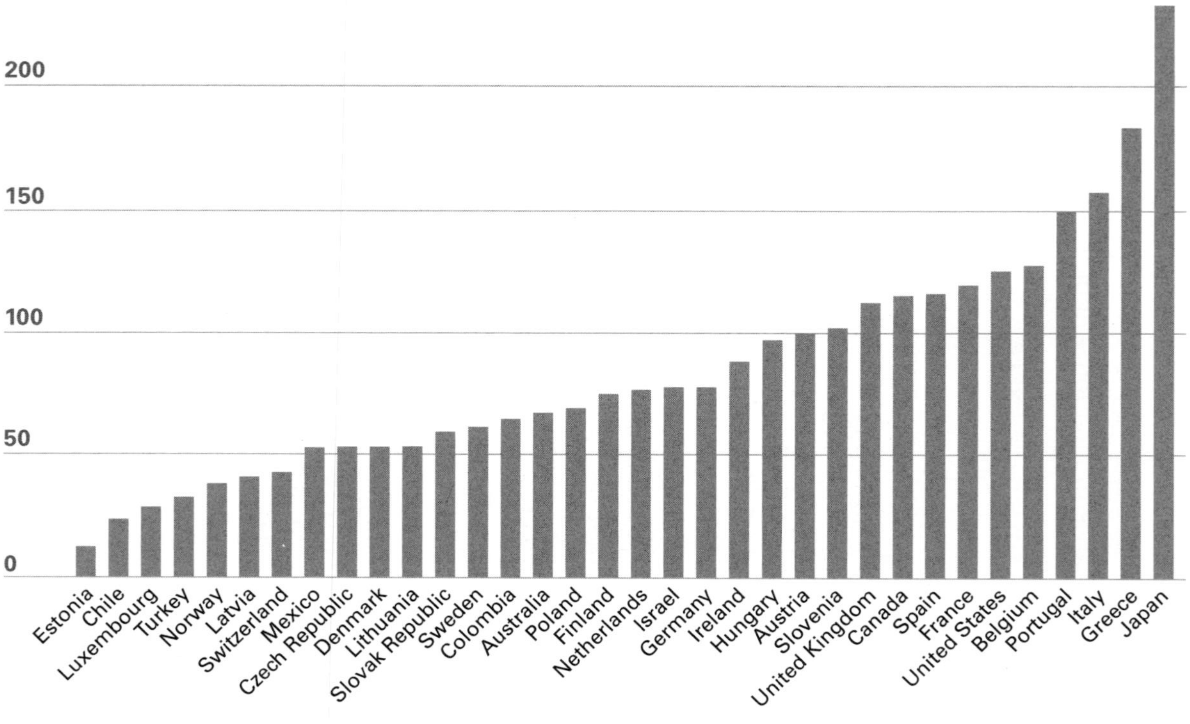

Source: OECD (2018) General government debt (indicator), doi: 10.1787 /a0528cc2-en (accessed 5 February 2018)

the former dwarves the latter because governments were forced to buy private sector banking assets to bail them out. There are some who think the debt does not matter. Others think governments are spending far beyond their means. Figure 2.1 shows a chart of government debt as a percentage of GDP, which is the usual measure of government indebtedness.

Bad leadership hides bad news

How on earth have our leaders allowed such a situation to occur? Well, because we incentivized them to do it. First, our political systems, especially democracies, do not incentivize their leaders for the long term. What is the point of making difficult decisions that will benefit another incumbent in the next term? Second, if politicians impose austerity to balance the books, they become unpopular and are voted out. The political moral of the story sounds the clarion call of Chapter 8 – embrace the paradox – only vote for politicians who are prepared and principled enough to be unpopular.

Consider how US debt is expected to jump in 2018 according to the US Treasury.[28] In Figure 2.2 we see a chart that reflects the US Treasury's expectations for 2018. They have assessed the current trajectory of spending and extrapolated the probable outcome as we see in the figure.

This is, of course, specific to the United States, but everywhere debt is the defining characteristic of our times. Why? Some say debt is always wrong, but to the leader it can be wrong while also being right. There's efficient and inefficient debt.[29] If interest rates are lower than profit levels percentage-wise, then debt is efficient. Where profitability is lower than interest rates, it's inefficient. In theory, in the former case, the more leverage, the more profit. The same can be said of national economies where GDP is growing ahead of interest rates. This only really applies in times when interest rates have been at record low levels. This

FIGURE 2.2 US national debt – $617 billion spike in five months

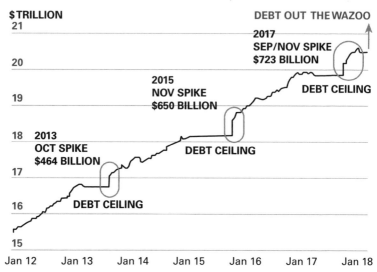

Source: US Treasury, Wolf Street, wolfstreet.com/2018/01/30/us-national-debt-will-jump-by-617-billion-in-5-months

is why some say borrowing at record low interest rates makes no sense if you already have a debt problem, while others say that it is crazy to not borrow more when interest rates are so low. Can you solve a debt problem by taking on more debt? Economists deeply disagree on this.

The problem with debt is that it's easy to get into and hard to get out of. This is especially true of governments with an essentially short-term view, ie to the next election. At the national economic level, there are several known methods for dealing with debt. Let's look at a few.

First, a nation can say it will never pay it back. This is called an Argentine-style default. No-one will ever lend to you again after this, unless it's at silly-stupid rates. Second, they can say the nation will pay it back, but later and less. This is called a haircut, and Greece has defaulted on much of its national debt this way. It pushes the payments further into the future, which means the original bondholders are defaulted upon. Third, nations can pursue austerity. This means the state will deliver less to their voters and/or tax them more. Fourth, the economy could simply grow its way out of debt. This is possible. It's what happened during the Industrial Revolution, but it is very hard to do.

Last, politicians can announce that they will permit higher inflation. This erodes debt. It is an implicit and surreptitious tax. This option means the lenders get their money back, but it's worth less than before. And now for the big one! We can abandon the entire system of money, currency and accounting altogether and introduce a new one. More about this possibility later in the chapter.

Nothing new under the sun

Creative thinkers always come with one simple conceit. They believe there's genuinely such a thing as a brand-new idea – there isn't. There's just the history they don't yet know. All ideas have been done before, but the context is often fresh.

This is not the first time countries have been in debt. For instance, the United States dealt with the accumulated debts from the American Revolution by inflating the value of the Colonial currency by printing ever more notes, which were known as the 'Continentals'.[30] So many were issued that all confidence in their value was lost. They became worthless, which led to the saying 'Not worth a Continental'. This happened again during the Civil War. The war debts disappeared when the United States effectively defaulted when inflation reached more than 5,000 per cent. Similarly, many investors believe the United States defaulted on the debts it accumulated in the 1960s. The cost of the war in Vietnam and the cost of the Great Society Program exceeded the capacity to repay. Figure 2.3 shows the various periods where the United States escaped a debt problem by inflating the currency.

FIGURE 2.3 US inflation from 1775 to 2015 – annual percentage change in overall US consumer-price index

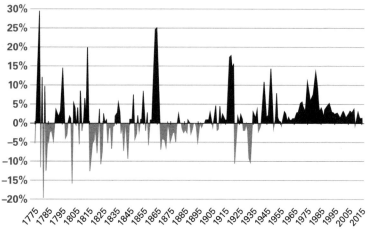

Source: Zumbrun, J (2015) A brief history of US inflation since 1775, *The Wall Street Journal*, 14 December, reprinted with permission of *The Wall Street Journal*, Copyright © (2015) Dow Jones & Company, Inc. All Rights Reserved Worldwide. License number 4282560442295

What's clear from the above is that the United States has embraced inflation much more than deflation and specifically around periods of debt burden, eg immediately post-war. When this happens the international lenders lose money. They may get paid back the say $100 they lent, but that same $100 buys far less once inflation is accounted for. Naturally, investors are nervous that the United States may choose this path again. Some would argue that it already has. After all, the solution to the financial crisis was simply to pursue inflationary policies, which would raise asset prices. This is exactly what happened. Following the United States' lead, governments around the world injected some $24 trillion into the world economy, most of which remains in place. Never in human history have so many nations injected so much capital, so consistently, for so long. According to *A History of Interest Rates* by Sidney Homer and Richard Sylla, interest rates post the financial crisis dropped to the lowest levels recorded since the Holy Roman Empire (Figure 2.4).[31]

The purpose was specifically to raise the inflation rate, in a bid to prevent further asset deflation from occurring. It has

FIGURE 2.4 Short- and long-term interest rates

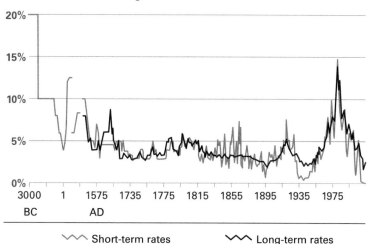

── Short-term rates   ── Long-term rates

Note: the intervals on the x-axis change through time up to 1715. From 1715 onwards, the intervals are every 20 years. Prior to the 18th century, the rates reflect the country with the lowest rate reported for each type of credit: 3000 BC to 6th century BC – Babylonian empire; 6th century BC to 2nd century BC – Greece; 2nd century BC to 5th century AD – Roman Empire; 6th century BC to 10th century AD – Byzantium (legal limit); 12th century AD to 13th century AD – Netherlands; 13th century AD to 16th century AD – Italian states. From the 18th century, the interest rates are of an annual frequency and reflect those of the most dominant money market: 1694 to 1918 this is assumed to be the United Kingdom; from 1919 to 2015 this is assumed to be the United States. Rates used are as follows: Short rates: 1694–1717 – Bank of England Discount rate; 1717–1823 rate on 6-month East India bonds; 1824–1919 rate on 3-month prime or first-class bills; 1919–1996 rate on 4–6-month prime US commercial paper; 1997–2014 rate on 3-month AA US commercial paper to non-financials. Long rates: 1702–1919, rate on long-term government UK annuities and consols; 1919–1953, yield on long-term US government bond yields; 1954–2014, yield on 10-year US treasuries
Source: Homer, S and Sylla, R (1991) *A history of interest rates*, Wiley; Heim, C and Mirowski, P (1987) Interest rates and crowding-out during Britain's industrial revolution, *Journal of Economic History*, 47, pp 117–39; Weiller, K and Mirowski, P (1990) Rates of interest in 18th century England, *Explorations in Economic History*, 27 (1); Hills, S, Thomas, R and Dimsdale, N (2010) The UK recession in context – what do three centuries of data tell us?, *Bank of England Quarterly Bulletin*, Q4; Bank of England, Historical Statistics of the United States Millennial Edition (https://hsus.cambridge.org/HSUSWeb/HSUSEntryServlet), and Federal Reserve Economic Database (https://fred.stlouisfed.or).

worked in the sense that asset prices have risen. Inflation has occurred in everything from property to paintings. Stock markets in the United States, Britain, all of Europe and across many parts of the world are at record highs in early 2018. The CPI data across most economies is now rising as well, albeit slowly and from a low base. In 2018, we now see inflation rising in the United States, the United Kingdom, the EU, Japan, China and elsewhere, but as we've established, it comes cleverly disguised.

In office, but not in power

Central bankers scoff at the notion that we might repeat severe inflationary episodes, especially considering the record debt burden. Some take the view that we should be lucky to get a bit more inflation. Others argue it may be the only way to escape the debt burden. Today's central bankers also have a high degree of confidence, even hubris, on this subject. They genuinely believe that they can control the temperature dial of inflation through interest rates. Dial it up and inflation drops, and vice versa. But what if they are reading the wrong dial? The problem is a lack of joined-up thinking. They only consider their policy tools and their areas of interest. They do not consider other contributing forces. Let's look at all the inflationary items that are not controlled by central bankers:

- Increased defence spending (which is a new wave of capital, just like quantitative easing)
- The Chinese investment in the Belt Road Initiative
- Rising wages in China
- New cryptocurrencies such as Bitcoin.

These are offset by some deflationary issues, which are also beyond their control, including:

- Falling energy costs
- Internet competition
- Debt (private and public sector)
- Countries holding US dollars in order to keep their currency competitive.

We know central bankers are more afraid of deflation than inflation. They prefer taking more risks with inflation to offset the risk of deflation. This means raising interest rates slowly and in small steps, while warning the markets well in advance. At best, the small and occasional rate hikes are a means of gently normalizing interest rates back to more typical levels. The markets tend to rise on such hikes because they confirm that economies are stronger.

Will such hikes save us from higher inflation? It is worth considering the opinion of Paul Volcker, Chairman of the Federal Reserve from 1979 to 1987. He slew the inflation dragon during that period by raising interest rates to 21 per cent – harsh medicine indeed. In May 2013 he told the Economic Club of New York: 'All experience amply demonstrates that inflation, when deliberately started, is hard to control and reverse.'[32] Today's central bankers seem to think Mr Volcker and his views are irrelevant.

The problem with their thinking is that things have changed since 2008. First, workers in China, and other emerging markets, are no longer willing to work for ever less pay. They have been demanding steadily higher wages, not lower ones. Asian workers are enjoying the highest wage increases anywhere in the world now.[33] According to Forbes, some Chinese wages now exceed European wages.[34] Today the only major emerging market that undercuts China on wages is Mexico. Its wages are 20 to 40 per cent lower than China and their quality control is US standard.

Manufacturers in emerging markets, other than Mexico, are increasingly moving their operations back to the West. In

September 2017, even Foxconn, the second-largest employer in China, announced its intention to build a manufacturing facility in Wisconsin.[35] When Wisconsin beats Shenzhen, something important is happening. The loss of competitiveness in low-value goods is forcing China to move up the ladder into products that can far better sustain long-term economic growth. It explains why they are keen to make higher-value products such as superfast trains and the railways associated with them, as well as small nuclear plants. On top of this, China is also investing $3 trillion+ in its Belt Road Initiative – another major injection of capital into the world's economy.

Is the internet deflationary or inflationary?

Most economists are very certain that the internet is deflationary. It encourages competition, and that brings prices down. It makes supply chains more efficient and makes it easier to find the lowest prices. It is obvious to them that the internet is deflationary because it increases productivity. The advent of the internet has also coincided with several other deflationary events and forces that may mask the underlying deflationary pressures.

For example, when Paul Volcker committed to higher interest rates in 1982, the shock slowed inflation. Then, in 1989, the Soviet Union ceased to exist and the Berlin Wall fell. This was a hugely deflationary event because workers from emerging markets began to systematically push down wages and prices. Shortly after this, the Cold War ended. This was an added deflationary force because defence spending was cut, the reverse multiplier effect kicked in. All that capital could now be redeployed from weapons spending into more productive uses.

Furthermore, the big expansion of the internet happened with the introduction of the iPhone in 2007. A 2016 headline from *Forbes* magazine declared: 'How the Internet Economy Killed Inflation'.[36] It's easy to see why people think inflation is over after such a long string of deflationary shocks. Also, it's now been over 10 years since governments added all that stimulus to the world economy. Many might say it simply didn't work. It may have staved off the possibility of another Great Depression but it has not unleashed inflation. So, there is little to worry about, right? Yet, in 2018, the Cambridge Analytica scandal revealed that Facebook makes its money from selling data. People were outraged. Mark Zuckerberg's response was simple. If we cannot make money on advertising, then we have to charge you to use Facebook. He was suggesting a potential price hike from zero to something. Remember that Facebook is a virtual monopoly. That's the internet showing it can be inflationary too. The point is that we find it very easy to assume that the internet is always a deflationary force, even though, sometimes, it might not be.

Time to get nerdy

But what do our economists really know? We know they missed most of the big events in the economy. We might also wonder whether they've measured the economy correctly. We know they use mainly historic data. We know they were wrong about the financial crisis, Brexit, the slowdown in China and many election results. So, here's a question. What if the internet increases the volume of money, its velocity and the number of transactions?

Economists use an equation, which is at the heart of quantitative easing and crude monetarism (known as the quantity theory of money), as follows:

$$MV = PT$$

Where,

M is the quantity of money in the system

V is the velocity that money flows around the economy

P is the level of prices

T is the number of transactions

You don't need to be an economist to work out that the internet is potentially inflationary in just about every way. This is because the volume of money (M) and prices (P) are both multiples of the speed of money (V) and the volume of transactions (T).

At a time when the internet is structurally changing the global economy, what have national governments been doing? They have been buying their own bonds. They have been spending on defence. This also has the effect of raising M, so if V was fixed, it would push up P or T or both.

QUICK TIP In economic terms, leaders should see the internet as transformational, not merely transactional. It's not just an infrastructure, it's also a way of multiplying money supplies through crowdfunding, mobile phone payments and internet currencies, for example.

The problem is that throughout history, it's been difficult to measure the volume and velocity of money. It used to be measured in savings and cheque accounts. Then, the measure included credit cards. Today, crowdfunding, mobile phone payment systems and cryptocurrencies are widely used but not included. Central bankers try to keep up by widening the definition of the volume of money. M1 was called narrow money and included notes and coins in circulation and bank deposits. Then we had M2 and M3, which added in longer-dated deposits and money market funds. The US Federal Reserve Bank stopped measuring M3 in 2006 because it was such a useless measure of reality. Today, the volume of money keeps expanding into entirely new and difficult-to-measure forms. So, now we tend to refer to MZM, which broadly means everything except what can't be measured. There's quite a lot of this, including all the forms of money that technology is creating.

We talked in Chapter 1 about a lack of joined-up thinking. Monetary policy, then, when viewed in isolation away from geopolitics and technical change, can be seen as an example of the worst type of narrow, analytical, reductionist thinking.

The ultimate solution to inflation – smash it up

Governments can, of course, hope the economy just grows its way out of the debt problem. This is what happened at the start of the Industrial Revolution. After decades of Napoleonic warfare, Britain had racked up debts that seemed entirely insurmountable. The government took a decision to radically change the system of money to stimulate the economy and erode the debt with inflation.

That system was based on tally sticks, which hardly anybody remembers now. These were wooden boards made of willow, pine or hazel, roughly cracked in half so that the two sides would perfectly and uniquely match. The matching grain in the wood served as a reliable watermark. Then every asset sale and purchase, tax payment and loan was recorded on both sides of the wooden ledger. The smaller and narrower side always went to the borrower and led to our phrase 'getting the short end of the stick'. The longer stick, or stock, always went to the lender, hence the terms 'stockholder' and 'stock market'. Holes in the boards indicated your worth. A palm-sized hole equalled £1,000. A thumb-sized hole equalled £100. We get the phrase to 'tally something up' from these sticks. They decommissioned the system in 1783 to introduce a new innovation – paper money. Why paper? Because it permitted inflation to help erode the war debts. Nobody trusted bits of paper, though. So, people kept making and using the sticks. By 1834, the government was frustrated, made the whole system illegal and confiscated the sticks. They were brought to parliament where they were burnt on the night of 16 October 1834. Unfortunately, it was one of those occasions where the event and metaphor fused. The fire got out of hand. Parliament burnt down. J M W Turner captured the event in his painting *The Burning of Parliament*. Shortly after that, the Industrial Revolution took hold and Britain grew its way out of the debt.

Cryptocurrencies

This is exactly what many governments are hoping to do today. We already know the name of the new system of money, called electronic money. The new system of accounting is already known as 'blockchain'. The combination of the two new technologies is set to radically transform the economy, just as in the early 1800s. Already central bankers are warning about the lack of control inherent in such cryptocurrencies. This may be because they are the ones who wish to issue and control them.[37]

There are now well over 1,000 new cryptocurrencies on the internet. By any measure, the creation of new money outside of the measured monetary base is inflationary. But e-money alone does not fix the debt problem. You need to move to blockchain for that. It is an entirely new ledger in which every single transaction is automatically recorded. In short, e-money and blockchain are the death knell of the black economy. Governments will be able to tax transactions at the exact moment they occur. While this will improve every government's finances positively and permanently, it may also punish those at the bottom all over again.

The internet is clearly changing the value of money. In the past, the value of money was tied to gold. That's because governments agreed that there should be some sort of proportional relationship between the volume of money and the value of gold they held in their reserves. The United States ended that policy in 1971 and many others followed. Ever since, the volume of money has been a function of the judgements made by economists at the Federal Reserve and other central banks. Naturally this has challenged the trust required for the public to place their faith in what are known as 'fiat' currencies such as the US dollar, the euro, sterling and so on. These are currencies declared to be legal tender, but not backed by a physical commodity. The value of fiat money is derived from the relationship between supply and demand rather than the value of the material that the money is made of. The fact that most governments have spent more than they have earned and now face record debt problems further undermines that faith and confidence. This increases the interest in shifting to the non-fiat e-money the internet facilitates.

A booming stock market

In addition to the stimulus of quantitative easing (QE), we now have the increased defence expenditure, the presidential tax cuts and the Belt Road Initiative (BRI). China is investing trillions of dollars into global infrastructure with the BRI, but that injection of capital is not necessarily picked up by traditional monetary aggregate measures. No one is adding up all the new BRI spending from Kazakhstan to Nicargua. In addition, Chinese wages are now consistently rising. Where once China was exporting deflation, it's now exporting inflation.

The internet has broken down national borders to create a global financial ecosystem, but insular national governments still measure the economy at national boundaries. Consequently, in 2018, inflation is materializing and everyone is looking for safe haven. Investors are being pulled into stock markets as inflation and innovation pick up. Small interest rate hikes confirm that growth is real. Inflation, even at low levels, compels investors to get out of cash. Inflation erodes the value of cash. It makes investors disinclined to buy more bonds because inflation hurts bonds.

We know that the US and other central banks are not especially worried about rising inflation. The leaders at the Federal

Reserve have intimated that we have been below the average inflation target for so long now that we should go above it for a while.

Meanwhile, we know that more money and faster money usually enable more leverage. In other words, more people can borrow against their collateral or take bets that are disproportionate to their actual capital. Could the internet be facilitating more leverage, more transactions and, therefore, more inflation?

What about underfunded pensions in a world where populations are ageing? Surely that is deflationary? Charles Goodhart, a greatly respected British economist, wrote a paper in which he argued that ageing populations may actually prove to be inflationary.[38] After all, there will be fewer young people around, so they will naturally want to raise the price of their labour. Also, older people are re-entering the work force at a record rate. This is giving them more disposable income and causing them to spend more of that disposable income. Maybe an ageing population is inflationary, not deflationary?

It's the same the whole world over/It's the poor what gets the blame/It's the rich what gets the pleasure/Ain't it all a bloomin' shame?[39]

Billy Bennett's music-hall ditty from 1930 could have been written for these times. The biggest issue of all remains debt. Everyone everywhere feels the problem. At the national and international levels, policymakers have encouraged consumption and penalized saving. That has been the purpose of record low interest rates. No-one can be surprised that the level of personal debt has risen. Personal debt is approaching all-time highs. This is worrying given rising interest rates and inflation. It doesn't take much imagination to see this is unsustainable. Neither are the consequences of personal economic failure difficult to see. Consumption has been encouraged by facilitating both consumer

FIGURE 2.5 Household debt (2015) – total debt as a percentage of net disposable income

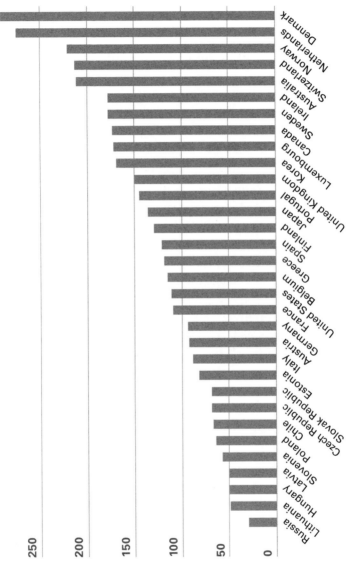

Source: OECD (2018) Household debt (indicator), doi: 10.1787/f03b6469-en (accessed 5 February 2018)

credit and spending. In Figure 2.5, we see the astronomic levels of personal debt, which echo those of the governments we saw earlier.

Living in the present, but destroying the future

Has there been wilful collusion by commercial, political and economic leadership in the process of indebting the poor? It would be too complex for an outright conspiracy, but it's difficult to conclude that this eventuality wasn't at least foreseen as an option by such intelligent leaders. Surely they knew that the purpose of their policies was to induce inflation. The process of impoverishing those least able to compete is hardly a new one. This time, though, it's different in terms of scale and location. It involves the Western democracies. This is the stuff of which political revolutions are made.

Not content to damage the present by unleashing a bit of inflation, leadership has arguably also conspired to destroy pensions and state retirement programmes. These are almost universally underfunded. This problem is slowly revealing itself. US pension funds in cities such as Dallas and Los Angeles are slowly admitting that they cannot make good on the promise of retirement because they are so woefully underfunded. Strikingly, this is occurring while stock markets hit record high valuations when you'd expect it to be easiest to meet performance and funding targets.

Pensioners globally are beginning to ask how and why their savings have evaporated. In some cases, low interest rates were the culprit. In others, it could be mismanagement or even theft. In the United Kingdom, we've seen examples of large firms where a new majority owner could strip all the cash out even when the pension fund suffered a shortfall. Business moguls are now being vilified for doing this. Witness Sir Philip Green, the founder of Topshop and owner of BHS, who was investigated for paying himself some £400 million (via his wife who is domiciled in Monaco, an offshore tax haven) while leaving the pension fund of BHS underfunded by between £70 million and £570 million at various points.[40]

All this brings forth demands that governments protect the public from the offshore banking system, from the greed of shareholders, from the tax consequences. Leaders may have yet to realize that pacifying their workforce is the least of their problems. Pacifying those who used to work for them may prove more intractable.

In addition, everyone in the financial world knows that pension funds everywhere are claiming that they are achieving performance that is vastly beyond reality. Why? Because the interest rate environment cannot achieve what pension funds need to meet current cash pay-outs. Pensions are claiming to achieve some 8.5 per cent returns in a world where equity and bond prices are high and not rising very much. They assure us that the returns will be there in 5–10 years. But can we trust this?

Perhaps this, then, is the triumph of Western Reductionism in its ultimate incarnation. We've perfected the art of financial analysis but forgotten to do the basics. Join the dots. Look after the elderly, the infirm and the poor. Live within our means.

It's fair to say that faith, trust and belief in economic leaders are at a historically low ebb. The cynicism and breakdown in trust have reached epidemic levels. The data about the economy and the story of the individual are two very different things. Leaders pay too much attention to the quantifiable, which leaves them vulnerable to the things that affect the quality of life of their followers.

How can they feel that deflation is certain even when the risks of inflation are becoming more apparent, even in the data? Could this be yet another surprise that will leave leaders blindsided and obvious? Perhaps engaging in scenarios about inflation and deflation would strengthen the ability to face an unknown future? Preparedness might be a better option than prediction.

Leadership implications of these economic changes

Leaders in the 21st century need to know not just where they are, but how their teams feel. They need to make sure they are navigating from the right spot and in the right way. This means more study. It means more listening. It means they must appreciate that the performance of the economy, as expressed by numbers, and the story about the economy, as expressed by feelings, may not match up. The perception and the reality may have profoundly diverged both in the mind of the leader and in the minds of their stakeholders. In response to such rapid economic change, it's easy but dangerous to fall back on old notions of what reality looks and feels like.

The paradoxes here are striking. Debt drives us apart even as the internet glues us together. Inflation pushes prices up, even as we expect the internet to drive them down. Data tell us one thing and people tell us another. We look at historic national data even when the internet has created a global economy. Perhaps the hardest aspect to make sense of is that the world is becoming more interconnected and more insular at the same time. It's another of the internet-driven paradoxes.

We try to address the pain but perhaps the world economy is already fixing many things all by itself? We engage in greater defence spending at the very moment that interconnectedness is producing ever more GDP. Many cry for nationalist solutions at the moment that globalization is redistributing wealth and power to many who have not had it before.

Conclusions

Leaders need to understand the forces that buffet people. Falling back on yesterday's truths about the world economy will quickly expose their lack of understanding. It's the classic Western

Reductionist mistake again. Historic data are linear but history is rarely linear at all.

This perception reality gap is the challenge leaders face when it comes to the world economy. Globalization is set to persist in the longer term, but it is occurring in new ways. The United States and Mexico are now able to compete against established emerging markets. China is entering the world stage as producer of global brands and high-end manufactured goods. The story of the world economy we like to fall back on no longer matches the story that is unfolding.

We cannot separate the economic from the behavioural, cultural, political or technical. We know that after 9/11, the political response was to cut worldwide rates of interest to zero and everyone was expected to borrow and spend. This created a huge credit boom which caused the banks and building societies to collapse under a mountain of bad debt. The political response to 2008 was to lower interest rates, in some cases to zero. Savers and citizens were punished while debtors and risk takers were rewarded. The big institutions got bailed out and the small citizens were left with the bill. There's a word that ordinary people had for the financial crisis response. Many called it 'nuts'. The shortfall in expert economic leadership was all too obvious. The leaders who pursued these policies say it would have been 'nuts' not to. The problem is that few saw these crises coming despite the indicators being there. Massive banks with brands were destroyed because of overconfidence that nothing could go wrong. Everything was logical, linear and just elegantly extrapolated into a fantasy future.

Let's suppose for a second that it is *all* nuts. Literally, it is nonsensical behaviour. Even nonsensical behaviour can be managed if there is confidence that somehow, nuts though it is, it still works. Confidence, though, isn't a conclusion. It's a feeling. It's an emotion lurking among all the data, the indicators, the analysis and the logic. This is one reason why leaders need to deal in feelings as well as facts. They need to assess confidence. They need to assess the confidence in them.

If worldwide economies were growing more strongly, the massive debt and historic technological changes would be less of a problem. From the United States to Europe to China, all the indicators are clear. The world economy *is* growing again. The world economy is picking up, at least so far. So, what leaders need to do is help guide people into the future by envisaging it, explaining it and understanding how people feel. It may be a more unstable world, but that brings opportunities that wise leaders can pursue. In part, they must dive deeper into technology. This is what underpins innovation and economic growth, and creates many of the problems, as we'll see.

Endnotes

1   https://www.forbes.com/quotes/6957
2   Strauss, W and Howe, N (1997) *The Fourth Turning: An American prophecy – what the cycles of history tell us about America's next rendezvous with destiny*, Broadway Books, New York
3   http://lyricsplayground.com/alpha/songs/s/shewaspoorbutshewashonest.html
4   Sinclair, U (1935) *I, Candidate for Governor: And how I got licked*, repr. University of California Press, 1994, p 109
5   https://www.wired.com/2002/03/schumpeter
6   http://www.businessinsider.com/henry-blodget-our-debt-will-kill-us-2009-10?IR=T
7   https://www.nytimes.com/2017/11/05/world/paradise-papers.html
8   https://www.ft.com/content/168c88f6-01c7-11e6-ac98-3c15a1aa2e62
9   https://tradingeconomics.com/united-states/inflation-cpi
10 https://www.ft.com/content/21dabb8e-f0d5-11e7-b220-857e26d1aca4
11 https://www.cnbc.com/2018/01/30/chart-of-surging-us-health-care-costs-explains-why-buffett-getting-involved.html
12 http://money.cnn.com/2018/01/30/news/companies/amazon-berkshire-jpmorgan-health-insurance/index.html
13 https://www.forbes.com/sites/joelkotkin/2017/10/19/rising-rents-us-housing-crisis/#502d293c1ef5
14 http://www.nydailynews.com/new-york/nyc-rents-soar-incomes-decline-article-1.1765445

15 https://www.cnbc.com/2018/01/19/how-rent-in-cities-like-new-york-and-san-francisco-changed-in-2017.html

16 http://www.pewresearch.org/fact-tank/2017/07/19/more-u-s-households-are-renting-than-at-any-point-in-50-years

17 http://www.pewresearch.org/fact-tank/2018/01/31/more-adults-now-share-their-living-space-driven-in-part-by-parents-living-with-their-adult-children/

18 https://www.bloomberg.com/news/articles/2017-10-18/xi-renews-call-housing-should-be-for-living-in-not-speculation

19 https://www.standard.co.uk/news/london/london-is-most-expensive-city-for-renting-in-europe-for-third-year-in-a-row-a3741731.html

20 https://www.globalagriculture.org/whats-new/news/en/32979.html

21 https://seekingalpha.com/article/125866-thinking-small-to-gain-big

22 http://www.latimes.com/business/la-fi-laz-shrinking-toilet-paper-20150121-story.html

23 https://www.iif.com/publication/global-debt-monitor/global-debt-monitor-january-2018

24 https://www.theguardian.com/business/2016/jun/16/chinas-debt-is-250-of-gdp-and-could-be-fatal-says-government-expert

25 https://www.theguardian.com/business/2017/aug/15/imf-warns-china-debt-slowdown-financial-crisis

26 https://www.cbsnews.com/news/most-americans-cant-afford-a-500-emergency-expense

27 https://www.msn.com/en-gb/money/personalfinance/seven-in-10-uk-workers-are-chronically-broke-study-finds/ar-AAv9tH3?li=AA54rU&;sa=U&;ved=0ahUKEwjWq-Ta-u3RAhWBwLwKHdTgDBIQFgiXATAW&%252525253Busg=AFQjCNGtalDGc78eftzTQy-u3Pbx5pqueg

28 https://seekingalpha.com/article/4141548-u-s-national-debt-will-jump-617-billion-5-months

29 https://www.wealthenhancement.com/blog/understanding-the-differences-between-efficient-and-inefficient-debt

30 https://allthingsliberty.com/2015/02/how-was-the-revolutionary-war-paid-for

31 http://www.businessinsider.com/chart-5000-years-of-interest-rates-history-2016-6

32 https://ftalphaville.ft.com/2013/08/06/1593422/guest-post-dual-mandate-right-goals-wrong-agency

33 https://www.kornferry.com/press/korn-ferry-2018-salary-forecast-smaller-real-wage-increases-across-most-parts-of-the-world

34 https://www.forbes.com/sites/kenrapoza/2017/08/16/china-wage-levels-equal-to-or-surpass-parts-of-europe/#5f4a34d53e7f

35 https://www.washingtonpost.com/news/fact-checker/wp/2017/09/08/president-trumps-repeated-claim-of-credit-for-foxconns-deal-in-wisconsin/?utm_term=.4351788c7c1e

36 https://www.forbes.com/sites/greatspeculations/2016/09/28/how-the-internet-economy-killed-inflation/#3f680489788b

37 http://www.bbc.co.uk/news/business-43254537

38 https://www.bloomberg.com/news/articles/2017-08-08/aging-populations-set-to-spur-higher-interest-rates-says-study

39 http://lyricsplayground.com/alpha/songs/s/shewaspoorbutshewashonest.html

40 https://www.ft.com/content/2b219156-0287-3419-b309-06d5bb3a4f6f

CHAPTER THREE

Understanding a New
Type of Behaviour

Immediacy and Impatience

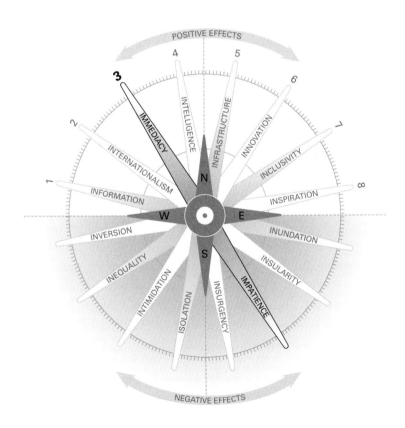

So far, we have looked at how information can overload leaders and create significant behavioural changes. Similarly, the internet is accelerating transactions and more cross-border trade, creating unparalleled opportunities. It may also be expanding the speed and volume of the money supply. At the same time, this internationalization is being countered by a rising tide of nationalism connected to economic inequality, overconsumption, migration and debt.

In this chapter, we'll explore further paradoxical behaviour changes caused by what seem, on the face of it at least, great technology efficiencies. These are, however, being partially offset by rising levels of negative behaviour.

We speed date. Eat fast food. Use the self-checkout lines in grocery stores. Try the 'one weekend' diet and pay extra for overnight shipping. We honk when the light turns green. Thrive on quarterly earnings reports. Speak in half-sentences. Talk in emojis and TLAs (three-letter acronyms). We tweet stories in 140 characters or fewer. We cut corners, take shortcuts. We txt and start things we don't fin...

We prefer to abandon, rather than wait. We often abandon reading what we want to read if it is not available at that moment. We are forgetting that we are part of the environment, and not the other way around.

The internet's primary feature is to link people and their devices. It is used for e-mail, research, downloading files, discussion groups, interactive games, education and self-improvement, friendship and dating, electronic newspapers and magazines, job-hunting and shopping.[1] In almost every instance these tasks were more expensive, difficult and slower than before the internet. Ostensibly, this change is a good thing, but in so doing we've lost something. The efficiency and speed created an expectation that everything else should now be as quick and easy.

The internet has contributed to an 'I want it now' web-driven impatience. We will see how this change has forced other changes and how impatience is percolating up to change expectations.

Web-fed impatience can be tracked all the way through its beneficial effects of efficiency and real-time information up to the erosion of trust and confidence at the strategic level.

Impatience is the reason many will never hear the ideas in this and other books. It is the reason why many long-term strategic goals will pass unrealized. It's the reason many careers and long-term relationships will fail. It is the reason why adults and children do not reach their potential. It is the primary reason that ignorance prevails. As Churchill put it: 'Men occasionally stumble over the truth, but most of them pick themselves up and hurry off as if nothing ever happened.'[2]

This is what we will cover:

- I want it now!
- How we have become Amazonified
- The consistent rise in disposable incomes
- Patience is not one virtue, but three
- Patience is a key factor in efficiency
- Impatience and stress
- Can patience be learnt?
- Impatience and relationships
- The effect on politics, leadership and trust
- The impatience of change, even just the perception of change
- Impatience *is* the source of division
- Conclusions

I want it now!

Patience has been one of the great unnoticed casualties of the 21st century so far. At a time when technology efficiencies are creating more leisure time and more income, we're also seeing a paradoxical effect. As we learnt in Chapter 1, an influx of communications is filling up the time-savings with overload. Now we feel busier than ever before, as we cram more into our lives. Impatience is defined as an irritation with anything that causes delay or a restless desire for change and excitement. The internet allows us to go so much faster and now we expect it of everything.

Well, who cares if we all want things to happen faster? It's hardly a new trend. In Figure 3.1, even before the internet, job tenure has been falling, especially for older men.

Between the ages of 25 and 44, the average tenure is between three and seven years. If we take the mid-point as five years, then we can say the average staff turnover is 20 per cent per annum. Workplace relationships are shortening. This might be because employees are not as loyal to employers or vice versa.

FIGURE 3.1 Male prime-age (25–64) workers' median tenure trends, by age (1951–2012)

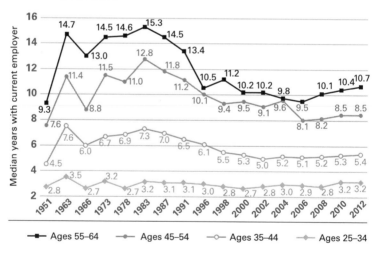

Source: Data (for 1951, 1963, 1966, 1973 and 1978) from the *Monthly Labor Review* (September 1952, October 1963, January 1967, December 1974 and December 1979) and from press releases (for 1983, 1987, 1991, 1996, 1998, 2000, 2002, 2004, 2006, 2008, 2010, and 2012) from the US Department for Labor, Bureau of Labor Statistics

FIGURE 3.2 The share of Americans living without a partner has increased, especially among young adults

ALL ADULTS   <35 YEARS   35–54   55–64   65+

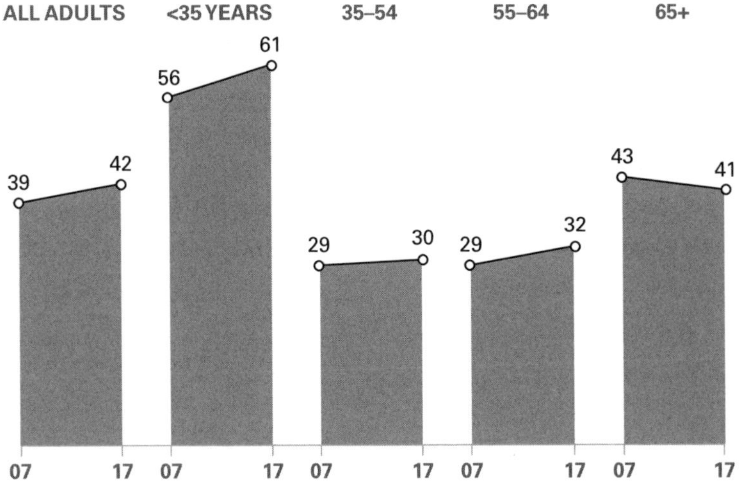

Note: Unpartnered adults are those without a spouse/partner present.
Source: Pew Research Center Analysis of 2007 and 2017 Current Population Survey, Annual Social and Economic Supplement (IPUMS), http://www.pewresearch.org/fact-tank/2017/10/11/the-share-of-americans-living-without-a-partner-has-increased-especially-among-young-adults

The same, though, is true for the share of people living in 'unpartnered' relationships. Figure 3.2 shows the rise of those in the United States, split into age group, over a 10-year period from 2007 to 2017. It is the graph of an atomizing society with more fluid and shorter relationships.

Why does any of this matter? Surely, if we're impatient, then we're 'go-getters' and 'high-flyers'? Certainly, that's the case, but this is a trend that cannot withstand much more linear extrapolation. When employee turnover reaches a certain level, the jobs become 'gigs' with little or no predictability or stability. Of course, this is fine, if you are in your first job, but for those with dependants, stability in all types of relationships is long-term efficient.[3] The standard 30-year US mortgage was designed around the average length of lifetime employment.[4] They were extended in length to allow middle-income earners to own property. The ability to plan and manage to a budget are linear relationships. Communities are built on patience. They look after the sick, elderly and infirm. So, any failure in an efficient short-term private sector relationship results in an inefficient, long-term relationship with the public sector. This creates the illusion of speed and efficiency, but often the actuality is the opposite.

> **QUICK TIP** Leaders should recognize that part of their role is protection of their teams and their communities. Flexibility may be valued by leaders, but it should be balanced with the benefits that stability brings. The latter is more long-term efficient.

The patient educate, feed and contribute to the community. All of these tasks become more expensive and less efficient when done by the state. This is especially true where families are involved. Relationship instability is also bad for business. An employer's staff churn knocks on to its ability to retain business and build relationships. If the average job tenure is five years, then this equates to an annual staff turnover of 20 per cent. Many firms manage only three years, thus are dealing with a churn rate of 33 per cent.

Uncertainty[5] makes it harder for leaders to engage with people. Leaders must work harder to emphasize vision and mission, to clarify expectations and communicate. The inescapable conclusion is that if the internet is destabilizing and undermining employment, then it is also disintermediating leadership itself. The time actually allowed for leadership to engage might become so brief as to undermine its effectivity.

As an aside, the same might even be said of parents trying to get the attention of iPhone-smitten teenagers. Many a parenting moment of insight has been lost due to teenage impatience to see what's new on their iPhone. This generation more than any other has expectations that the offline world should more closely match the online one.

The only group that is living with a partner more frequently are those over 65. Well, who cares whether you live with a partner? This again is a matter of efficiency. People living with partners tend to be healthier, live longer and can afford better accommodation.[6] The more households, the more pressure on house prices.

This trend towards shorter, more rapidly churning internet relationships is clear. Half of British singles have never asked someone out on a date face-to-face. Forty-six per cent of singles had never broken up with someone in person; it was done online or via texting.[7] The internet has therefore facilitated both the forming of new and the ending of old relationships. In this respect, dating apps have performed a similar role to recruitment software.

Uncertainty makes it harder for leaders to engage with people. Leaders must work harder to emphasize their vision and mission, to clarify expectations and communicate.

The majority of online daters also admitted that dating apps have made them more judgemental of people's looks and more likely to choose a partner more quickly.[8] This growing impatience is a trend also recognized by Professor Ramesh Sitarman at the University of Massachusetts in Amherst, who showed that the majority of internet users would, for instance, give up waiting for a video to load after only 10 seconds.[9] The majority of visitors to a website have even less patience. They will leave unless the page loads within only three seconds.[10] Therefore, we know that where choice is involved, people will move on rapidly to another alternative. This increases the number of relationships in total.[11]

> **QUICK TIP** Leaders should be careful to review their online presence, whether it be personal or corporate. If anything takes too long to find, or takes too long to load, it will be discarded.

How we have become 'Amazonified'

The technology change over the past 15 years has been only one contributory factor. And it doesn't just encompass the iPhone. On 4 February 2004, Mark Zuckerberg launched Facebook and it now has 1.7 billion users. On 15 October 2009, Amazon announced same-day delivery in the United States. Last year, the company developed $6.4 billion sales.[12] On 12 September 2012, a little-known app called Tinder was launched. At March 2018, it had made over 20 billion matches.[13]

Now you can get all your banking online. No-one waits for photography. You can get most government services online. You are connected everywhere – travelling, in the bathroom, in bed, in school, even at the top of Mount Everest. You can see anyone and anywhere in the world via Skype, FaceTime, Zoom and so on. You can monitor security and control the temperature in your home remotely. You can use WebMD to diagnose your symptoms online without having to book a doctor's appointment, so why can't all doctors do that?

We mentioned Metcalfe's Law briefly in Chapter 1, but we need to revisit it here to understand that the speed at which we're now moving may well be counter-productive. If we go back 15 years, new office technologies such as e-mail and teleconferencing contributed to a significant boost in productivity. Information flows were accelerated as co-workers collaborated. The knock-on effect on productivity was significant. Productivity thus grew faster during the 1990s and early 2000s than in previous years and then it suddenly stopped growing as fast.[14]

Since 2007 it has stagnated. The iPhone was launched in the same year. Could this be the reason?

If Metcalfe's Law holds good, then the utility and value of a network increase exponentially as the technology reaches its maturity. Two telephones add no value. Everyone having a telephone adds huge value. The problem comes when examining the cost/usage relationships. It's easily understood that usage increases as cost falls. But what happens when the cost falls so far that everyone interacts in real-time?

> **QUICK TIP** Tech is loved by the impatient. It is helpful to a point but it can and does deliver diminishing returns. New tech is not always better, it's just different.

When previously the productivity technology was confined to the workplace, this represented, in Metcalfe's terms, a smaller number of nodes. When the nodes expand to just about everyone and all waking hours, the number of connections expands exponentially. This is what would logically happen if everyone were given an iPhone. Under these circumstances, the productivity then is replaced by paralysis as everyone communicates with everyone, in real-time, all the time. When this is linked to impatience, it becomes a recipe for overload, as we saw in Chapter 1. This is almost certainly why office productivity has declined dramatically since 2007. In Figure 3.3 we can see the consistent acceleration in productivity from 1973 through to 2007, when technology gain began to be offset by Metcalfe's Law and overload. Now, it is no longer certain that more information and more technology will improve productivity.

Companies, though, have continued to invest in new technologies, under the sometimes misguided assumption that productivity would improve automatically. The new systems, however,

FIGURE 3.3 Productivity change in the non-farm business sector (1947–2016)

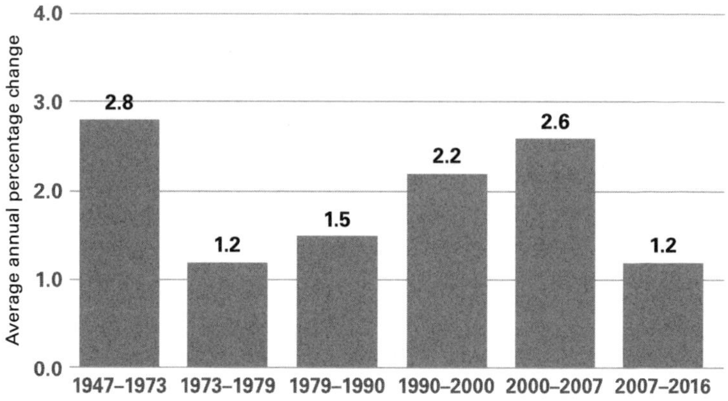

Source: US Bureau of Labor Statistics, https://www.bls.gov/lpc/prodybar.htm

may not be *better* or more productive, they may just be *different*. The technology has become so swamped by other communication technologies that it's starting to have the opposite effect. The net result is that leadership is now dealing with one of the most distracted audiences ever in the history of leadership. Our very capacity to concentrate has become eroded by the constantly declining attention spans. Worse, leaders are competing for attention with the best directors of video and graphic designers, all of whom have the capacity to make the material more stimulating.

Now management communications take longer because we first need to get attention, then maintain it, then check that everyone has the information. On top of this, leadership now has compliance checks to periodically check that the amnesia caused by overload has not expunged the previous information.

Leadership must up its game as far as communications are concerned. It cannot rely on spreadsheet and PowerPoint decks; it must go further to include greater brevity, entertainment, humour, graphics and so on.

QUICK TIP Leaders should never confuse communication with conversation. They should take every opportunity to talk to as wide a group of stakeholders as possible. They should use every opportunity to back up what they say with compelling online graphics and videos.

So, Metcalfe's Law clearly has a dark side: as the cost of communications decreases, the number of interactions increases exponentially, as does the time required to process them. The principle applies to meetings as well. As the cost of video conferencing technology such as *Zoom* decreased, the number of meetings increased. As a consequence, the number of meetings has increased and the number of attendees per meeting has exploded. Now some 15 per cent of an organization's collective time is spent in meetings – a percentage that has increased every year since 2008, according to the *Harvard Business Review*.[15]

When the cost of communication was much greater, more time was invested in careful and thoughtful communication. The quantity of communications has increased but the quality has fallen. The low cost and abundant communication have now passed tipping point and, as we learnt in Chapter 1, have given us overload. Worse still, all the technology has one thing in common. It's faster than what it replaced. Well, of course, this is one of the great positive effects of the internet. You can have everything faster than ever before. There's no need to wait. There's no need for delayed gratification. This creates an expectation not just for applications, but for everything else.

For example, why do we need shops and shop assistants? If the shop is on my laptop and can deliver this afternoon, why do I need shops? This is having a profound impact on urban centres. When Tinder allows you to swipe right for an alternative partner, it creates an expectation that relationships are that easy to dissolve and easy to replace. There are plenty of alternatives. Why should I put up with this partner when I can have another one? This is having a profound effect on the longevity of relationships domestically and in the workplace. When Facebook allows you to *like* something, it hears your view and creates an expectation that maybe all of life should be like that, too. For instance, why can't someone who's so obviously guilty just be convicted right away? Why do we need to give politicians a mandate? Why can't we take all the votes ourselves? Why can't we have direct democracy?

Impatience is changing behaviours and expectations in many areas. Now let's look across to the economic consequences of this level of impatience.

The consistent rise in disposable incomes

In Chapter 1 we saw that the abundance of facts provided by the internet is not necessarily correlated with their uptake. Fantasy is always much more entertaining than fact – hence the arrival of fake news. In much the same way, the greatest period of material wealth improvement ever has coincided with a greater debate on income inequality. This is because it doesn't matter what the average or overall numbers say, there are winners and losers. These groups can also shake out into sub-groups by age, gender, ethnicity, residential area, education and so on.

Consistently rising disposable incomes for the rich have also contributed to the impatience and vice versa both in the UK[16] and the United States.[17] Impatience, overconsumption and debt are thus reflexive relationships.

The speed at which internet commerce operates online means that purchases can be made without consent or hidden, for example Amazon Quick Buy, in-game purchases, roaming data rates, online gambling with fixed odds betting terminals (FOBT), Apple Pay and so on. Sometimes, variable pricing according to demand can increase costs without formal consent. Under these circumstances, we're not choosing what we want to buy at the price we want to buy it. We're being given the illusion of choice and price. We're asked which item we'd like to consume, rather than having the option of not to consume at all. All of this is fed by targeted (and re-targeted) programmatic advertising designed to constantly remind us of missed purchases and reinforce awareness of the novel and the abundance.

Patience is not one virtue, but three

One definition of patience is 'waiting without complaint';[18] to be patient is to endure discomfort in silence. This enfolds three other virtues such as self-control, humility and generosity. Therefore, patience is not necessarily a single virtue, but an amalgam of others, and the lack of it has profound social consequences.

Patience is required in just about every walk of life. Patience is also inherently tied to justice. It takes time for a court to listen to witnesses, consider the facts and ask questions. It takes time to assemble a jury. Media justice is all the swifter but, unfortunately, all the more frequently found to be lacking. For a just decision to be reached, all witnesses need to be consulted, all statements read. The lawyers and solicitors must work together to agree the correct charge. If any conviction is made, then it must be subject to a right of appeal, sometimes at several levels.

Democracy depends on patience. Candidates must campaign. Policies must be drawn up and costed. The electorate needs to hear both sides of the argument. Then, after the election, the representatives must work patiently to draft legislation. Changing statute law is an especially painstaking process. Laws must pass through several consultation stages so that all those who are to be governed by them agree.

Construction requires patient planning of all environmental considerations. It needs to be authorized by all relevant safety representatives. Each trade must be carefully coordinated to ensure they work in sequence. Sometimes engineering projects, in particular, encounter unforeseen difficulties requiring a change of plan.

Teaching requires an understanding that not everyone learns at the same pace or in the same way. There are many different ways of learning and it doesn't stop after school or college. Nursing recognizes that healing is not a straight-line process. There are good days and bad. To employ someone, an employer must have patience to allow a job to be learnt and for mistakes to be made. This is patience as tolerance. There are of course many types of patience. Some leadership tasks can be boring but many of the most important are repetitive and require persistence. This is patience as determination, perhaps one of the greatest – and most underrated – of all leadership skills. Leaders are also subjected to the problems of the whole team in addition to their own. Good leaders learn to subordinate their own problems to those of the team. This is patience as self-sacrifice to put others first.

The human virtues of caring, nurturing, even parenting itself all depend on patience. The very fabric of our society is therefore being undermined by the increased speed of technology, so highly valued and so highly prized by so many. This, of course, is another paradox where what looks to be a gain is merely a short-term improvement at the expense of long-term efficiency.

Patience as a key factor in efficiency

In *Too Fast to Think*, we examined the difference between the illusion and the reality of speed. Moving along a zig-zag line fast may feel quick. You can get to the destination in a straight line, faster. To do this requires patient planning rather than immediate departure for the objectives. Impatience for action, in its crudest form, then represents wasted energy which might be better applied to planning a solution to a problem.

Patience is not only required for carers. It's required for inspiring leadership as well. Demonstrations of patience can be powerful. When a leader reveals a long-term goal, every setback is a way of renewing the determination to achieve the goal. Victory without setbacks is not as inspirational.

In a similar way, when a leader waits in line with their team or even goes to the back of the queue, they demonstrate that all those who are waiting are equally as worthy to get what they wait for. This is patience as democracy. This is patience as manners and a demonstration of self-discipline which shows strong leadership. The best way for a team to identify with a leader is to see them sharing the same difficulties. This demonstrates that the leader is not just aware of their own thoughts and needs, but those of others, too.

Power and patience walk hand in hand. Rushes to judgement and short-term displays of power do not project anything other than weakness. Less is more. Therefore, patience in leadership is important, but it's surprisingly absent in other areas. For instance, among shareholders. Depending on country, some stock markets around the world insist on immediacy and on investees reporting back to investors every 90 days. This is where patience and trust are linked.

QUICK TIP Do not confuse the illusion of speed with the actuality of it. The speed of decisions is usually inversely proportional to the actions implemented.

Impatience and stress

It comes as no surprise that impatience and stress are linked. The remedies for dealing with stress are well developed and include exercise, meditation, yoga, mindfulness and so on. Classes to develop patience, though, are not so well developed, but they might help address how impatience causes so much stress in others. It would seem, however, that the systems that create so much efficiency are also encouraging our expectations that all things should be as quick and easy. We recognize and deal with stress, but seldom address its real cause – our own impatience to cram in as much as the internet will allow, then use any time-savings resulting to cram in even more. We need to stop, create space and then see what happens.

Can patience be learnt?

It's often said that leadership is a natural talent. You either have it or you don't. Patience, though, is at the centre of good, long-term, unifying leadership. Can this be learnt in a business school? Most business schools concentrate on putting leaders under time pressure and then subjecting them to complex problems. This, of course, is perhaps a more realistic situation. Real-world leaders are often required to make decisions under stress, deprived of sleep and often with inadequate information, usually with conflicting priorities.

The first experience of this can be frustrating, isolating and stressful. The first place leaders have to learn patience is with their own performance. This requires perseverance. You can't demonstrate endurance and empathy in others without first applying it to yourself. This is sometimes why failure can be an excellent spur to success. Those with the patience and determination to try again have a better chance of succeeding.

This then highlights one of the dividing lines between a leader and a manager. The latter concentrates on doing things right. The former on doing the right things. This requires courage and personal responsibility to absorb the notion of failure and re-frame it positively. A bitter or resentful approach to failure is the hallmark of incompetent leadership.

In *Strength of Will and How to Develop It*, author E Boyd Barrett offers the following:

- Scatter 50 coins on the floor. Then quietly and slowly pick them up and place them in a pile. The author suggests doing this once per day for several days, increasing the number of coins as you go.
- Take a book of at least 150 pages and turn the pages one by one quietly and slowly, making a pencil mark on each page as you go.
- Beginning with the number one, count out loud slowly and distinctly for 10 minutes.

If this sounds pointless, then you've understood it. This is the same perseverance required for incremental physical improvements such as dieting or exercise. Mental discipline is the parent of patience.

QUICK TIP Patience is an amalgam of being disciplined, considerate, unselfish. It is long-term efficient. It fosters long-term unity and trust. Impatience atomizes teams. It is difficult to respect long-term values with impatience.

The whole point about patience and self-discipline is highlighted by the so-called 'Marshmallow Experiments' done by psychologist Walter Mischel in the early 1960s at Stanford University in California.[19] Mischel gave children the choice between a reward (like a marshmallow, pretzel, or mint) they could eat immediately or a larger reward (two marshmallows) for which they would have to wait alone, for up to 20 minutes. This was a longitudinal study followed up years later which found that children who had waited for the second marshmallow generally fared better in life. For example, studies showed that a child's ability to delay eating the first treat correlated with higher academic scores and a lower body mass index (BMI). Researchers showed that parents of 'high delayers' even reported that they were more competent than 'instant gratifiers', without ever knowing whether their child had gobbled the first marshmallow.

Impatience and relationships

Not all relationships go well from the start. All emotional partners can attest to that. Sometimes it takes time for people to grow together. Could it be that the increased divorce rate and the decline of patience are linked? The presence of alternatives is also a factor. Those who are impatient trigger impatience in others. This is the chain reaction, which seems to be both accepted and accelerating. According to The UK Office of National Statistics, a quarter of children are in single parent families.[20] Every parent of teenagers knows the 'phases' of adolescence can be challenging, which also takes time and forbearance. This is love as an allotrope of patience.

The effect on politics, leadership and trust

Above all, it's impossible to develop trust where there is no patience. Therefore, it may not be the representatives who are at fault but the electors. Could it be that the root cause of the lack of trust is not so much that human nature has changed, but that expectations have been raised beyond the realistic?

In Jean-Jacques Rousseau's 1762 work, *Of the Social Contract*, the idea of the sovereignty of the people and their relationship with political leadership was established. 'Man is born free; and everywhere he is in chains. One thinks himself the master of others and still remains a greater slave than them. How did this change come about? I do not know. What can make it legitimate? That question I think I can answer.' He goes on to discuss the relationship between the leaders (in this case government and monarchy) and the people. Rousseau's work is relevant here because it was echoed by the social media of the time – cheaply printed pamphlets which stirred up hatred for the monarchy planted the seeds for revolution.

The impatience for change, even just the perception of change

Let's look at impatience as the provenance of political change. Whether politicians like it or not, they are civic leaders. The first job of any leader is to protect and serve their followers and their political systems. Brexit and the rise of nationalism both in Europe and the United States are signals that large groups don't feel leaders have done enough to protect them. This applies to their perceptions of fairness, healthcare, education, and law and order. Things haven't changed fast enough in their eyes.

Shortly after the US election in November 2016, *The Guardian*[21] asked a sample of US citizens why they voted for the President. Some said they didn't want the Clinton legacy continued in the White House, citing Bill Clinton's impeachment. Others admired the presidential candidate as a self-made man. Some wanted to change the United States to serve the people instead of a political system that wants to serve itself. 'He tells it how it is' was another reason.

The United States, and the world, was strongly split between those who think the new President is a disaster and those who think he is an unmitigated success. Part of the picture here is that there are now two impatient Americas, both of which want change, but both of which have differing models. One is made up of coastal cities and known to the rest of the world, including New York, Boston, DC, Los Angeles, San Francisco. Some refer to this as the 'Clinton Archipelago'. The other is the wider interior which is less well known to the world, including Wyoming, Utah, Idaho, Kansas, Montana, Alaska, Alabama, Nebraska and North Dakota. This 'Core America' vote won the presidential race, the Senate, the House and most of the Governorships and they intend to turn the country in their direction.

How many leaders think they know the United States just because they spend time in New York City? Travelling is not necessarily understanding. It is too easy to make judgements about a brief experience. Assumptions need challenging in the new world.

Impatience *is* the source of division

The new President will in no way soften his stance and many in core America love this. Therefore, even as the headlines read one thing, his approval ratings with his supporters remain steady. Therefore, it's no use any more talking about the President's popularity or unpopularity. The United States is divided by its impatience with the other tribe. Many people would now have a problem with their offspring marrying outside of their political party.[22]

It's easy to become caught up in the media chorus of opprobrium of President Trump. No doubt, some find his manner alone to be offensive. It may be, though, that there is more of a global anti-establishment movement than is realized. It's easier to pin it all on one man who is easy to dislike than to accept that this wave of populism (or popular impatience) is wider and more global. Part of the campaign message was about voter impatience with Washington. This was manifest specifically as a pledge to return government to the state, rather than Federal, level. His repeated assertions that he wanted to 'drain the swamp' indicated to some that he wanted a smaller government overall.

In a similar way, the wave of sexual harassment allegations that rocked entertainment in Hollywood and politics in

Westminster in 2017 also shows the growing impatience with the judicial system. Many allegations against individuals were made and repeated by media. This resulted in cases of significant reputational damage being done to individuals, despite no convictions being secured.

Conclusions

The very thing we most like about doughnuts is how good they make us feel instantly, right now, in the short term. Maybe that's why the United States is consuming record amounts of them?[23] This is also true of the internet. It feels great to have instant gratification for every whim. Ultimately, both are bad for us because they create an expectation that these short-term pleasures have no long-term consequences.

The immediacy of online environments raises expectations of performance in offline environments such as politics, electoral systems and the judiciary. The ever-increasing levels of impatience are impacting every aspect of human relationships. Consumerism and consumption are driven up as job tenure and average relationship lengths are driven down. Although household incomes are rising, so are the levels of debt as people struggle to keep up by changing jobs. This is causing greater stress and instability which itself impacts upon relationships. This atomizes and multiplies the number of households. This increases more consumption and drives yet more debt and inequality. In sum total, we pay a high price for the immediacy and short-term efficiency we get from technology. In the long term, it creates great inefficiency, inequality, unhappiness and waste. This further erodes trust in both national and international leadership. This, combined with other factors, is resulting in an erosion of traditional politics which is leading to a radically changed world.

The conclusion is that there is a causal link between impatience engendered by the internet and the risk of a breakdown in relationships on a personal, domestic, corporate and political level. The new technologies, if they are applied like their predecessors, will only exacerbate these trends.

Impatience is a hidden killer of potential and is probably the reason that many will never read these words.

Endnotes

1 https://www.edn.com/electronics-news/4351406/Top-10-uses-of-the-Internet
2 http://www.bbcamerica.com/anglophenia/2015/04/50-churchill-quotes
3 http://ftp.iza.org/dp1470.pdf
4 https://bebusinessed.com/history/history-of-mortgages
5 http://westernct.dalecarnegie.com/assets/70/15/Engaging_Employees_During_Times_of_Uncertainty.pdf
6 https://www.theguardian.com/lifeandstyle/2016/apr/17/couples-healthier-wealthier-marriage-good-health-single-survey-research
7 https://www.datingsitesreviews.com/staticpages/index.php?page=Online-Dating-Industry-Facts-Statistics
8 https://www.datingsitesreviews.com/staticpages/index.php?page=Online-Dating-Industry-Facts-Statistics
9 http://digitalmarketingphilippines.com/the-age-of-impatience-interesting-things-you-must-know
10 http://www.bbc.co.uk/news/business-37100091
11 http://www.telegraph.co.uk/news/health/news/7450868/Young-women-have-three-times-as-many-sexual-partners-as-grandmothers-did.html
12 http://www.telegraph.co.uk/technology/2017/06/27/facebook-now-has-2-billion-users-mark-zuckerberg-announces
13 http://www.news.com.au/finance/business/the-real-story-behind-hugely-successful-dating-app-tinder/news-story/81c7d4587ea0d7f6f7aea7e20dcd4027
14 https://www.bls.gov/lpc/prodybar.htm
15 https://hbr.org/2014/05/your-scarcest-resource
16 http://webarchive.nationalarchives.gov.uk/20160107023650/http://www.ons.gov.uk/ons/rel/social-trends-rd/social-trends/social-trends-41/index.html
17 https://fred.stlouisfed.org/series/DSPIC96
18 http://www.christianitytoday.com/biblestudies/articles/spiritualformation/virtue-of-patience.html?start=7
19 https://www.theatlantic.com/health/archive/2014/09/what-the-marshmallow-test-really-teaches-about-self-control/380673

20 https://www.ons.gov.uk/peoplepopulationandcommunity/
    birthsdeathsandmarriages/families/bulletins/familiesandhouseholds/2015-
    01-28#lone-parents
21 https://www.theguardian.com/us-news/2017/oct/26/no-regrets-one-year-after-
    they-voted-for-trump-has-he-delivered
22 https://www.pri.org/stories/2016-02-15/people-don-t-date-across-political-
    party-lines-any-more-why
23 https://www.statista.com/statistics/283198/us-households-consumption-of-
    donuts–doughnuts-trend

CHAPTER FOUR

Understanding a New Philosophy

Intelligence and Insurgency

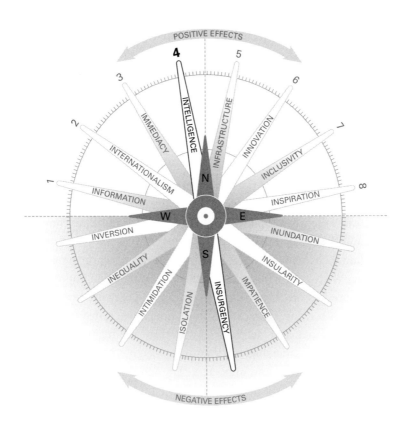

So far, we've seen how even current technologies are driving vast amounts of information and changing behaviour. This has resulted in greater transparency, understanding and enlightenment which has, in turn, driven cooperation, wealth and a better understanding of challenges. As per the pattern we've established, it's had the exact opposite effect as well – the overload can blind us. We've also seen how technology has accelerated economics, causing massive opportunities, and how at the same time it has caused overconsumption, debt and isolationism. We've also seen how the efficiencies brought by 'on demand' internet technologies raise expectations that we should demand the same speed from all other areas of our lives. The death of patience is upon us and with that comes the potential for great ignorance. Learning and listening require patience. When that is lost, experience and knowledge are also undermined and we enter a modern age of educated ignorance. We become fast-forgetters, where yesterday is gone, tomorrow hasn't arrived and all that matters is now.

This plague of ignorance shows itself first as impatience. It that goes unchecked, it becomes anger, the parent of hatred and, eventually, violence. This is the negative consequence of the connectivity we enjoy. The more into the interrupted present we move, the more we're pushed towards greater division and atomization driven by ever more left-brained thinking.

Great leaders cannot understand how to lead unless they first understand these dynamics. This also means investigating and understanding their own right-brain ability. You can never create a team at peace with itself with a leader who's unaware of its importance. People need to feel they belong in the team. There are no psychometric tests for this. How can you measure patience, determination, sense of humour and character? All of these are highly correlated with successful leadership, but they are subjective, irrational and intangible, but nonetheless, important. The acquisition of these skills is more of an indicator of true intelligence than mere intellect.

In the 20th century, the provenance of so much mainstream thinking on physical health and well-being came from the fringe, for example homeopathic medicine, organic foods and environmentalism. In the 21st century, it will be no different in the philosophical and spiritual sphere. Meditation, mindfulness and holistic thinking will enter the boardroom not because it's fashionable or weak-minded, but because it's effective in defending organizational and community culture and values and in mitigating the atomization that we're seeing.

This is what we will cover:

- What is intelligence?
- Intelligence as enlightenment
- The axis of leadership challenge
- Why (the f**k) is everyone so angry?
- How bad is the problem?
- The leadership opportunity
- A new commercial opportunity, too?
- Mainstream media make us angry
- Social media make us angry, too
- Disintermediation
- The leader's critique
- Rule 34
- The case for mindfulness
- Resolving conflict
- Greed is good?
- The ultimate selfishness
- Empathy
- The process of non-doing
- The role of humour
- Creative provenance
- Conclusions

What is intelligence?

There are many definitions of intelligence but most include simply the ability to acquire and apply knowledge. The problem that intelligence faces is the rubric within which it works. Intelligence

FIGURE 4.1 Howard Gardner's eight signs of intelligence

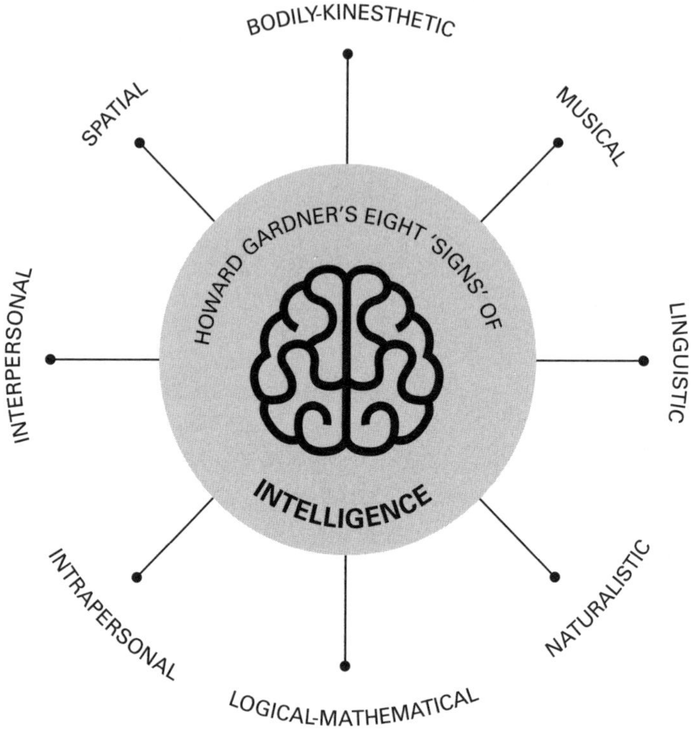

Source: Gardner (2006)[1]

is usually synonymous with Western Reductionist thinking. The evidence of intelligence is codified in exam passes and degree awards but some, like Howard Gardner[2] for instance, have begun to advance alternative theories. He said there were several types of intelligence (Figure 4.1).

As you can see, few if any of these qualities are referenced or codified in the traditional models of primary, secondary and tertiary education. The orthodox emphasis is much more on the logical-mathematical (science) or linguistic-historical (arts) vectors. Bestselling author and educationalist Sir Ken Robinson has also pointed out the limitations of this model and emphasized how educational paradigms are shifting.[3] As he says, it's a world where 'there's a right answer and it's at the back of the book'.

QUICK TIP The leader's job is not to be the most intelligent person in the room. The leader should make everyone else feel as if they're the most intelligent person in the room. So, if you're the most intelligent person in the room, you're in the wrong room!

This is fine so far as it goes, but intelligence is not necessarily required for leadership. Sure, it helps, but leadership is also strongly correlated with many more basic personal skills and qualities, such as determination and tenacity. These are also qualities that increase the likelihood that other skills will be acquired. Sometimes they also dictate whether the over-educated will also become the under-achievers. The problem is that some of these qualities are difficult to spot. Stubborn determination and stupidity are almost indistinguishable.

Intelligence as enlightenment

The educational establishment that currently prevails was created in the model of the Enlightenment. This was a European intellectual movement of the late 17th and 18th centuries that emphasized reason and individualism rather than tradition. This is where Western Reductionism came of age. In the early 21st century a new Enlightenment is under way, which harnesses mindfulness as its intelligence. A lot of what it espouses amounts to balance and self-awareness.

The axis of leadership challenge

One of the great benefits of parenthetic thinking is the ability to spot imbalance. The model shown in Figure 4.2 was evolved for

FIGURE 4.2 Axis of leadership challenge

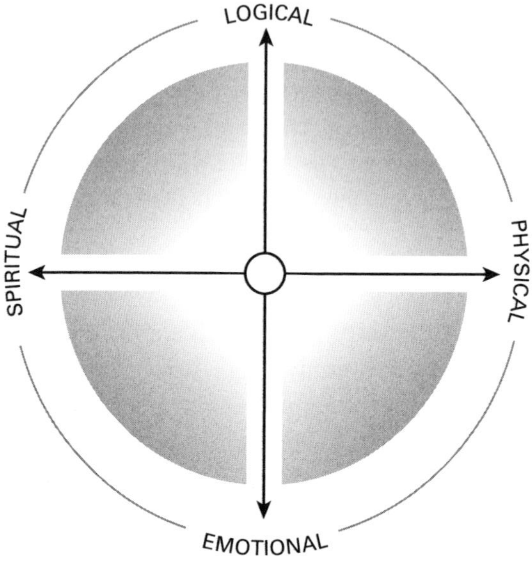

Source: LEWIS Rise Academy

personal balance, but it has useful applications in an organizational sense. The objective is to keep as close to the origin of the axes as possible.

Stress in one quadrant of the model is balanced by full and opposite application on the other. So, for instance, if the organization is going through a period of intensely challenging, long work hours developing a new product with a lot of challenges, this might be placed on the Logical/Physical quadrant. A Spiritual/Emotional balancing item for this challenge might be a social event such as a family day or night out with the team. The loss of a major client might be a Spiritual/Emotional challenge which could be met by a Logical/Physical response, for instance additional intensive training. A logical challenge such as a set of professional exams might be balanced with something emotional, eg time with family or watching a favourite sports team.

This balance model is important in that it recognizes that overemphasis of one area – typically the logical axis – is, of itself, destabilizing to the overall balance. Of course, the world of logic dominates leadership challenges. We live in a world of rules and regulations which also logically delineates spheres of activity and behaviour. Perhaps the rise in emotional reaction is the equal and opposite effect of this?

Why (the f**k) is everyone so angry?

The 20th century killed more people more violently in more countries than any previous century. Whether the 21st century is an angrier place than any other century is therefore debatable. What is clear, though, is that we can hear and see it more than ever. Social media are full of it. We see it in schools with online bullying. We see it at sports stadiums, on airlines and in hospitals. In the UK, physical assaults on NHS staff rose from 67,864 in 2014/15 to 70,555 in 2015/16.[4] We see it in bars and cars. In California, drivers even started to aim their cars at construction workers widening the highway because they were angry about delays.[5] We see it in political debate. The more atomized we become, the more frustrated we become with 'the other'. It is so much easier to be angry and violent towards those with whom we feel we have no connection. Atomization and anger are also reflexive.

QUICK TIP Leaders must make sure their team knows each other. It's easier to be angry with people you don't know. The more of a social unit it is, the more effective it becomes. They should take time to introduce people and get them working together. Ignorance and fear are the real provenance of anger.

What's making people angry could be any one of many things – fear, stress, powerlessness, frustration, pain, exhaustion, trying to get attention or just a bad habit they've got into. Let's not forget also that some people like being angry and will pay money for the pleasure (see New York City's Wrecking Club later). What we do know is that it's getting worse.

How bad is the problem?

The British Association of Anger Management[6] (yes, there is such a thing) says almost a third of people have a friend or family member with trouble controlling their anger. More than one in four people say they worry about how angry they feel. A fifth of people say they have ended relationships when angry. The majority agree that people are getting angrier. Almost half of us regularly lose our temper at work and confess to 'office rage'. A third of all NHS nurses have been attacked at work. The majority of absences from work are caused by stress. A third of British people are not on speaking terms with their neighbours. There were 10,854 air rage[7] incidents reported by airlines worldwide in 2016, up from 9,316 incidents in 2014. The UK has the second-worst road rage in the world after South Africa.[8] More than 80 per cent of drivers say they have been involved in road rage incidents. Twenty-five per cent have committed an act of road rage themselves. Seventy-one per cent of internet users admit to having suffered internet rage. Fifty per cent of us have reacted to computer problems by hitting our PC, hurling parts of it around and or abusing colleagues. More than a third of the UK population are losing sleep from anxiety.[9]

According to an *Esquire/NBC* News Survey published in January 2016, half of all Americans were angrier than they had been the previous year.[10] If we look at this more closely, women report a greater rise in anger than men. The #metoo and

#timesup movements are examples of this trend. Could it also be that women empathize more than men about the treatment of others? To answer, we need to look at what anger represents. It could be the response of someone who has high expectations which have not been met. It could be the behaviour of someone who is stressed. We've already established in Chapter 1 that people are under greater stress. When we interrupt people constantly we prevent them from concentrating on the task in hand. The anger could also be about a set of perceived injustices, such as income inequality, gender unfairness, sexual harassment or racism.

The leadership opportunity

Leaders across the political spectrum are defined by the way they handle anger and conflict. Nelson Mandela,[11] Mahatma Ghandi and Martin Luther King turned non-violent protest into a major part of their campaigns. The latter said: 'Non-violence is a powerful and just weapon. Indeed, it is a weapon unique in history, which cuts without wounding and ennobles the man who wields it.'[12]

Effective leaders can harness anger and use it productively. The worst situation to face is universal apathy.

Effective leaders can harness anger and use it productively. It is a leadership opportunity. The worst situation any leader can ever face is when they are met by universal apathy. When people are angry, at least they are sufficiently emotionally involved to demonstrate their feelings. The leader's job is to make sure this is done productively and positively. If it goes unchecked, anger leads to hatred. It is the leader's job to recognize this and lead people away from hatred either by example or through conversation. The leader must have a narrative of better times. You can't lead with pessimism.

The first thing to realize is that the anger is really nothing new. The scale is now greater because technology has removed the filter. This is where we need to be careful not to confuse communication with conversation. It is harder to have a prolonged angry conversation.

A new commercial opportunity, too?

Believe it or not, the anger phenomenon is now so widespread that it attracts entrepreneurs.[13] In 2017, 1,500 people paid to break crockery, electronics and furniture in two reinforced rooms in a basement in Manhattan called the Wrecking Club.[14] Here, you can buy 30 minutes of mayhem (music is optional) where you can wreck pretty much whatever they have there. It takes 15 minutes to put on all the safety gear. Anyone can take part, from the age of 12.

It's not the first rage-based enterprise. The Anger Room opened in Dallas in 2008 to allow clients to batter effigies of Hillary Clinton and Donald Trump. The Rage Room, which first opened in Toronto in 2015, now has licensees in Budapest, Singapore, Australia and Britain. Anger is becoming big business. Perhaps commercializing anger helps legitimize it?

Mainstream media make us angry

To some extent, the level of anger is a learnt process. The influence of mainstream media has had an effect, says Edward Wasserman, Knight Professor in Journalism Ethics at Washington and Lee University. He says that it sets a bad example. 'Unfortunately, mainstream media have made a fortune teaching people the wrong ways to talk to each other, offering up Jerry Springer, Crossfire, Bill O'Reilly. People understandably conclude rage is the political vernacular, that this is how public ideas are talked about. It isn't.'[15]

Social media make us angry, too

Social media have changed behaviour because they confer the authority to communicate without responsibility and often without identity, too. Wherever people can hide their identity, they can behave irresponsibly and, in many cases, with no fear of punishment. Godwin's Law is an illustration of this. It states that the longer an online argument, the greater the likelihood that one of the participants will liken the other to a Nazi. Funnily, another is the Exclamation Law. This states that the more exclamation marks an online comment has, the more mentally unbalanced the writer is. More internet rules later.

The propensity to shout online is known as disinhibition. Most of what people say, when unidentified, they would not dream of doing if their name were attached. It's a common form of bullying which is surprisingly widespread. It's partly this aggression that drives traffic and click-thru rates. Many *Daily Mail* readers from all over the world actively participate in shouting in the comments section of stories. Could this be a reason why it is the most popular online newspaper in the world?[16]

Social media have changed behaviour because they confer the authority to communicate without responsibility and often without identity.

This environment has terrible consequences for online bullying. This is not just confined to children. In the UK in June 2016, Labour MP Jo Cox was murdered by a constituent who had gathered information online. Hundreds more are subjected to death and rape threats daily. The impunity with which this happens is worth examining because it's not just MPs who are subject to it. Increasingly, most leaders will have to contend with online criticism, which often appears worse than it is because of its anonymous source.

Internet psychologist John Suler[17] has written about six characteristics of the internet which lead to radical changes in online behaviour:

Anonymity

Online people feel they can't be identified in the same way they can when they're in public. Ironically, though, some people are far less anonymous online than offline. Because of the online disinhibition effect, some share too much on their social networking profiles, sometimes even things they wouldn't admit to their closest friends.

Invisibility

When others know they can't be seen online, they don't have to worry about their facial expressions. This can allow people to open up about things that they can't discuss face-to-face. Online support groups rely on this openness to allow members to discuss their deepest hopes and fears. This is one of the potentially positive aspects of the online disinhibition effect, as long as users protect their privacy and identity.

Stop/start communication

Face-to-face, people's reactions can be seen immediately. Online there are no such restrictions: because of online *synchronicity* it's possible to say something and wait 24 hours before reading the response, or never read it at all. This cuts both ways. So-called 'internet trolls' are people who post to discussion forums or other online groups with the express purpose of stirring up controversy. They may not mean their criticism personally. They are just experts in a kind of emotional hit-and-run.

Voices in your head

The very act of reading online creates a surprisingly intimate connection. While humans have been reading novels and letters for centuries, these are relatively formal modes of communication, and it's only in the past decade that online communication has brought the intimacy of a letter to informal, everyday conversation.

The imaginary world

The anonymity, invisibility and fantasy elements of online activities encourage participants to think that the usual rules don't apply. The problem is that when life becomes a game that can be left behind at the flick of a switch, it's easy to throw responsibility out of the window.

No police

This imaginary world appears to have no police and no authority figures. Although there are people with authority online, it's difficult to see them. There is no internet government, no one person in charge. So, people feel freer online away from authority, social convention and conformity.

Disintermediation

Disinhibition is magnified because social media also disintermediate the messages. Now you can talk to anyone and they can respond. It's never been easier to make people hear. Because social media are so personal, it's easy to get to people with sometimes intimidating results.

The latent anger lurking on Twitter, for instance, can be devastating to those who inadvertently trigger it. In July 2012, shortly after the #aurora theatre shootings, Celeb Boutique, an online clothes store that allows people to fashion themselves after celebrities, tweeted that: '#Aurora is trending, clearly about our Kim K inspired aurora dress.'[18] Needless to say, it received thousands of e-mail complaints plus significant adverse broadcast coverage. Of course, this was a tweet in bad taste, and there are many examples of this.

QUICK TIP Social media are swords with two edges. They can be powerful for leaders to use, provided they have the judgement to use them wisely. They are most powerful when used as a listening tool.

The leader's critique

Because of the above, leaders can be subject to a deluge of criticism, some anonymous, some not. This is especially the case in publicly represented positions or companies that are traded. In the 21st century, to the uninitiated, this can come as a shock. Spend a day tracking social coverage for any Congressman, MP or public figure and the level of abuse is shocking. One UK Labour MP, Jess Philips, reported that she had 600 rape threats in one day.[19] It takes a certain type of courage and determination to continue in a public position when you, your family and co-workers are subjected to this.

Leaders often have no prior warning of this sort of public criticism and it can be bewildering to those that experience a crisis, for instance. It can come from named or unnamed sources and the volumes can be surprising, sometimes running into thousands of e-mails a minute. It is, though, useful to remind leaders of the words of the 25th President of the United States, Theodore Roosevelt:

> It is not the critic who counts; not the man who points out how the strong man stumbles, or where the doer of deeds could have done them better. The credit belongs to the man who is actually in the arena, whose face is marred by dust and sweat and blood; who strives valiantly; who errs, who comes short again and again, because there is no effort without error and shortcoming; but who does actually strive to do the deeds; who knows great enthusiasms, the great devotions; who spends himself in a worthy cause; who at the best knows in the end the triumph of high achievement, and who at the worst, if he fails, at least fails while daring greatly, so that his place shall never be with those cold and timid souls who neither know victory nor defeat.'[20]

Leaders, at some point, can expect to find themselves on the receiving end of anger, whether it be from customers, shareholders, constituents, colleagues or the public. You can deal with anger in a straightforward way. Remember that when a fight breaks out in a bar, people often go to hit the person they've been wanting to hit, not the person who started the fight. Despite the provocation, it's important to stay calm (or at least act it). This means speaking slowly and clearly. What you put into someone is what you get out. Anger begets anger. You should ask yourself if the anger is justified. Ask what role you have played in causing the anger and whether there's anything you can immediately do to fix it. Sometimes the person is so angry, you may need to withdraw for safety and come back to them when they've calmed down.

Rule 34

Rule 34 of the internet, as it has become known, states that for every conceivable subject, there's pornography for it. Belinda Luscombe, writing in *Time Magazine*,[21] said: 'Porn is so ubiquitous, it has spun off memes, including Rule 34,[22] which states, "If it exists, there is porn of it." (Leprechauns? Check. Pterodactyls? Check. Pandas? Check.) The internet is like a 24-hour all-you-can-eat buffet restaurant that serves every type of sex snack.'

It's the same for anger. If it's a thing, there's anger for it. There's another effect here as well. The profoundly opinionated, grossly intolerant and deeply ignorant are no longer isolated voices. They can find connections and form groups to create some sort of hate norm. This creates a mingled reality between what we hear in the real world and what we hear online – some of it fact and some of it most definitely fiction. Is it so hard to understand the rise of the extremes in such an environment? The same process swirls around good and bad causes online, driven by 'Armchair Activism'. This is where people don't get involved in good causes, but support them at a distance. It can be quite close to Slacktivism, a term that refers to those who use simple measures to support an issue or social cause which involves virtually no effort on the part of participants. Slacktivist activities include signing internet petitions, joining a community organization without contributing to it, copying and pasting social network statuses or messages and altering one's credentials on social network services. Clicktivism is also similar and involves the use of digital media for facilitating social change and activism. The idea behind it is that social media allow for a quick and easy way to show support for a cause. Its focus has become inflating participation rates by asking less and less of their members.

The case for mindfulness

OK, so we've established there's a lot of anger and ignorance out there. Perhaps it's always been there? Perhaps the internet has just facilitated it? What can leaders do about it? They can seek to mitigate it as above. Leaders are logical, practical and resourceful people, not easily persuaded by the intangible, the illogical and the spiritual. They are also, however, made of flesh and blood, not necessarily given to seeking open confrontation to achieve objectives. Sometimes, they need to be able to absorb the pressures of an angry world.

In Chapter 1, we encountered Professor Ian McGilchrist who summed up the power of the analytical mind:[23] 'The left hemisphere's talk is very convincing because it shaved off everything that it doesn't find fits with its model and cut it out. This model is entirely self-consistent largely because it's made itself so. The right hemisphere (the imagination) doesn't have a voice and it can't make these arguments.'

There's been much talk about mindfulness in leadership[24] and many companies such as Google, Aetna and General Mills have implemented schemes.[25] This is the right brain writ large. It's about paying attention to ourselves, being aware of the present and avoiding self-deception. It's recognizing that thoughts are thoughts and not beliefs. It's also recognizing that the very busyness leaders indulge in causes them to lose connection with others and themselves. Saint Augustine was an expert on this area: 'Do you wish to be great? Then begin by being. Do you desire to construct a vast and lofty fabric? Think first about the foundations of humility. The higher your structure is to be, the deeper must be its foundation.'[26]

Many employees have gone through these sorts of programmes and the data show that there's a definite impact on leadership skills in the areas of productivity, decision-making, listening and in reducing stress. Jon Kabat-Zinn is a scientist, writer and Professor of Medicine Emeritus at the University of Massachusetts Medical School. He describes mindfulness as: 'Paying attention in a particular way: on purpose, in the present moment, and non-judgmentally.' It's about being more in the present and thereby being able to do everything with more discipline and focus.

Making the case for mindfulness, Monica Thakrar,[27] writing in *Forbes Magazine,* says: 'the biggest benefit of mindfulness is its direct impact on the development of emotional intelligence.' Daniel Goleman, a leading expert on emotional intelligence, recently made a direct connection between it and mindfulness,[28] saying that: 'Emotional intelligence builds attention and focus and these are the cornerstones in enhancing self-awareness, as well as empathy. In turn, these are critical skills to enhancing emotional awareness.'

Mindfulness techniques are manifold but often appear under familiar names, eg meditation, breathing, yoga, walking, music, nature and so on – anything that allows you to come back to the present moment. Whatever focuses on the present moment is a mindfulness tool.

Megan Reitz and Michael Chaskalson,[29] writing in the *Harvard Business Review,* say that mindfulness works because it improves resilience, the capacity for collaboration and the ability to lead in complex conditions. They say, however, that the techniques need to be practised and ingrained: 'Simply attending one or more workshops might help strengthen resilience by sharing some useful tools and techniques, but other improvements require practice.' They identified three areas of leadership perspective. The first they called Metacognition or 'the ability to simply observe what you are thinking, feeling, and sensing so you can actually see what's going on'. Second, allowing for 'the ability to let what is the case, be the case. It's about meeting your experience with a spirit of openness and kindness to yourself and others.' Finally, they identified curiosity, 'or taking a lively interest in what has shown up in our inner and outer worlds'.

Resolving conflict

In Jeffrey Krivis' book *Improvisational Negotiation: A Mediator's Stories of Conflict*,[30] he points out how conflict is resolved. His process itself is worthy of note. He describes negotiation as: 'reframing a situation in order to get people to shift their positions in a way that makes a resolution possible'. This is more than just dealing with anger. This is a process similar to mindfulness which is based around paying attention. This involves acting out the role of a neutral player who just wants to get the problem resolved. He says there are five stages to the process:

Convening: Here the negotiator needs to work out whether all parties can be spoken to or whether the process needs to involve separation.

Opening: This involves coaching both sides to make sure they make the best use of the time. It usually begins with an opening statement from both sides.

Communication: This is where legal and/or personal arguments are made. These are to be laid out as logically as possible.

Negotiation: This is the core of the process, which involves flexibility and imagination to come up with ideas that might meet the requirements of both sides.

Closure: This is where agreements are codified and ratified by all parties.

An important point to conflict resolution is to check the reliability of the assumptions that both parties are making. In an age of social media half-truths, this can be significant. The ability to empathize and to be creative are important qualities here. This is especially the case when appealing to emotions for compromise.

The ability to resolve conflict relies heavily on the right-brain process. This is the ability to look for similarities rather than differences, alignments rather than contrasts and mutuality rather than conflict. In the future, leaders will find themselves called upon more frequently to resolve conflict, whether it be individual or group-based. The key to this is to understand the primary cause of the conflict. There may be secondary issues, but we're interested in the principal concern.

As settlement agreements are sometimes improvised, it's possible they need to be 'tried on'. Where this is the case, some may be an immediate mismatch. Humility and an acknowledgement of misunderstanding can be useful skills here.

Krivis points to the right-brain skills: 'Intuition can be a powerful mediation tool. It is especially useful in situations where you're dealing with preconceived notions and need to improvise. Remember effective improvisation is a product of skill (education plus experience) and intuition.' Sometimes, leaders also need to accept that resolution is not always possible. He says: 'Get comfortable with the idea that when it comes to mediating your employees' problems there are no hard and fast rules. Negotiation is all about going with the flow and seizing opportunities as they arise.'

Greed is good?

It might have been a great line, but it was a lie. There's nothing good about greed. It divides people. It perpetuates injustice.

It doesn't create happiness or resources. It also comes in many forms. We often just think of it as a greed for money or food, but greed for power, control and the limelight and media attention is just as bad. A well-known story arc is based upon the psychology of the unexpected, man bites dog and so on. Once a successful leader is known and admired in the media, then the story waiting for them is that they are no longer a successful leader.

QUICK TIP In any meeting the true leader is always the one who facilitates the discussion and searches for the truth. When summing up and providing their view, they should speak last, if at all.

Greed is just another form of selfishness and, make no mistake, it provokes anger. The simple desire for something, such as wealth, power or food, is an attempt to fill a hole that cannot be filled. Leadership is wanting what you have, not having what you want.

The ultimate selfishness

There is a lesson in joined-up thinking here. Let's take national political leadership as an example. Voters will not be denied. Nor will they accept deferred gratification. We saw earlier that politicians are fearful of the entitlement and impatience of electorates. This, in turn, places pressures on them and on economists to stimulate the economy through quantitative easing, thus creating inflation. This reduces the debts caused by living beyond the means, but undermines everything else. The internet accelerates that impatience and greed by fulfilling requirements faster than ever before. This does not make people more patient, nor does it make them less selfish. When they are denied what they have been so used to getting, the result is anger. This is the ultimate in selfish behaviour because it automatically assumes injustice and righteousness. It takes no heed of the target's feelings. It has no empathy.

Empathy

In the 21st century, empathy is more powerful than authority. This is not a faith or belief in itself but an ability to tap into the other person's situation. The Rev Alasdair Coles[31] has a great deal of experience as a Chaplain in a number of institutions: 'I spend a lot of time listening to people and it's clear that for many, it's a novel experience', he says. The ability to solve problems through individual dialogue is spiritual leadership at its best. Leaders can learn a lot from this, but they need to learn how to listen. This requires patience (in short supply) but it also requires time. It's surprising how obvious the required actions are when listening happens. In one report by the *Harvard Business Review*,[32] empathy was defined as: 'a deep emotional intelligence that is closely connected to cultural competence. Empathy enables those who possess it to see the world through others' eyes and understand their unique perspectives.'

The process of non-doing

Nobody does nothing. If anyone asks you what you did at the weekend, it's usually a tumble of events, as if to admit that doing nothing made you a loser. It was Einstein who said: 'Creativity is the residue of time wasted.'[33] The problem is that leaders are busy people. They got to where they are by doing stuff, and, as we're beginning to see, that's not enough. They must swap their 'to do' list for 'to be' lists. They must learn to be something.

This is not easy, because to do so requires mindfulness. This means making time for yourself and others. It means finding new ways of solving old problems. Above all, it means making time to see the interconnectedness of things.

The role of humour

We live in serious times. Perhaps that's all the more reason for us to take humour seriously. We can use all sorts of techniques to handle stress and anger in our teams but by far the easiest, quickest and most accessible is humour. It's easily dismissed as a concept, because it doesn't fall into the Western Reductionist model. We need to be on guard against the notion that only intellect and logic matter in leadership. This can easily turn us into what Nassim Taleb calls the IYI (Intellectual Yet Idiot[34]). Humour, when correctly executed, can signal a number of vital qualities, such as judgement. It takes real skill to use humour. When it's used badly it's worse than not being funny. It's disastrous. We've all seen and heard a badly timed joke. The courage, skill and timing required to make a well-received joke are real leadership qualities. On top of this, leaders with a sense of humour tend to be more relaxed. Their teams tend to acquire skills more easily because competence always follows preference. People get good at what they like doing. If they're having fun, it makes them more likely to repeat tasks and acquire new skills.

> **QUICK TIP** It sounds like a stupid idea, but remember to smile when you greet people. So much of the tone of a meeting is set by how the leader looks.

Will McInnes is co-founder of Brighton-based social media firm NixonMcInnes. He advocates using the 'Church of Fail'[35] technique. This is where a forum is created for anyone to stand up and talk about the ways in which they have failed. This is quasi-support group cum church congregation and it's an interesting idea. Of course, leadership has to commit to it and participate, but it also highlights how failure is a part of success. Leaders need to study failure and also the fear of failure, because this is often something that makes teams resistant. It may not be the change that is the problem; it may be what the change brings that is feared.

QUICK TIP Deal with anger in the team by organizing a 'Church of Fail'. It can be funny but with a serious outcome to see what people consider to be failure.

Creative provenance

In *Too Fast to Think*,[36] many senior leaders were asked where they were and what they were doing when they had their best ideas. The responses were uncannily similar: they were most often away from their workplaces, alone and, importantly, not trying. Could it be that we have a subconscious mind which is working away in the background, joining the dots and spotting the patterns? Is it coincidence that it reminds us of its output only when the left-brain process is either preoccupied or switched off? Not one of the leaders interviewed ever reported anger as being the provenance of insight, but some did report that they discovered ideas when a suggestion was made as a joke. The conclusion here is clear – anger and fear can inhibit individual as well as team performance. It can make teams dysfunctional and waste resources on internal conflict that should be used on more positive outcomes.

Conclusions

Intelligence in leadership is about much more than mere academic attainment. This is particularly acute when it comes to harnessing intelligence. This appears in many different forms, and leaders need to find time to connect with team members to locate and develop these skills. Maintaining balance and general awareness themselves, as well as the team, is another factor in success.

The promulgation of one type of hierarchical intelligence (short-term, drill-down, academic, data-based and so on) creates vulnerabilities. It shuts out potential and imagination. It excludes the long-term, diversity and opinion, which destroys hope and creates a causal chain of frustration, impatience and anger. The logical extrapolation of left-brained thinking is damaging to leadership because it notices the difference, but not the similarity, in people.

As we've seen already, the Kythera has a dark side which includes impatience, ignorance and anger. It is the online environment itself, with its ease of connectivity, that is leading to record levels of online abuse and bullying. This has fostered a climate offline where attacks on nurses, car drivers and airline staff, for instance, have become often irrational yet commonplace. This rising epidemic of atomized behaviour, ever more geared to individuals rather than a wider community, is something that leaders need to notice.

Above all, they must recognize the growing tide of frustration and cynicism and work to create more harmonious outcomes. This means recognizing and resolving conflict and focusing teams on shared goals and values. Mindfulness is an important tool in this respect. Even to consider it, though, requires a leap of faith. We need to suspend our left-brain judgement long enough to consider the intangible. Anger and rage are not logical, so maybe the solutions to them aren't either?

Endnotes

1   Gardner, G (2011) *Frames of Mind: The theory of multiple intelligences*, Basic Books, New York

2   Gardner (2011) *Frames of Mind: The theory of multiple intelligences*, Basic Books, New York

3   https://www.youtube.com/watch?v=zDZFcDGpL4U

4   http://www.independent.co.uk/news/uk/politics/nhs-staff-violent-attacks-government-blind-spot-hospital-assaults-nurses-unions-doctors-a8009441.html

5   https://www.npr.org/templates/story/story.php?storyId=12370592

6   https://www.angermanage.co.uk/anger-statistics

7   http://www.iata.org/pressroom/pr/Pages/2016-09-28-01.aspx

8   http://www.iata.org/pressroom/pr/Pages/2016-09-28-01.aspx

9   http://www.iata.org/pressroom/pr/Pages/2016-09-28-01.aspx

10 http://www.esquire.com/news-politics/a40693/american-rage-nbc-survey

11 https://www.youtube.com/watch?v=skdvlysoL68

12 https://www.nobelprize.org/mediaplayer/index.php?id=2586

13 https://www.nytimes.com/2017/08/09/style/anger-rooms-the-wrecking-club.html

14 http://www.wreckingclub.com

15 https://www.scientificamerican.com/article/why-is-everyone-on-the-internet-so-angry

16 https://thenextweb.com/media/2012/01/25/the-daily-mail-is-now-the-most-popular-newspaper-website-in-the-world

17 http://www.spring.org.uk/2010/08/six-causes-of-online-disinhibition.php

18 https://www.pushon.co.uk/blog/social-media-in-2012

19 http://www.independent.co.uk/news/uk/home-news/labour-mp-jess-phillips-rape-death-threats-one-day-social-media-attacks-training-a7915406.html

20 http://www.theodore-roosevelt.com/trsorbonnespeech.html

21 http://ideas.time.com/contributor/belinda-luscombe/?iid=sr-link1

22 http://ideas.time.com/contributor/belinda-luscombe/?iid=sr-link1

23 https://www.ted.com/talks/iain_mcgilchrist_the_divided_brain

24 https://hbr.org/2016/12/how-to-bring-mindfulness-to-your-companys-leadership

25 https://hbr.org/2016/12/how-to-bring-mindfulness-to-your-companys-leadership

26 Garrison, B (2016) *Leadership by the Book: Lessons from every book of the Bible*, Elevate Faith, Farmington, MO

27 https://www.forbes.com/sites/forbescoachescouncil/2017/06/28/how-to-create-mindful-leadership/#26d0cdac342a

28 https://www.eqsummit.com/dr-martyn-newman-interviews-godfather-emotional-intelligence-dan-goleman-prior-eqsummit2017

29 https://hbr.org/2016/12/how-to-bring-mindfulness-to-your-companys-leadership

30 Krivis, J (2006) *Improvisational Negotiation: A mediator's stories of conflict about love, money, anger – and the strategies that resolved them*, Jossey-Bass, San Francisco, CA

31 Lewis, C (2016) *Too Fast to Think: How to reclaim your creativity in a hyperconnected work culture*, Kogan Page, London

32 https://hbr.org/2015/09/empathy-is-still-lacking-in-the-leaders-who-need-it-most

33 https://www.barnesandnoble.com/review/the-residue-of-time-wasted-jonah-lehrer-talks-creativity

34 https://www.zerohedge.com/news/2016-09-16/nassim-taleb-exposes-worlds-intellectual-yet-idiot-class

35 https://www.inc.com/magazine/201311/leigh-buchanan/nixonmcinnes-innovation-by-celebrating-mistakes.html

36 Lewis, C (2016) *Too Fast to Think: How to reclaim your creativity in a hyperconnected work culture*, Kogan Page, London

CHAPTER FIVE

Understanding Geopolitics and the New Infrastructure

Infrastructure and Isolation

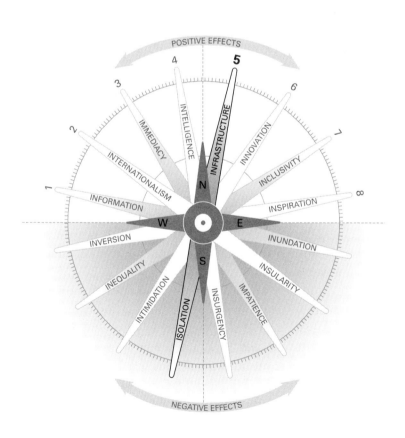

This book is intended to be used as a guide to modern global leadership. So far, we have looked at some of the paradoxical qualitative trends which are driving leadership change.

We've already established that it's vital for leaders to look at the world with parenthesis as well as analysis. We established in Chapter 2 that inflation fundamentally changed when the Berlin Wall fell. While this was a political event, it was also a financial event. The Cold War dictated the policy of economic intervention and government spending. Militaries suddenly became less important, where previously they'd been a normal aspect of governance.

Historically, leadership had to consider geopolitics, but since the Berlin Wall fell a generation has grown up unconcerned by it. Now geopolitics is back and in this incarnation it is freighted with commercial as well as military considerations. Defence spending is on track to hit a post-Cold War record in 2018. Defence spending has become the new quantitative easing. It's a backdoor stimulus to the economy. The new defence spending is also more technological and rather less military than before. It has immediate commercial dividends. Now it's about military altitude satellites rather than new aircraft carriers. Governments and their militaries remain large, influential players. They fundamentally reshape the leadership environment and the economies that surround them. Their decisions affect citizens in many ways. It's worth noting that conscription is being brought back across many European countries and that private organizations are increasingly being asked to fulfil intelligence tasks on behalf of their governments.

What do leaders know about the landscape of geopolitics? Many leaders travel the world with such ease and comfort that they think they understand the countries they visit. They may spend time in China and India and yet be surprised when the headlines reveal strategic security tensions between the two countries. Leaders often comment that the manufacturing centre of the world is Shenzhen and the coding centre is Bangalore.

They may refer to oil-producing countries as rich. But is all this still true? The truth is that countries are in constant flux, just as technology, economics, prices and relative competitiveness are changing, too.

QUICK TIP Just because you've been to a country, it doesn't mean you know it. Going is not knowing. Good leaders need to talk to local players and understand what's changing. In any case, some countries are changing so fast they must be periodically 'sampled'. Leaders need to be plugged in, switched on and clued up. Local geopolitics needs to be checked as frequently as the weather. Local is on the rise. A large proportion of Trump voters have never left their hometowns.[1]

Leaders endanger themselves and their teams by falling back on old notions and overconfidence. They must not only keep up with today, they also need to anticipate tomorrow because they're constantly asked to allocate resources. For instance, do countries still matter as much as individual cities? Cities are on the rise as centres of population. Mayors are sometimes more important than prime ministers. Is China still the future or is the United States a better place to invest time and capital? Is Britain finished as a result of Brexit or is it embarking on a stronger future? Is the EU aligning more strongly or heading towards fragmentation? How will the Middle East look now that Saudi Arabia and Israel seem to have aligned and other neighbours are intensifying old rivalries?

The overlay of geopolitics is making the commercial land-scape more complex. Governmental policy is responsible for vast capital flows, so understanding the way they behave is important for leaders. Being on the side of the future can make a big difference. For instance, organizations such as the Council on Foreign Relations and NATO make ever more reference to the possibility that we might be stumbling into some kind of new Cold War.[2]

Everyone assumes that the post-war international rule system can be depended upon to prevent conflict. Leaders in the 21st century, however, cannot afford to take anything for granted. They need to think about the competition for scarce resources, the rise in defence spending and the seeming loss of trust in the international rule system.

All this begs a key question. What do we really know about the world's geography? In this new environment, everything we assume needs to be subjected to hard questions. Being a long-time expert on a location no longer confers authority. There are no experts anymore. There are just those who are more or less ignorant. The provenance of certainty is now mediocrity not excellence.

This is what we will cover:

- Geography is destiny
- One Belt, One Road, One Circle (BRI[3]) – a brand-new global infrastructure
- The biggest infrastructure project the world has ever seen
- Defence spending is rising
- Old and new causes: but what about the wall?
- A new multipolar world with walls
- Conflicts cause migration and vice versa
- Resource infrastructure
- Environment in its widest sense
- Protein
- Energy and the end of oil
- Centralization versus decentralization
- Infrastructure is the new politics
- Rules
- Diplomacy
- Conclusions

Geography is destiny[4]

In 2015, Henry Kissinger told the US Armed Services Committee of the US Senate that: 'The United States has not faced a more diverse and complex array of (foreign policy) crises since the end of the Second World War.' Every nation must face this problem, he said, because 'the existing international order itself is being redefined'. In other words, the geography of the international rule system itself is changing. The physical geography of the world is changing as well. Countries like China are building new transport connections and the United States and Europe are building new walls. Some places are becoming more competitive and others less so. People are on the move. Migration continues to be one of the most important defining features of the geopolitical landscape, as is the ongoing competition for scarce resources. Borders are fluid and moving, too.

One Belt, One Road, One Circle (BRI) – a brand-new global infrastructure

Westerners have become used to their version of the world. The British foresaw the importance of the international date and time system, so they put the dateline through Greenwich. London thus became one of the few cities that could make a same-day announcement for the majority of the planet. Heathrow has only recently been overtaken as the busiest international airport in the world. No longer, though, will infrastructures automatically point at New York or London or Singapore. Instead, China is dramatically re-orienting the world in its direction. China needs resources from around the world to sustain its growth. It can no longer rely upon the infrastructure built by Western nations and the territorial certainties of the 20th century.

The biggest infrastructure project the world has ever seen

Infrastructure is geopolitics. Many leaders have not truly clocked the magnitude of the so-called Belt and Road Initiative. In China, though, it is real and happening. The world doesn't know much about it because it's happening in obscure places. Leaders might easily dismiss the BRI because they believe new infrastructure in, say, Kazakhstan is not relevant to their interests. It would be easy to think that this plan simply upgrades the Old Silk Road that runs from China through Central Asia. That, though, would be a mistake. According to *The Economist*, the BRI 'is the kind of leadership the United States has not shown since the post-war days of the Marshall Plan in Western Europe'. BRI is in fact seven times larger financially.

The BRI is not really a plan. It is a series of discrete infrastructure deals with different purposes, financing arrangements and participants. Together, though, they add up to one massive network. Specific routes and pathways being established or strengthened, for instance:

- A railway will link Yiwu in Eastern China to London and Madrid via Kazakhstan, Russia, Belarus, Poland, Germany, Belgium and France. This link will also connect Yiwu with Rotterdam via Moscow and Urumqi in China.
- It will connect with regional railway networks such as those in South East Asia. Trains from Kunming, China will link to Vietnam, Laos, Thailand, Cambodia and Myanmar. In East Africa, the BRI will connect Ethiopia, Djibouti, South Sudan, Kenya, Tanzania, Uganda and Rwanda.[5] In each case, ports are also being built or upgraded.
- In the Himalayas, China is building railway and highway links in both Pakistan and Bangladesh to connect China to the sea via both countries via the China–Pakistan Economic Corridor and the Bangladesh–China–India–Myanmar Corridor.[6]

The Himalayan Economic Rim project will connect Nepal, India, Bhutan and Tibet.[7]

- In the Middle East, China seeks to link Turkey, Lebanon, Syria, Iraq, Iran and Jordan. The railway routes in the region will be supplemented by new or upgraded ports in places like Oman, all the way to Athens.

- The road and maritime links (the belt) go thousands of miles. The 'Circle' applies to the Arctic part of this. The Arctic Circle is now a fast way to China's western markets, going from Dalian at the southern tip of China's Liaoning Province. This will allow goods from Eastern China to arrive in Rotterdam in 26 days via the Arctic or more likely, in the opposite direction.

- A proposed new port will be built on the east coast of Mexico at Lazaro Cardenas.[8] This is expected to be bigger than Long Beach in California (the second largest in the United States[9]). This will allow Chinese ships to bypass US West Coast ports for those with deeper water on the US Gulf Coast and East Coast. Some suggest that as much as a quarter of the approximately 60 million tons of cargo that Los Angeles and Long Beach handle each year could be diverted.[10] Mexico will get new ports and upgraded railways and highways in the effort to ensure that commerce from the East and West coasts of North America can reach China ever more easily.

- This will be matched with another two proposed Panamax-sized canals, the first in Nicaragua – The Grand Nicaragua Canal,[11] the second across the Kra Peninsula in Thailand – The Thai Canal.[12] China is also moving closer to Malaysia in its BRI projects and has invested 14 billion Singapore dollars (US[th]$10 billion) in the Melaka Gateway project, a port that could replace Singapore as the main entry point in the region.

- In Latin America, the BRI will take the form of an ocean railway that will run from Brazil to Chile and the Trans Amazonian Highway across Brazil.

- The Arctic aspect of the BRI is a maritime route that runs from Dalian in Eastern China through the Arctic Circle to

Rotterdam and then south through the Suez Canal back to China. The widening of the Suez Canal to accommodate two-way traffic and Panamax-size tankers is one of the biggest projects of all within the BRI.

All this investment will add at least a further $5 trillion to global investment. When you add this to the $18 trillion already invested by global central banks, you can see that this is not insignificant.

The BRI is ambitious even inside China. According to the official *China Daily*, '29 of China's 31 provinces and regions are now served by high-speed rail, with only the regions of Tibet and Ningxia in the northwest yet to be connected.'[13]

China's efforts to manage geography are not just physical. They are also occurring in the Data Sphere (see Chapter 6). China's leaders are increasingly compelling the world to communicate on Chinese platforms such as WeChat. They are creating the infrastructure for quantum telephone calls which are said to be unhackable. The communications infrastructure may be less connected to the West, but the West is being more connected (physically) to China.

Defence spending is rising

The Kythera shows us that there is always a dark side to the trends. No discussion of geopolitics and the geography of the world today can avoid reference to the fact that defence spending is rising. This is a different but equally important kind of global infrastructure. The Jane's Defence Budgets report projects that 'Global defence expenditure is set to increase again in 2018 to reach its highest level since the end of the Cold War.'[14] The same technological advances that benefit the world economy are also perfecting new weapons. For instance, China, the United States, Russia and some others are moving to hypersonic weapons that travel at Mach speeds and can cross the planet in very little time.

New naval vessels and aircraft that operate without humans are being invented. Superpowers are in a new space race, spending money on speed and accuracy.

This raises questions that leaders should consider. After all, even the Council on Foreign Relations, an independent, non-partisan think tank, writes about the possibility of 'a new cold war'.[15] While everyone wants to avoid such an outcome, it is hard to ignore the incidents between superpowers. There are air and sea incursions between many nations. The Japanese complain about the build-up of the Russian presence in the Kurile Islands, just as the United States complains about China's increasing presence in the Pacific. Russia and NATO member states regularly accuse each other of engaging in provocative acts in the air and under the sea. One of the reasons here could be that all other former members of The Warsaw Pact, except Russia, are now part of NATO.[16] Given that the Berlin Wall fell in 1989, it was unthinkable that by 2005, just 16 years later, all former Russian allies would be allied to the West.

From Russia's perspective, the United States and NATO have been encroaching. A key battleground for this is what happens in Ukraine. Support in the country has been growing for it to join as well. This has accelerated since Russia took control of the naval base in Sevastopol that it leased from Ukraine for many years. The West may have taken the view that not taking action to support Ukraine would, in the long term, force it closer to NATO. Allowing Russia to continue using the port was no more than the status quo. The Russian Navy cannot sortie in war time because it would still need to navigate the Bosporus, which is controlled by Turkey, a NATO member.

Meanwhile, senior NATO leaders refer to Russia's 'Arc of Steel',[17] which implies that Russia is building a strategic security presence from the Baltics to the Mediterranean and into the Middle East. It also implies a hardening of nuclear capabilities. Russia sees the same thing in reverse. It sees the United States and China expanding nuclear arsenals and security capabilities.

Regional superpowers are engaged in new conflicts. The Saudi/ Yemeni conflict now threatens to spread to other locations. The North Korean nuclear issue keeps drawing our attention to the Korean Peninsula. Russia and NATO[18] have accused each other of simulating war in various military exercises. China and its neighbours seem to be in arguments involving military vessels and aircraft more often. It feels as if the 'Peace Dividend' is diminishing. The solution is, of course, greater diplomacy and dialogue, but as we've established, the behaviour change is not confined to either governments or civilians. Both communicate but don't converse. The tone is often angry and impatient. Often, neither side demonstrates empathy.

Leaders from the private and third sectors are well placed to influence dialogue. They have less national pride and political prestige vested in the process. They do need greater awareness of the geopolitical pressures, but in some cases, it might be easier for them to manage dialogue. The tendency to avoid or suppress the subject might contribute to worse outcomes.

Old and new causes: but what about the wall?

What is causing this? The simple answer is that geopolitics has always been a feature of the global landscape. Its retreat in the decades following the fall of the Berlin Wall was the exception to the historical rule.

Economic policy has helped encourage the return of geopolitics. When central banks are under scrutiny for injecting stimulus and QE, defence spending is a way of adding more money without attracting economic criticism. It is a form of economic stimulus and popular with voters in times of financial crisis. One of the reasons given for promoting defence sales is that they create so many jobs in key political constituencies.

In a time of division and recession, militaries are also the employers of last resort. Governments can prop up economies and political prospects by expanding military spending. It is also true that the presence of a foreign opponent can help unite the public during difficult economic times. Domestic politics in many countries benefit from the allegation that foreign powers somehow were the cause. This is not new in history. Leaders, however, are in a strong position to choose positive outcomes if they can see the patterns and embrace collaboration over combat.

Consider the Korean Peninsula. After frightening headlines suggesting that there was a real risk of a nuclear event, we see China and the two Koreas fostering greater dialogue. The two Koreas arrived at the 2018 Winter Olympics under the same flag. Many cultural exchanges have been announced. For all the hectoring between the United States and China, the two superpowers seem aligned in their desire to prevent the worst possible outcome on the North Korean issue.

A new multipolar world with walls

A natural instinct when faced with unresolvable conflict is a wall. There is little use denying that Russia and its neighbours rattle each other. Poland and Lithuania are both building a weaponized wall around Kaliningrad,[19] while Russia is increasing its naval presence and expanding its arsenal of missiles there.[20] Sweden and Lithuania have both reintroduced military conscription as a result of their concerns about the escalation on all sides in the Baltic Sea.

Saudi Arabia has engaged in something not seen for decades – a naval blockade. Its target is its neighbour, Qatar. Most people had assumed that the Gulf States were all aligned. It turns out that they are not. What else might surprise us? Some parts of the world are worth paying more attention to. Russia is re-establishing its naval presence in the Mediterranean[21] now that it has control over warm water ports in Syria. New gas fields have been found in the Eastern Mediterranean and many regional nations will lay claim to them as their value increases. As North Africa becomes less stable,[22] it would be no surprise if nations from afar became interested in its oil and gas assets.[23]

Conflicts cause migration and vice versa

While China connects the world, others are building new walls. Everyone knows about the wall between the United States and Mexico. There are, however, many more. The historian Timothy Garten Ash says: 'Europe's walls are going back up – it's like 1989 in reverse.'[24] He talks of the 'razor and barbed wire fences, like much of the old iron curtain', which now cross European borders. Elisabeth Vallet, the author of *Borders, Fences and Walls: State of Insecurity?*, says: 'There are now five times as many border walls as there were at the fall of the Berlin Wall in 1989.'[25] Walls are going up in North Africa and across parts of the Middle East, including between Saudi and Yemen, between Israel and the West Bank and between Turkey and Syria.

Immigration seems to be the principal driver of the new mentality. In 2015, António Guterres, the UN High Commissioner for Refugees, made the case plainly: 'In 2014 we had 59.5 million people displaced by conflict in the world.'[26] His numbers were stark. 'In 2010, there were 11,000 new people displaced by conflict per day. In 2011, it was 14,000. In 2012, it was 23,000. In 2013, it was 32,000. In 2014 it was 42,500 people displaced by conflict per day.'[27]

That does not include economic migrants who are simply looking for a better life. The United States now hosts a higher number of foreign-born migrants than at any stage in its history (Figure 5.1).

Some have already decided that a wall between the United States and Mexico would be a disaster. Yet, something interesting has happened that may have escaped their attention. Mexico's economy has become very competitive. Wages in Mexico

FIGURE 5.1 Foreign-born population and percentage of total population for the United States (1850–2010)

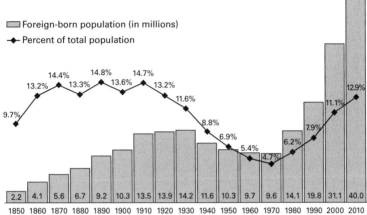

Source: US Census Bureau, Census of Population (1850–2000) and the American Community Survey (2010)

are substantially lower than in China now. Quality control in Mexico is US standard and deeply entwined in the United States' supply chains. As a result, Mexicans are no longer moving north, because there are good jobs at home. If anything, US business leaders are moving south, shifting operations into this competitive location. Similarly, China does not see Mexico as a threat, more as an investment opportunity, as it is now upgrading Mexican infrastructure, including airports, ports and rail links.

European economies are profoundly affected by immigration flows. The strife in the Middle East and the lure of European life have together attracted war, economic and political migrants. Europeans are divided on the issue. Some leaders want freedom of entry for all refugees and not only for moral reasons. Europe has an ageing population and needs the infusion of youth. Others feel Europe's slow growth and limited job creation capacity will leave such immigrants without resources and opportunities while threatening the lives and livelihoods of existing citizens.

For the United States and Europe alike, the question comes down to the two cardinal points on the Kythera: Infrastructure and Isolation. They either embrace the opportunities created by migrant flows or they put up walls against them.

Resource infrastructure

Access to raw materials such as water, protein and energy continue to drive geopolitics because they shape the behaviour of nations and migrants alike. Even in an era of unprecedented technological advancements, these resources still matter. China, for example, lacks enough water and arable land to feed itself. It has 20 per cent of the world's population but only 7 per cent of the water. The problem is the Heihe–Tengchong Line.[28] West of this line is 57 per cent of China by area, but only 6 per cent of the population. East of the line is 43 per cent of the area, but 94 per cent of the population. Even after 80 years, the area west of the line remains underdeveloped and poor compared to the east. Much of this is desert. This is why water provenance really matters. Despite energy costs falling in the long-term forecast,[29] desalination cannot yet provide water supplies to the hinterland of China. This is because the process needs a plentiful supply of seawater plus an ability to dispose of heavily polluted residues without causing environmental damage. China's leaders understand it can't have Western standards of living without an increase in water consumption. Here's the problem. Only 2.5 per cent of all the water on the planet is fresh water and, of this, 2 per cent is frozen in glaciers. This is illustrated in Table 5.1.[30]

China is not alone when it comes to water problems. The Middle East, India, Africa and even the United States suffer from a lack of water. This is one reason leaders worldwide are fo-

TABLE 5.1 World water reserves

Water source	Water volume, in cubic miles	Water volume, in cubic kilometres	Percent of fresh water	Percent of total water
Oceans, seas, and bays	321,000,000	1,338,000,000	–	96.54
Ice caps, glaciers, and permanent snow	5,773,000	24,064,000	68.7	1.74
Groundwater	5,614,000	23,400,000	–	1.69
Fresh	2,526,000	10,530,000	30.1	0.76
Saline	3,088,000	12,870,000	–	0.93
Soil moisture	3,959	16,500	0.05	0.001
Ground ice and permafrost	71,970	300,000	0.86	0.022
Lakes	42,320	176,400	–	0.013
Fresh	21,830	91,000	0.26	0.007
Saline	20,490	85,400	–	0.006
Atmosphere	3,095	12,900	0.04	0.001
Swamp water	2,752	11,470	0.03	0.0008
Rivers	509	2,120	0.006	0.0002
Biological water	269	1,120	0.003	0.0001

Source: Gleick, P H (ed) (1993) Water in Crisis: A guide to the world's fresh water resources, Igor Shiklomanov's chapter 'World fresh water resources', Table 2.1, by permission of Oxford University Press, USA

cused on solutions that lessen the reliance on water. These include growing methods that require less of it and more efficient harvesting.

Environment in its widest sense

China's economic success has also created new problems. It lost 6.2 per cent of its farmland between 1997 and 2008, according to a report by the United Nations' Food and Agriculture Organization and the OECD.[31] In an era of spiralling property prices, local governments are incentivized to sell agricultural land to more profitable real-estate developments. This trend, combined with the fast transition to manufacturing, has resulted in so much environmental degradation that China's leaders have now made it a top priority. At the start of President Ji Xinping's second term, at the 19th Party Congress in 2017, he announced that the nation is now 'at war' with pollution.[32]

No discussion of the world's geography and infrastructure is complete without some reference to the environment. To date, we have defined the world environment too narrowly. If the environment is to be saved, there needs to be civil dialogue. The ultimate environmental catastrophe might be not global warming but conflict. Leaders might ask if they are paying more attention to plastic waste than the possibility of apocalyptic military events. Both might be important.

Protein

This is one reason why China is especially focused on the freedom of the seas. It sees a world in which protein is in short supply. The *Washington Post* writes:[33] 'China's per capita fish consumption was estimated by the Food and Agriculture Organization at nearly 80 pounds in 2010, nearly double the global average, and is growing by roughly 8 percent a year.' This helps explain the incidents between China and its neighbours in the South China Sea, and is one reason why China is committed to the South China Sea. 'Fish, the overlooked destabilizer in the South China Sea', as one research group put it.[34]

Pork is also important to China. This is the single most important food item for Chinese households. In recent years, the price of pork has risen by as much as 300 per cent in a single year. So, China is focused on acquiring not only more pork but better pork-growing know-how. That is why one of the largest acquisitions China has announced was the 2013 deal in which the Chinese giant Shuanghui International acquired US company Smithfield Foods.[35] Smithfield processes 27 million pigs, producing over six billion pounds of pork per annum. It owns the world's largest slaughterhouse and meat-processing plant. It was acquired at a premium of 30 per cent to its market price, which was, at the time, the largest Chinese acquisition of a US company ever.

Energy and the end of oil

China also lacks energy resources, which is another reason for the physical and diplomatic links into the Middle East – although, as we'll see, even those oil producers are moving away from oil. Energy resources play a large part in understanding geography. Nations that depend on oil for their income have seen it dramatically damaged by falling oil prices. The Kingdom of Saudi Arabia (KSA), Russia, Norway, Nigeria and Iran all saw their budgets damaged by lower revenues. This coincided with a backdrop of rising costs and higher inflation as government subsidies fell away. Many in the tech world anticipate that alternative energy advancements may reduce the value of a barrel of oil to historically low levels over time.

The KSA has changed its leadership in response to the cash crunch caused by a falling oil price. It has skipped several generations to empower the new Crown Prince, Mohammed bin Salman (or MBS). He has recognized that the Kingdom can no longer afford to provide the traditional subsidies for housing, petrol and food. Saudi is embarking on radical reforms to diversify its economy away from oil dependency. The new leadership is now promoting entrepreneurship and encouraging a wide range of business sectors to the country. Like Norway, Saudi is also selling oil assets. The plan is to float Saudi Aramco and then use the proceeds to support the reform programme rather than reinvest in oil infrastructure.

The Kingdom is expanding its universities and greatly promoting a new culture of entrepreneurship. It has unveiled plans to spend $500 billion creating an entirely new economic zone called NEOM on the country's North West Red Sea coastline. The 26,000 km^2 zone will link to Jordan and Egypt and is expected to contribute $100 billion to GDP by 2030.

Nigeria has also suffered from falling oil prices. The public there have been demanding ever-greater accountability about oil revenues and how they're spent. Nigeria, too, is diversifying away from oil and to entirely new sectors of the economy.

Saudi,[36] Norway,[37] Russia[38] and Nigeria[39] are all promoting entrepreneurship. They all want to strengthen the small and medium-sized business culture. All are introducing new sectors. Nigeria has emerged as the new coding centre for the world. Mark Zuckerberg has backed a firm called Andela that specializes in training young male and female Nigerians with world-class coding skills.[40] As a result, some argue that Lagos is fast replacing Bangalore as the world's coding centre. This is a major change on the geographic landscape that leaders should know about. Andela is now spreading into Uganda and Kenya, building this same human tech infrastructure across the continent.[41]

Russia is also moving away from oil and gas and into high tech. This is one reason that we have heard President Putin say that the nation that leads in artificial intelligence (AI) 'will be the ruler of the world'.[42] Russia sees a strong future in pursuing the 'colossal opportunities' that AI affords. China agrees and continues to diversify its economy in this direction as well.

Suddenly, we can see why leaders need to rethink their understanding of the geography of the world. Every place has its own story. We've long known of the Africa that is blighted by famine and poverty. Does that blind us to the Africa that is becoming connected and tech driven? Some of the fastest-growing economies in the world are now in sub-Saharan Africa.[43] We think of the Middle East as a place that is being torn apart by wars, but it, too, is changing its orientation on the Kythera. It has chosen to have better infrastructure and more connectedness to the world economy.

Centralization versus decentralization

A common theme has been unfolding as populism has increased. People are asking whether the solution to global and national problems is to centralize or decentralize power. The Brexit vote in the United Kingdom can be seen in these terms. The political leadership in the EU seems to be moving towards more centralization, for instance, with a single European Army and a single Foreign and Finance Minister. While some love

Leaders need to ensure the structures they operate in are as flexible as possible.

this direction of travel, others harken back to the concept of subsidiarity. They want more power to reside at the state level. Leaders should be aware of this dynamic. They will see the same trend in their own organization.

Europe is caught in this debate, seeking something halfway between capitalism and socialism. Can German capitalism or Rheinische Capitalismus combine free market capitalism with social policies in an acceptable way? This is a question faced by many nations. Japan is trying to balance between the two extremes. Even the United States has an audience for a third way: witness the supporters of former US presidential candidate Senator Bernie Sanders, who exemplifies this position. China, too, wants to encourage capitalist incentives and payoffs while ensuring that income disparity and the decentralization of power are not destabilizing forces.

The question is whether Brexit was the end of that debate or whether it was the first sign of further fragmentation in Europe. Leaders must think about these questions because they will be asked to choose between the UK and the EU, just as they are being asked to choose between the United States and China or even between China and Africa. Britain's success does not mean the EU's failure or vice versa. Both have different political and business models. China's success does not ensure the Unites States' failure or vice versa. Instead, leaders can look for the synergies between the parts of the world and leverage the relationships between them. There is room in each case for both to succeed, but flexibility is important. Leaders need to ensure the structures they operate in are as flexible as possible.

The Unites States may be undergoing a similar phenomenon. Both Presidents Obama and Trump were elected on a change mandate. The public want to change Washington, DC. Some want the capital and the Federal government to be bigger, others want it to be smaller. This is the same centralization argument again.

QUICK TIP Leadership needs to be self-aware of the balance between centralized and decentralized decision-making. This is a dynamic measure which should alter depending on economic conditions, being usually more centralized in recession.

Infrastructure is the new politics

China has cleverly dealt with the centralization issue by introducing the BRI. The new infrastructure ensures that the country will have new markets both to buy from and sell to. All roads, though, lead back to China. It is ensuring that China is increasingly the centre of the world, while also allowing for great diversity in the internal and external economies it interfaces with. The BRI both centralizes and decentralizes simultaneously.

Truth be known, when the British established the Prime Meridian or the sea lanes or when the United States and Germany built their freeways and autobahns, they were doing the same thing. This is simply a lesson from history being redeployed.

Rules

The greatest challenges on the global geopolitical landscape involve the rules of the game. Since the Second World War, the United States has backed a global rule system that was designed to benefit all those who signed up to it. It came with clear goals – free trade, the freest possible movement of capital, goods, services and human capital, and free transmission of ideas. Institutions were built to support and facilitate these outcomes – The World Bank, the IMF, the UN and other international organizations – but new developments and scandals have weakened faith and trust in the rules and in all institutions.

China and Russia have become ever more sceptical, fearing that they could never get a seat at the table that was commensurate with their power.[44] China, in particular, tried to repair and reform these Western institutions and ideals in the aftermath of the financial crisis. It was rebuffed. Instead, it has decided to create its own global institutions, such as the Asian Infrastructure Investment Bank which now rivals The World Bank. Both Russia and China feel the United States has been too cavalier with the rules and the institutions, seeking to fulfil its own interests first. Emerging-market nations have long complained that these organizations unfairly offer all the senior roles to staff from the founder nations, so they can never have any influence.

Meanwhile, the public are expressing increasingly populist views. They lean towards the isolation side of the Kythera. They are not interested in trade rules that never seem to benefit them. Public support for free trade has waned. Everyone seems to want greater protection from globalization at the very moment, ironically, when globalization seems to be spreading jobs and wealth more widely than ever. Where all the jobs used to go to mainly China, the world economy is distributing job creation more widely. Perhaps the public will catch up and decide that this benefits them? Their leaders across every sector will be called upon to contribute to these debates. The geopolitical landscape is changing fast, reconfiguring itself in real-time. Everything is affecting everything else, so the need for parenthesis is fundamental.

Diplomacy

Carl von Clausewitz said: 'War is the continuation of policy by other means.'[45] If that's true then diplomacy is now more important than ever, but it's not just something that happens between nations. It also occurs between leaders. International organizations, whether private or public, have a part to play, too. The problems described here are difficult enough. They become almost impossible in a world where anyone who disagrees is labelled either as evil or as an idiot. Leaders can play their part in restoring civility and returning to the language of diplomacy. They can see win–win solutions instead of binary outcomes.

Leaders need to infuse their thoughts and actions with this positive and enlightened attitude. This is because the rise in defence spending combined with the imperative for resources are together likely to produce more geopolitical trouble spots. Leaders cannot allow themselves to be surprised by this. They need to study the true state of geopolitics proactively, not assume it has been unchanged since the Berlin Wall fell.

Conclusions

Despite many feeling as if this period is the 'end of days', there are many other periods in history that could lay greater claim to this. The Cuban missile crisis, the dropping of the first atomic bomb, the Blitz or even the Great War might have been worthier of this epithet. The world may be a more dangerous place but not necessarily when compared to other periods in history. It is possible that we can manage this.

We are being driven to defence spending for economic and nationalistic reasons. Sometimes this is to gain access to resources. More often, it's because the original 20th-century infrastructure benefitted only the nations that established it. These new links will create new important geographies, often in areas where there were none before.

Governments are being torn in two directions. First, they are having to deal with a new nationalism, with its implied threat of isolation and tariff barriers. This comes from an old world of sovereign parliaments and defined boundaries. At the same time, the trend towards internationalism is clear and the global economy is redistributing wealth and economic power at an unprecedented rate, based on ever more open trade. Leaders of all types therefore need to be internationally and geopolitically fluent at the same time as being aware of the pain caused by economic change. This is quite some balancing act.

Endnotes

1 https://www.theatlantic.com/politics/archive/2016/10/trump-supporters-hometowns/503033
2 https://www.cfr.org/interview/perils-new-cold-war

3 Belt Road Initiative

4 Verghese, A (2009) *Cutting for Stone: Forbidden love, family secrets and a country in turmoil*, Vintage, New York

5 https://qz.com/996255/kenyas-3-2-billion-nairobi-mombasa-rail-line-opens-with-help-from-china

6 https://thediplomat.com/2017/05/reviving-the-comatose-bangladesh-china-india-myanmar-corridor

7 https://thediplomat.com/2016/08/tibet-and-chinas-belt-and-road

8 http://gcaptain.com/mexicos-900-million-mega-container

9 http://www.inboundlogistics.com/cms/article/top-10-us-container-ports

10 http://www.inboundlogistics.com/cms/article/top-10-us-container-ports

11 https://www.smithsonianmag.com/science-nature/new-canal-through-central-america-could-have-devastating-consequences-180953394

12 http://www.theindependent.sg/the-real-threat-to-spore-construction-of-thais-kra-canal-financed-by-china

13 https://www.reuters.com/article/us-china-railway-yunnan/china-completes-high-speed-rail-links-from-southwest-yunnan-idUSKBN14I07I?il=0

14 http://www.janes.com/article/76463/global-defence-spending-to-hit-post-cold-war-high-in-2018-jane-s-by-ihs-markit-says

15 https://www.cfr.org/interview/perils-new-cold-war

16 https://www.nato.int/cps/ua/natohq/topics_52044.htm

17 https://www.defensenews.com/naval/2015/10/06/us-russia-building-arc-of-steel-from-arctic-to-med

18 http://www.independent.co.uk/news/world/europe/russia-nato-zapad-simulated-full-scale-war-against-west-vladimir-putin-riho-terras-commander-estonia-a8146296.html

19 http://www.bbc.co.uk/news/world-europe-38635737

20 http://www.independent.co.uk/news/world/europe/russia-nuclear-missiles-kaliningrad-baltic-sea-poland-lithuania-nato-a8199011.html

21 https://www.thetimes.co.uk/article/putin-expands-naval-presence-in-the-mediterranean-hq3rhhzdh

22 http://www.ozy.com/opinion/as-the-caliphate-collapses-extremists-eye-north-africa/83749

23 https://www.thecairoreview.com/essays/russias-new-energy-gamble/

24 https://www.theguardian.com/commentisfree/2015/nov/29/europe-2015-walls-1989-paris-refugee-crisis

25 http://www.middleeasteye.net/fr/node/1011

26 http://www.unhcr.org/en-us/admin/hcspeeches/55ba370f9/global-conflicts-human-displacement-21st-century-challenges-delivered-antonio.html

27 http://www.unhcr.org/en-us/admin/hcspeeches/55ba370f9/global-conflicts-human-displacement-21st-century-challenges-delivered-antonio.html

28 https://en.wikipedia.org/wiki/Heihe%E2%80%93Tengchong_Line

29 https://www.eia.gov/outlooks/aeo/pdf/0383(2017).pdf

30 https://water.usgs.gov/edu/earthhowmuch.html

31 https://www.bloomberg.com/graphics/2017-feeding-china

32 https://www.reuters.com/article/us-china-congress-pollution/chinas-president-xi-says-will-continue-years-long-war-on-smog-idUSKBN1CN0CI

33 https://www.washingtonpost.com/world/asia_pacific/fishing-fleet-puts-china-on-collision-course-with-neighbors-in-south-china-sea/2016/04/12/8a6a9e3c-fff3-11e5-8bb1-f124a43f84dc_story.html?tid=a_inl&utm_term=.4e272a879109#https://www.washingtonpost.com/world/asia_pacifi

34 https://worldview.stratfor.com/article/fish-overlooked-destabilizer-south-china-sea

35 https://www.wsj.com/articles/SB10001424127887324412604578512722044165756

36 https://www.ft.com/content/fd4b10c0-b8b7-11e7-8c12-5661783e5589

37 http://www.bbc.com/news/business-35318236

38 http://www.bbc.co.uk/news/world-europe-41904509

39 http://www.bbc.co.uk/news/av/world-africa-35801064/nigeria-s-efforts-to-diversify-economy-and-be-less-dependent-on-oil

40 https://qz.com/754847/the-co-founder-of-nigerian-startup-andela-is-leaving-to-start-a-payments-company

41 https://yourstory.com/2016/04/m-pesa-ushahidi-andela-africa-startup-movement

42 https://www.theverge.com/2017/9/4/16251226/russia-ai-putin-rule-the-world

43 https://www.nasdaq.com/article/5-fastest-growing-economies-in-the-world-cm773771

44 http://foreignpolicy.com/2016/10/03/imf-officially-gives-china-a-seat-at-the-adult-table-of-world-economies

45 https://www.clausewitz.com/readings/OnWar1873/BK1ch01.html

CHAPTER SIX

Understanding the Data Sphere

Innovation and Intimidation

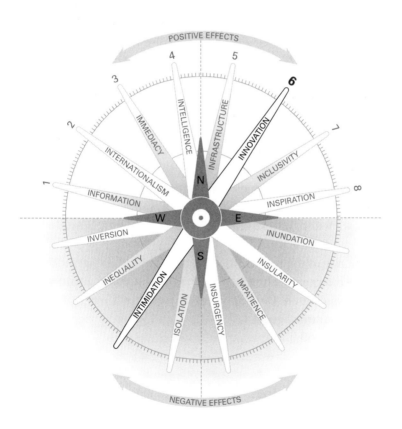

We've already seen how information has impacted behaviour by interrupting and inundating us. The technology has affected so many of the changes we've talked about so far. In this chapter, we'll look into the future to see the changes coming over the horizon. You'll recognize the pattern by now. We face potentially two super-positioned outcomes. The first is innovation, where we'll see wonderful new developments that will benefit our communities, extend our lives, make them more fulfilling and allow us greater efficiencies.

Equally, we'll see how these will be used to cause great changes which have the potential to be negative. In banking and finance the technology change is likely to result in significant restructuring. On top of this, the technology could be used as a social control, to monitor and report on us and to invade our privacy.

The inception of these new technologies could also be matched by a growing fear and incapacity as depicted in Ken Loach's 2016 film *I, Daniel Blake*. In this docudrama film, an unemployed, technologically illiterate man with health problems is confronted with a welfare system that only uses technology. The story covers Blake's frustration and alienation with a world that seems to have left him behind.

We will gallop through a number of imminent technologies to give an overview of the depth and breadth of change. This is what we will cover:

- The rise of the robots?
- The Internet of Things
- Introducing the Data Sphere
- Artificial intelligence (AI)
- The bodyNET
- Autonomy
- Drones
- Energy and batteries
- A new currency
- Green stuff replaced by not very green stuff

- Super computing
- The dark web
- Model citizens?
- Peer group ratings
- Human qualities
- The end of the affair?
- Conclusions

The rise of the robots?

The future has always been in need of better PR. Popular dystopian depictions include everything from Fritz Lang's *Metropolis* through to *Westworld*, *The Stepford Wives*, *Terminator* and *Bladerunner*. Why? Because change is always perceived as a threat to the community and therefore makes a great story. Fear sells.

The truth is more prosaic, of course. Just look at the miracles all around you, robots for example. You're likely to have already interacted with a robot without even realizing it. Google uses software robots, so does Facebook and many sources of online help. They're already here.[1] You can see them in the form of 'chatbots', which are simply AI-led programs that interact with messaging applications. They do this by maintaining a database of likely input questions that are matched to output answers. They use AI and fuzzy logic and computational linguistics to read the questions and interpret meaning.

Chatbots, backed by machine-learning technology, can remember conversations and learn from new ones, building up data over time to respond to a range of queries. A common application, for instance, is with Twitter bots which appear like normal identities but pick up on key phrases to respond to or retweet messages. 'Just in terms of engaging audiences who can't handle complex user experiences, they're brilliant,' says Pete Trainor,[2] who is director of human-centred design at Nexus, a digital agency that created an AI assistant called Luvo for RBS bank. Chatbots on Facebook Messenger and other apps are unashamedly artificial and focused entirely on providing information and/or completing tasks for the humans they interact with.

Perhaps the best known of all chatbots is Amazon's Alexa app. This voice-activated robot is being used in conjunction with other technologies that, for instance, can control many domestic applications such as heating, security, shopping and so on.

The Internet of Things

Most people have begun to experience the Internet of Things (IOT) through the network of physical devices, vehicles, home appliances and other items connected to the internet. These are embedded into electronics, software, sensors, actuators and other connectivity that enable devices to connect and exchange data. This might be how you use a health app such as Fitbit to measure your heartbeat or steps. Or the way your smartphone connects your car to the internet. Or how you control your heating and ventilation via an app.

IOT devices are two-way. Your kettle makes hot water but it can also broadcast the fact that you are boiling water. It may also broadcast your conversations as you drink your coffee. Some devices keep a record of your conversations; for instance, in 2017, an Amazon Echo was subpoenaed in an Arkansas murder trial because it was a witness.[3] IOT devices are now everywhere. Some fridges now deploy Tizen, which is software that permits the interior cameras to gather information about the contents and independently assess whether you need more milk.[4] Some fridges will even automatically alert you, so that you can order more.[5]

IOT can also be used with radio-frequency identification (RFID) chips, which are tags built into clothing, for instance, that use electromagnetic fields to automatically identify and track objects.[6] The tags contain electronically stored information. Naturally, all these data are going to end up somewhere.

Introducing the Data Sphere

We're entering a new dimension where everything is connected, virtualized and triangulated. For example, in the Data Sphere, it will soon be nearly impossible to lie about your whereabouts. Consider the man who claimed to have been elsewhere when his house burnt down. The pacemaker in his heart gave away his location. It also revealed what was happening to his heart as he splashed gasoline around and set his home alight. The prosecutors triangulated upon him using the Data Sphere. Your smartphone tracks your walking gait and this reveals many things about your health, your state of mind and your location.[7] Cameras increasingly populate every environment. After the Houston hurricanes in 2017, insurance firms that deployed drones were quickly able to detect fraudulent claims because they could see the damage. The cameras and sensors at the shopping mall, in the walls of your office space, on public transport, in your clothes and in the home will capture everything, including transactions, actions and emotional reactions.

Artificial intelligence (AI)

Artificial intelligence and machine learning are the glue that brings these technologies together. It connects the dots, gathers data from IOT and other sensors and then drives algorithms that make the choices in our lives. Jeff Bezos, founder of Amazon, says we are in the golden age of AI: 'it is a horizontal enabling layer, it will empower and improve every business, government organization, every philanthropy... there is no institution in the world that cannot be improved with machine learning.'[8]

AI was employed by online retailer shoes.com early on in November 2015 to create personalization on its website on a scale never seen before.[9] Using AI technology around visual perceptions and natural language processing, it allowed customers to interact with products and features. The brand could then create personalized interactions to enhance the customers' experience.

Today in China, Alibaba's Taobao[10] delivers mass personalization at scale. In 2016, on its annual online shopping bonanza Double 11 (or Single's Day), 6.7 billion personalized shopping pages were generated. This resulted in a 40 per cent increase in year-on-year sales. AI knows what the customers want before they do. It can uncover customer insights and trends to deliver predictive service. Netflix is also a good example of this, serving us refined content recommendations based on our usage behaviour.

In advertising, AI can personalize advertising to change parts of it, depending on the audience, to include different music or other content. Technologies that deliver appropriate advertising for specific customer types will become even more sophisticated. Programmatic creative platforms will allow brands to change content to target different user demographics, resulting in an unprecedented precision.

One of the main issues here isn't lack of data. It's making sense of them. In Salesforce's study of 3,500 marketing leaders ('"State of Marketing" Report – Marketing Embraces the AI Revolution'[11]), high-performing brand leaders are twice as likely to be using AI. Further, the majority of marketing leaders plan to use AI in the next two years, the highest among all other technological tools. Leaders recognize that AI could bring value to consumers by anticipating future needs. We've seen this before. iTunes, Netflix and Uber all changed the way we consumed the product. The perception is that brands follows consumers. For the successful brands, it's the other way around.

The Washington Post is using an AI software system called Heliograf,[12] which has published hundreds of news articles for them since 2016. *Wired* magazine calls this 'the most sophisticated use of artificial intelligence in journalism to date'. Those stories will feed into automated polling systems and reveal that the politician in question has just lost a large percentage of their voters' support.

AI will know you were the person in seat 12A at the cinema and connect it to the analysis of your emotional reactions to the film. Your phone, your Alexa, your automatic vacuum cleaner, your IOT fridge and kettle and the RFID chips that are in your clothes will all broadcast data. The Data Sphere is already able to know your sexual orientation before you do.[13] This is how Target figured out that a teenage girl was pregnant before her father knew, back in 2012.[14] Banks today use data analysis and algorithms to assess the spending patterns in a family. Small purchases here or there by spouses begin to reveal that there is trouble at home. The Data Sphere automatically issues the instructions for the algorithms to reduce the credit balance of the lower-earning partner. The bank knows you are about be divorced[15] before you do. It acts before you know your life is about to change. The Data Sphere knows more about you than you do, whether you are an individual, a community, a company, a family or a country.

Sophie Hackford[16] at *Wired* describes this as: 'Perfect information – you can access any information about anything, at any time, in real time.'[17] This is almost a new dimension fuelled by the most valuable commodity in the world, data – 'the new oil'.[18] Instead of being grounded in a physical location, data exist in a new dimension. It is almost as if we are entering a fourth dimension which has its own geography. This is not a continuation of the old 20th-century 'black box' approach to mathematical modelling. That approach was linear, opaque and usually assumed that there was a single correct answer to any given question. A 21st-century leader needs to understand how the Data Sphere heightens transparency and vastly improves clarity. The holographic data-filled dimension of reality is literally more accurate than reality itself. Leaders will need to learn how to conjure forth answers from this more crystal-clear approach to data. The answers won't be black and white or binary any more. Instead, the Data Sphere will give us a rainbow of scenarios and options that are constantly dynamic and permanently tested. This mirror image of reality will also reveal us to the world more precisely. You will see but also be seen.

The bodyNET

The bodyNET is another part of the Data Sphere which allows communications from devices in your body, from pacemakers to hip replacements to ingested pill-sized robotics and brain prosthetics. This may sound far-fetched, but these so-called haptic technologies are already with us. Elon Musk is so sure of it that he has launched a firm called Neuralink, which aims to implant electrodes into humans so that they don't need screens or devices to communicate. Instead of speaking or typing into a phone or computer, we will be able to simply project our thoughts directly onto the internet.

In the future, wearables will be merged with our bodies. We will have elastronic sensors[19] made from stretchy, flexible circuits that move with our bodies and both receive and convey information.[20] We already have biomedical tattoos that permit monitoring and the delivery of data to the body.[21] Ingestible origami-like robotics can now perform targeted surgeries inside the human body.[22] The first such surgery on the human eye was successfully undertaken in the UK in 2016.[23]

We have computer chips that can take human DNA and process it on a microchip[24] to cure diseases that were never curable before.[25] This is why we see nations racing to beat each other in coming up with a cure for cancer.[26] A synthetic synapse will process information millions of times faster than an organic brain, but use less energy. Furthermore, we will be able to just print them.[27]

Neurology is also already part of the bodyNET. In addition to Neuralink's efforts, brain prosthetics are emerging to help Alzheimer's patients.[28] Knowledge itself may soon be ingestible. We already have digital biometric data that allow a doctor to administer medicines remotely. Johnny Matheny of Port Richey, Florida, lost his arm to cancer and is now the first person to have a mind-controlled robotic arm.[29] Science is now looking at memories to establish if they are chemical sequences that we can edit[30] or even implant.

Perhaps the most astonishing development, and another that shows how the internet is disintermediating human relationships, is the rise of teledildonics.[31] The Fourth International Congress on Love and Sex with Robots was held in 2018.[32] David Levy, its founder, is also the author of *Love + Sex with Robots*. He says that the first human–robot marriages will occur by 2050.[33] The Congress also showcased some new gadgets. These included the 'Teletongue', a pair of ear-shaped lollipops programmed to react to the user's licking sounds. There was also a device named Kissenger, which connected two mobile phones for a 'real-time Internet Kiss Communication Interface'. Its creator, Emma Yann Zhang, explained that such haptic devices helped convey feelings and emotions to evoke a sense of presence in a remote environment. According to her, the importance of physical interaction to the quality of our relationships is still grossly underestimated. Ghislaine Boddington is Creative Director of an interactive design collective in the East End of London and Reader at The University of Greenwich. She says that so-called 'body technologies' have potential to connect people romantically, emotionally, physically and sexually. She coined the term 'Internet of bodies' to describe the way that such devices could eventually enable us to network our responses. 'Physical intimacy goes way beyond sex, or even romance', she said. 'It's rather about attachment, and this includes how we feel about each other, our environment and all the objects that surround us. What excites me now is actually the convergence of these technologies and bringing them into our bodies to create new types of intimacy and hyper-enhanced sensualities.'

Autonomy

With AI, suddenly, the idea of a truck without a driver makes sense. We can comprehend that this might mean lower pollution, safer roads, fewer car owners, fewer cars and car accidents, and less energy consumption. Some estimates[34] say that the overall volume of cars will decline to a tenth of what they are today. But none of this really captures what is happening. Driverless cars are just electronic sensors. They are nodes in the Data Sphere that send data and pull them down from this new world.

The changes will be dramatic. Ford, Mercedes, BMW and Tesla have already released self-driving features. According to a briefing paper by BI Intelligence, there will be nearly 10 million cars with some degree of autonomy within the next 10 years.[35] The biggest benefits of self-driving cars are that they will help to make roads safer and people's lives easier. In the UK, KPMG[36] estimates that self-driving cars will lead to 2,500 fewer deaths by 2030. It will herald the end of the designated driver. People on a night out will be able to just call their car or car club from a smartphone.

By 2021, Ford will be mass producing cars without a steering wheel, accelerator pedal or brake pedal. The company believes that the future of the market lies in producing vehicles where a driver is not even required. It has announced a $1 billion (£800 million) investment in Argo AI, an artificial intelligence company that will produce the software needed for a new generation of self-driving cars.[37] This will have profound effects on car design; for instance, the occupants will no longer have to face the same way. All four seats will face each other in the new generation of Ford people carriers. Ford says it expects to profit not only from having its own autonomous car on the road in 2021, but also by licensing the technology to other companies, including rival manufacturers. Ford believes that the cost of owning, maintaining and parking a car in a city means that people will look for an alternative way of getting around, and that is where its vision comes in.[38] Leaders should seek out this sort of transformational change and ask how it applies to their businesses.

In June 2017, General Motors (GM) announced that it had completed 10 self-driving test vehicles of its Chevrolet Bolt electric vehicle (EV). GM believes the achievement could position the company at the head of the autonomous car race. 'The autonomous vehicles you see here today are purpose-built, self-driving test vehicles', GM's chairman and CEO Mary Barra says. GM has the platform and the technology to back up its claim: it's the first car manufacturer to mass produce self-driving vehicles.[39]

Autonomous vehicles are still a niche market but some studies show the market could grow to $87 billion by 2030.[40] The data that these cars throw off about each of us individually, and all of us collectively, can hardly be estimated, but they will clearly be valuable for road maintenance, insurance, weather and so on.

Drones

Drones are remote-controlled aerial robots. Today, most are toys. We're just beginning to deploy drones for industrial tasks. Goldman Sachs estimates that the global drone market is set to reach $100 billion.[41] Drones will generate extraordinary cost savings. They can detect and deter attacks on oil pipelines that today result in hundreds of days lost to shutdowns and loss of oil and gas assets. They can help manage toxic waste from mining sites and keep the logistics at building sites under control. They can be used to survey aquaculture and to manage the migrations of animals and even human refugees. Drones will probably not be used for delivery very much, despite the hype. Amazon made a big splash with their drones for delivery announcement. It's clear, however, that no-one wants a cold pizza or to have packages dropped on the heads of children and dogs playing in suburban neighbourhoods. Regulators are increasingly uneasy if they fly near people or buildings or a thousand feet above the legal height limit (usually 400 feet) and in the way of aircraft. This can be easily fixed with code that prevents drones from bypassing the legal height and distance laws. Drones will, however, increasingly deploy the ever more sophisticated cameras and sensors that fill the Data Sphere with information.[42]

Energy and batteries

Closely correlated with the development of autonomous vehicles is battery development and renewable energy. Solar roads are on their way.[43] Cochin airport[44] in India is entirely powered by solar energy: it has 46,150 solar panels spread over the equivalent of 25 football fields. Wind farms are generating ever more of the power on national grids worldwide. Energy storage is advancing fast, too. On 14 December 2017, the coal-powered energy plant at Loy Yang in Australia had a sudden loss of 560 megawatts of power at 1:59 am.[45] Luckily, Elon Musk had already built the Hornsdale Power battery system, which is the world's largest battery. It was 620 miles away and only just completed some two weeks before the event. It shot 7 megawatts into the grid, which led to the restoration of electricity to the 170,000 homes that had been affected.[46]

Leaders need to think about a world that might not be dependent on oil and gas. Norway is Europe's biggest energy producer and has earned so much that it now has the world's largest sovereign wealth fund. The government used oil and gas to create a trillion-dollar public entity called the Government Pension Fund Global. It owns 1 per cent of all global equities. It rocked the energy and equity world by announcing in late 2017 the sale of all its oil and gas stocks.[47]

The Kingdom of Saudi Arabia seems to be taking a similar view. It is seeking to diversify away from energy sources, investing in other kinds of energy production. The Kingdom announced a commitment of $7 billion for renewable energy projects in 2018.[48] It is now planning for at least 10 per cent of its energy needs to be met by renewables within only five years.[49] It is well documented that the Kingdom is also planning to float

Saudi Aramco[50] to raise funding for other ventures. This, too, is another form of diversification.

A new currency

As we learnt in Chapter 2, we live in inflationary times. Historically, the response to this has been to introduce inflation or a new currency. Or both. We've seen it many times in history, most recently with decimalization of sterling in 1971 and the euro in 1999.

With Bitcoin, the lack of intermediaries such as governments, banks and other third parties will drive down the cost and transaction time of business. Furthermore, because the technology is available on any mobile device, no-one ever need go into any bank again. This limits the banks' ability to sell further added-value financial products. This is likely to lead to more retail banking outlet closures and less real-estate occupancy.

At the height of the banking crisis, in January 2009, a man claiming to be called Santoshi Nakamoto[51] (he was never seen again) published a paper entitled *Bitcoin: A Peer-to-Peer Electronic Cash System*. He then released the first Bitcoin software, which launched the network and the first units of the Bitcoin.[52] New Bitcoins are issued every 10 minutes and the supply is limited, so there will only ever be 21 million Bitcoins, a hard-money rule like the gold standard. Bitcoin is here, it's real and it works. It will make a major difference to financial transactions in the future, making them faster, more secure and less costly. It could entirely replace the security, safety and trust role of the banks, which in any case were badly damaged by the financial crisis. This will affect every aspect of organizational life because it will address many of the rogue elements of technology, such as identity theft and security breach.

Bitcoin shows how a new, decentralized, automated financial system works. It provides the currency, the transaction and the regulatory framework (essentially an in-built audit). At present, there's a low transaction volume when compared to conventional payment systems, but the public interest in them has risen almost as fast as the price. Bitcoin is only one of more than 1,000 different cryptos. Others worthy of note include Ethereum, Ripple, Stellar, NEM, NEO and EOS. Bitcoin is just the most robustly tested of them all so far.

The underlying technology, blockchain, is even more significant than the currencies themselves. Blockchain software allows a set of transactions to be built up in a series of links. Each of them validates the previous one and provides a key which is encrypted. Blockchains can be established in finance, property or stock markets. The implications are profound. It allows peer-to-peer, one-to-many or many-to-one transactions which are instant, secure and need no intermediary. This will do to the banks what the internet did to music. It will shift wealth from publishers to the tech companies. Under that model, the artists made less money than ever. Ironically, blockchain raises the prospect of new artists being able to garner wealth directly without having to do a record deal of any sort. 50cent, the rap artist (aka Curtis Jackson), proved this in 2017 when he was paid some $8 million for his 2014 album *Animal Ambition*. He agreed to accept Bitcoins, which were worth $657 at that time, giving him sales worth about $460,000 at the time. By late 2017, the value of his Bitcoin had leapt to nearly $8 million.[53]

These new forms of accounting, money and property were all made possible by the Cloud, which Microsoft[54] defines as, '... the delivery of computing services – servers, storage, databases, networking, software, analytics and more over the Internet'.[55] Blockchain is simply an automated accounting ledger in the Cloud which allows individual transactions to be verified using cryptography. Everything is digitally recorded, chronologically and incorruptibly. The data are then uploaded into blocks. Each contains a timestamp and a cryptographic hash mark of the previous block, so all data are tied together. Since each block is verified by the blockchain community, nobody can go back and alter it. It is worth, however, remembering that there are people, leaders included, who still have not quite worked out what the Cloud is, let alone properly understood blockchain.

Green stuff replaced by not very green stuff

Today our use of cash is declining rapidly. In 2015, cashless payments accounted for the majority of transactions. The use of cash is set to decline by a further 30 per cent over the next 10 years, according to The Payments Council.[56] The first cash to disappear will be coin. From 2014 to 2017, Victoria Cleland, Director for Banknotes and Chief Cashier of the Bank of England, said there was a 46 per cent increase of notes in circulation.[57] Combine blockchain with crypto and mobile telephone systems and there's no need for banks or currencies. Mobile phone payment networks already move money around without intermediaries. This is permitting many of the world's poor to join the world economy, for example.

For instance, in Shanghai, street hawkers and beggars routinely accept electronic payments using apps such as Alipay which has 520 million users in China alone.[58]

Cryptos, it turns out, are energy intensive. *Wired* magazine said that measuring this is complicated but equals the energy consumption of a 'medium sized country'.[59]

For this reason, some 81 per cent of the world's Bitcoins have been mined in China, primarily because the price of energy is so cheap there. The country has ordered banks to stop financing crypto operations and trading for this and other reasons.[60] It's not environmentally friendly and it facilitates capital flight.

The question is whether moving to blockchain and e-money will improve public and private finances. Governments will be able to tax transactions at the exact moment they occur. This will improve every government's cash flow positively and permanently. They will, however, also force governments to reveal far more about how they spend and what they waste.

Super computing

Fast computing is the power station that fuels AI. As we discovered in Chapter 1, we're experiencing a data explosion. The accumulation of data is rising at the rate of almost 400 per cent per annum. By the year 2020, we will have gathered 44 zettabytes. By 2025, we will have gathered another 180 zettabytes.[61] This is what is known as 'big' data. Even this is becoming passé as it is replaced by 'fast' data.[62] The monumental scale of data is such that they can only be digested by AI. Yes, we're acquiring more data, but we're also getting more powerful processors. In addition to the sensors described above, organizations are acquiring data from multiple sources: customer relationship management (CRM), transactional data, websites, marketing and social media. AI can ingest all these data using machine learning and algorithms to segment customers. This can then be used to show predictive data, uncovering new insights and trends to reach these consumers more comprehensively.

All this takes massive processing power, which is why the new space race is for quantum computers. The Russians currently are leading the field with a 51-qubit quantum computer. China is building the world's largest quantum facility. When complete, it will have a million times the computational power of the entire planet today.[63]

Qubits are quantum bits that underpin this new technology. A normal computer has a memory made up of bits and bytes. Each bit is represented by either a one or a zero. A quantum computer maintains qubits which can be represented as a one, a zero, or a super-position of two qubit states. The upshot is that they are exponentially faster.

They provide something other computers can't handle because a qubit can be in both states at the same time.

The dark web

We still have parallel web universes, such as Tor ('The Onion Router'), which are like the Wild West of the internet. Tor is a not-for-profit organization dedicated to the protection of personal privacy, as well as the freedom and ability to conduct confidential communication. Ironically, the bulk of the funding for Tor's development came from the US military, specifically from The Office of Naval Research and The Defense Advanced Research Projects Agency (DARPA). For this reason, attacks against Tor are welcomed because they improve the security of the network. Tor is now frequently used by criminal organizations for illegal activities, for example to gain access to censored information, to organize political activities or to circumvent laws against criticism of heads of state. It channels user traffic through a free, volunteer network consisting of more than 7,000 relays or layers (hence onion). This hides the user's location and usage from anyone conducting network surveillance or traffic analysis. It protects the user's personal identity and privacy, as well as their freedom and ability to communicate confidentially by keeping their internet activities in the dark. For instance, someone might want to edit their own Wikipedia entry without revealing the identity of the author. Of course, Wikipedia has added Tor blockers to prevent this.

There are no reliable figures for the user numbers of Tor but it is heavily used. In theory, the access is anonymous. In practice, regulators have software that counters that.[64] It is endorsed, however, by the Electronic Frontier Foundation (EFF) and other civil liberties groups as a method for whistleblowers and human rights workers to communicate with journalists.

This means that if someone believes they are whistleblowing, they can take confidential data and leak them with impunity and anonymity. Tor can therefore be used for just about anything: anonymous defamation, unauthorized news leaks of sensitive information, copyright infringement, distribution of illegal sexual content, selling controlled substances, weapons and stolen credit card numbers, money laundering, bank fraud, credit card fraud, identity theft and the exchange of counterfeit currency.

Model citizens?

The Data Sphere is also a scoring mechanism. Of course, we score people now.

Credit scores have been around since Bill Fair and Earl Isaac invented credit scores (Fair Isaac Company) in 1956. Today, FICO scores are used to determine many financial decisions, including the interest rates on mortgages and loan approvals. But what if this information was linked to other social media sources? Supposing these data could be aggregated so that governments could rate behaviour as either positive or negative to create a template of a model citizen? This could create a Citizen Score and tell everyone about your creditworthiness for a mortgage or a loan. Some governments have already developed social credit systems (SCSs) to rate citizens.

Governments around the world are using these data, for instance in travel security. In 2015, the Transportation Security Administration (TSA) proposed expanding the PreCheck background checks to include social media records, location data and purchase history. This expansion of credit scoring into 'life scoring' could lead to what Kevin Kelly in his book *The Inevitable*[65] called 'coveillance'. This is where participants in such schemes are also allowed to see the algorithms used to monitor them.

In an era of big data, this will go further. A person's own social score could also be affected by what friends say and do, beyond their own contact with them. If they're connected to negative online posts, their own score could also be dragged down. This is why transparency on the methods is important. Why would people sign up for a publicly endorsed government surveillance system? For the same reason they sign up to loyalty schemes or low-risk drivers' premiums – cost and benefit.

China has introduced a national credit scoring system and believes that citizen scores are much needed. This is because China suffers from a lightly regulated market where the sale of counterfeit and substandard products is a problem.[66] The OECD says the majority of all fake goods, from watches to handbags to baby food, originate from China.[67] China's trust system is working well and having consequences. In February 2017, the Supreme People's Court said 6 million citizens had been banned from taking flights so far because of social misdeeds.[68] This, though, is still very much at an early stage. The benefits of the SCS are, for instance, cheaper loans, car rentals and use of the VIP check-in at Beijing Airport. By 2020, everyone in China will be enrolled in this database.

Professor Wang Shuqin[69] refers to 'China's Social Faithful System'. She points out that because half of signed contracts are not honoured, doing business in China is risky: 'Given the speed of the digital economy it's crucial that people can quickly verify each other's creditworthiness', she says. 'The behaviour of the majority is determined by their world of thoughts. A person who believes in socialist core values is behaving more decently.'

Social credit systems reflect a paradigm shift. In an increasingly materialistic and connected society, gamifying obedience is an easier alignment tool than 'top-down' control. It's possible these systems may become subject to illicit or unwanted ways of gaming the data in the same way that Facebook likes and Twitter followers can be bought.

Peer group ratings

Employers are already used to anonymous rating services such as Glass Door and Checkatrade, but what if this was applied to everyone, irrespective of their employment status? Peeple is an app launched in March 2016, which has been described as a Yelp for humans.[70] It allows you to rate and review everyone you know – friends, family, neighbours, doctors, bosses and even former partners. The app rates you with a 'Peeple Number' based on all the feedback and recommendations you receive. This has proved controversial, not least because once you're on the system, you can't get off.

> **QUICK TIP** Imagine a world where everything is a data-gathering node? How could leaders use this? How could this be used against leaders?

Human qualities

Humans are being weighed and measured, sized up and assessed by the Data Sphere all the time. This is producing data that result in scores and opinions and real outcomes. However, perhaps leaders need to ask what is happening to our humanness in this new Data Sphere. It is not only that humans are going to become more robotic through various implants and prosthetics. Are humans becoming less humane and being treated less humanely? Are we using all the data to find efficiencies at the expense of other qualities that are worth protecting and preserving, such as community building, empathy and compassion? We may be entering a new dimension of knowledge, but the old mob mentality may follow us into the Data Sphere and try to digitally lynch people. The Data Sphere will give us new identities, but it can also take them away. It will rank us and give us all social credit scores based on our social behaviour but not value our humour or our kindness.

Leaders need to learn to use this sophisticated tool, but that is not enough. They must also decide where we are navigating to.

What kind of society will result from the directional choices leaders make?

> **QUICK TIP** Technology creates profound opportunities but also vulnerabilities. Leaders need to ask how they would work without the most fundamental components. What if we lost power? Or data? They need the imagination to prepare for failure.

The end of the affair?

The love affair with technology is beginning to slow as awareness of its dark side develops. In 2018, former employees[71] of Google and Facebook, alarmed over the ill-effects of social networks and smartphones, are challenging the companies they helped build. The Center for Humane Technology plans an anti-tech addiction lobbying effort together with an ad campaign targeted at 55,000 public schools in the United States. Entitled *The Truth About Tech*, it will be funded with $7 million from non-profit media watchdog Common Sense Media. It's aimed at educating students, parents and teachers about the dangers of technology, including the depression that can come from heavy use of social media. The group says that: 'Our society is being hijacked by technology. What began as a race to monetize our attention is now eroding the pillars of our society: mental health, democracy, social relationships, and our children.' Its goal is to move away from technology that extracts attention and erodes society, towards technology that protects our minds and replenishes society.

Leaders must encourage an attitude that experiments and anticipates new ideas.

It says that 'Humane Design', which protects the vulnerable from getting overwhelmed, stressed or outraged, is the goal. The group points out that we are vulnerable to micro-targeted persuasion using 'messages that use our personality and traits against us'. It points out how we are vulnerable to the expectation of being available to each other 24/7.

Salesforce CEO Marc Benioff[72] offered up an analogy to treat social media like a health issue, similar to tobacco and sugar. 'I think that you do it exactly the same way that you regulated the cigarette industry. Here's a product: Cigarettes. They're addictive, they're not good for you', Benioff told CNBC in 2018. 'I think that for sure, technology has addictive qualities that we have to address, and that product designers are working to make those products more addictive and we need to rein that back.'

Conclusions

If we thought the changes so far were substantial, then we must prepare for more of the same. We're likely to see technology become more pervasive and more joined up to the point that the data generated constitute an entirely new and more accurate dimension of reality than reality itself. It will be possible to know and analyse everything and learn new insights into our behaviour.

Our enemies are fear and prejudice. Our weapons are understanding and familiarity. Leaders can make this happen by ensuring their teams feel the technology is serving them, rather than the other way around. This means the leader must encourage an attitude that experiments and anticipates new ideas and looks for ways to apply it.

It is typical of humans to think of new technology in terms of old ideas. We remain wedded to the notion of cars and drones and kettles. But, increasingly these are all just electronic nodes in the Data Sphere. As technology changes, so must our way of thinking about it.

If history teaches us anything, it's that the future of technology has always been viewed darkly. It usually turns out to be wrong. The emerging Data Sphere offers extraordinary opportunities, but leaders must understand the conflicting forces at work.

Fear of the new can drive us into an incapacitated state, unable to make decisions and fearful of the future. Familiarity and awareness of the opportunities could have the opposite effect. This could also be a moment of inception, holding up a lantern above a darkened pathway that leads to a more enlightened future. This is where we must rekindle our curiosity and imagination. Learning and leading must go hand in hand.

Endnotes

1 https://www.forbes.com/sites/gilpress/2016/07/20/artificial-intelligence-rapidly-adopted-by-enterprises-survey-says/#673601a012da

2 https://www.theguardian.com/technology/2016/sep/18/chatbots-talk-town-interact-humans-technology-silicon-valley

3 https://www.wired.com/2017/02/murder-case-tests-alexas-devotion-privacy/

4 https://www.theverge.com/2016/1/5/10708380/samsung-family-hub-fridge-mastercard-app-groceries-ces-2016

5 https://www.usatoday.com/story/tech/reviewedcom/2017/01/04/finally-a-fridge-with-alexa-that-orders-groceries-for-you/96155086

6 http://www.wired.co.uk/article/thoryn-stephens-american-apparel

7 https://www.health.harvard.edu/blog/a-sluggish-unsteady-walk-might-signal-memory-problems-201207235047

8 https://www.geekwire.com/2017/jeff-bezos-explains-amazons-artificial-intelligence-machine-learning-strategy

9 https://venturebeat.com/2017/05/05/3-ways-retailers-are-using-ai-to-reinvent-shopping

10 https://www.forbes.com/sites/ahylee/2016/11/07/how-alibaba-turned-chinas-singles-day-into-the-worlds-biggest-shopping-bonanza/#313a01bc76c0

11 https://www.salesforce.com/blog/2017/06/fourth-annual-state-of-marketing-report.html

12 https://www.washingtonpost.com/pr/wp/2016/10/19/the-washington-post-uses-artificial-intelligence-to-cover-nearly-500-races-on-election-day/?utm_term=.d15788828c4a

13 http://americablog.com/2013/03/facebook-might-know-youre-gay-before-you-do.html

14 https://www.forbes.com/sites/kashmirhill/2012/02/16/how-target-figured-out-a-teen-girl-was-pregnant-before-her-father-did/#1ac91efd6668

15 https://www.thedailybeast.com/how-visa-predicts-divorce

16 http://www.howtoacademy.com/conferences/how-to-change-the-world-2015

17 B2B Online Summit 2016

18 https://www.economist.com/news/leaders/21721656-data-economy-demands-new-approach-antitrust-rules-worlds-most-valuable-resource

19 https://www.nature.com/news/bring-on-the-bodynet-1.22643

20 https://www.prnewswire.com/news-releases/global-printable-flexible-and-stretchable-sensors-and-electronics-market-report-2018–over-250-in-depth-company-profiles-300591985.html

21 https://news.harvard.edu/gazette/story/2017/09/harvard-researchers-help-develop-smart-tattoos

22 http://www.telegraph.co.uk/science/2016/05/13/origami-robot-can-be-swallowed-in-pill-and-then-sent-on-missions

23 http://www.bbc.co.uk/news/health-37246995

24 https://www.prnewswire.com/news-releases/nano-global-arm-collaborate-on-artificial-intelligence-chip-to-drive-health-revolution-by-capturing-and-analyzing-molecular-data-in-real-time-300559508.html

25 https://www.prnewswire.com/news-releases/nano-global-arm-collaborate-on-artificial-intelligence-chip-to-drive-health-revolution-by-capturing-and-analyzing-molecular-data-in-real-time-300559508.html

26 https://www.npr.org/sections/health-shots/2018/02/21/585336506/doctors-in-china-lead-race-to-treat-cancer-by-editing-genes

27 http://advances.sciencemag.org/content/4/1/e1701329

28 https://alzheimersnewstoday.com/2015/10/06/brain-implant-help-people-memory-loss

29 https://futurism.com/mind-controlled-robotic-arm-johnny-matheny

30 https://www.sciencealert.com/new-discovery-could-allow-us-to-edit-memories-to-make-them-less-traumatic

31 https://gizmodo.com/teledildonics-the-weird-wonderful-world-of-social-sex-1516075707

32 http://loveandsexwithrobots.org

33 Levy, D (2008) *Love + Sex with Robots: The evolution of human–robot relationships*, Duckworth, London

34 https://www.fastcompany.com/3027275/car-sharing-means-there-are-already-500000-fewer-vehicles-on-the-road

35 http://uk.businessinsider.com/report-10-million-self-driving-cars-will-be-on-the-road-by-2020-2015-5-6

36 http://uk.businessinsider.com/report-10-million-self-driving-cars-will-be-on-the-road-by-2020-2015-5-6

37 http://www.telegraph.co.uk/technology/2017/08/17/ford-patents-removable-steering-wheel-driverless-cars

38 http://www.telegraph.co.uk/business/2017/02/27/ford-seeks-pioneer-new-generation-driverless-cars

39 https://www.usatoday.com/story/money/cars/2017/06/13/general-motors-we-can-mass-produce-self-driving-cars-now/102805626

40 https://www.forbes.com/sites/oliviergarret/2017/03/03/10-million-self-driving-cars-will-hit-the-road-by-2020-heres-how-to-profit/#216603277e50

41 http://www.goldmansachs.com/our-thinking/technology-driving-innovation/drones

42 http://www.goldmansachs.com/our-thinking/technology-driving-innovation/drones

43 https://futurism.com/chinas-first-solar-highway-complete-soon-charge-electric-cars

44 https://www.scienceabc.com/innovation/indias-cochin-airport-worlds-first-100-percent-solar-powered-airport.html

45 http://reneweconomy.com.au/tesla-big-battery-outsmarts-lumbering-coal-units-after-loy-yang-trips-70003

46 https://qz.com/1165314/elon-musks-giant-tesla-battery-in-australia-proves-it-can-power-the-grid-when-coal-plants-fail

47 https://www.ft.com/content/611c2e9e-cad9-11e7-aa33-c63fdc9b8c6c

48 https://www.bloomberg.com/news/articles/2018-01-16/saudi-arabia-plans-up-to-7-billion-of-renewables-this-year

49 https://www.forbes.com/sites/mikescott/2018/01/18/saudi-arabia-plans-to-source-10-of-its-power-from-renewable-energy-within-5-years/#6c97136e485f

50 https://www.theguardian.com/business/2018/jan/05/saudi-aramco-takes-key-step-towards-ipo

51 http://time.com/money/5002378/bitcoin-creator-nakamoto-billionaire/

52 https://bitcoin.org/en/faq

53 http://www.bbc.com/news/business-42820246

54 https://azure.microsoft.com/en-us/overview/what-is-cloud-computing

55 https://azure.microsoft.com/en-gb/overview/what-is-cloud-computing

56 https://www.paymentsuk.org.uk/news-events/news/uk-set-make-120-million-payments-day-2024

57 http://www.bankofengland.co.uk/publications/Documents/speeches/2017/speech978.pdf

58 https://intl.alipay.com

59 http://www.wired.co.uk/article/how-much-energy-does-bitcoin-mining-really-use

60 http://www.scmp.com/business/banking-finance/article/2129645/pboc-orders-banks-halt-banking-services-cryptocurrency

61 https://whatsthebigdata.com/2016/03/07/amount-of-data-created-annually-to-reach-180-zettabytes-in-2025

62 https://www.entrepreneur.com/article/273561

63 https://www.wsj.com/articles/the-computer-that-could-rule-the-world-1509143922

64 https://www.theguardian.com/world/2013/oct/04/tor-attacks-nsa-users-online-anonymity

65 Kelly, K (2017) *The Inevitable: Understanding the 12 technological forces that will shape our future*, Penguin, New York

66 http://shanghaiist.com/2016/10/11/substandard_online_goods.php

67 http://www.oecd.org/industry/global-trade-in-fake-goods-worth-nearly-half-a-trillion-dollars-a-year.htm

68 http://www.wired.co.uk/article/chinese-government-social-credit-score-privacy-invasion

69 http://www.wired.co.uk/article/chinese-government-social-credit-score-privacy-invasion

70 https://www.cbsnews.com/news/peeple-the-yelp-for-people-app-launches

71 https://www.nytimes.com/2018/02/04/technology/early-facebook-google-employees-fight-tech.html

72 https://www.cnbc.com/2018/01/23/salesforce-ceo-marc-benioff-says-regulate-facebook-like-tobacco.html

CHAPTER SEVEN

Understanding Gender

Inclusivity and Inequality

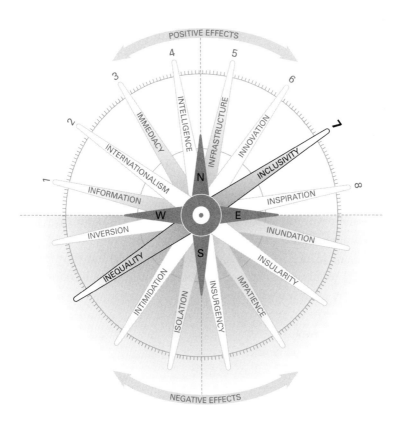

Leaders need to create the conditions under which collective endeavour can be maximized. They need to be able to unify people in the pursuit of common goals and create a collective identity, cohesion and efficiency.

For this reason, good leadership concentrates on things we have in common. Our future, a vision and shared ambition. Qualities that unify. Take the motto of the United States, for example, *E Pluribus Unum* (out of the many, one). It is one of the greatest leadership statements of all time. The United States doesn't care where you're from. It cares where you're going.

To unify groups, one must first understand them. One of the largest of all group sub-identities in the workplace is gender. This has become a hotly debated issue for a number of reasons, so we should be careful to generate light rather than heat. We're not interested in judgements. We're searching for the truth.

Our motivation in understanding gender is to allow leaders to create effective, modern, aspirant and representative teams that liberate potential. This chapter is not therefore just about gender. We're interested in both masculine and feminine thinking traits. We're not just concerned with whether someone is male, female or transgender. All genders can be the provenance of both thinking traits. Women can think in a masculine way and vice versa. This is about potential and how to access it. If we're going to embrace 21st-century leadership, we need to understand the issue of gender.

The gender debate in leadership is frequently framed as a matter of justice to women. It certainly is that, but that justice belongs to all those who feel the impact of leadership failure.

This is what we will cover:

- Assumptions
- Understanding gender
- Problems with the playing field
  - Height and authority
  - Confidence and loudness
  - Are women more agreeable?

- Is a 'hidden' patriarchy to blame?
- More interrupted, less listened to
- More judged on looks
- The cult of the individual
- Are women more emotionally intelligent?
- Do women collaborate more?
- Introducing the LAB Brain Model
- What is androcentricity?
- Who was the internet built by and for whom?
- Gender differences on social media
- Overconfidence as a cause of our problems
- Could it be the faster we move, the more superficial our perception becomes?
- An inherent bias against diversity?
- A war on men?
- Training for confidence
- Techniques for boosting confidence
- Techniques for breaking the circle
- Conclusions

Assumptions

We will start from a principle of stating some assumptions. Of course, these are open to question, but we state them nonetheless as a starting point.

First, we believe there is such a thing as Western Reductionism or analytic thinking. If we believe this, then it follows that an alternative way of thinking is also possible. This is synthetic or parenthetic thinking. This joins up the dots rather than analyses the difference between them. We refer to this as the left-brain process and the right-brain process. We know that neuroscientists such as Ian McGilchrist[1] have shown that these processes are not located in those hemispheres. Instead, he and others have shown us that distinct processes in each are meant to work together. That is our goal here – not to choose between the two approaches, but to become more skilled at both.

Another assumption is that there are gender traits embodied in the two types of thinking. Drill-down, short-term, tactical, quantitative left-brain thinking is often associated with masculine traits. Big-picture, compassionate, empathetic, qualitative right-brain thinking is often associated with feminine traits.

Here we make another assumption. We separate gender traits from gender identity. We will not use the terms 'male' and 'masculine thinking' interchangeably. We're only interested here in masculine and feminine thinking, not in male or female genders. Why does this matter? Because leadership needs both sets of skills. It needs both left- and right-brain thinking. Like playing a keyboard, it needs to be able to play all the notes and not just part of the keyboard.

Understanding gender

Debates about gender are depressingly predictable. This is often because they are about gender differences rather than the desired outcome. Is there evidence of gender inequality? Yes. Only 7 per cent of the FTSE 100 companies have female CEOs.[2] Is there also evidence of a gender pay gap?[3] Yes. The reasons for both, though, are complex.

If males are water and females oil, we need an emulsion created by a vigorous and energetic leadership culture.

Investors are increasingly demanding that firms create more gender diversity. BlackRock, the world's largest asset manager, has said it will divest from firms that have fewer than two women on their boards.[4] Most organizations remain hierarchically structured irrespective of the gender of board directors.

Why is this so entrenched? To understand, we need to explore further. What we're trying to get to is the three values of modernity, aspiration and representation. These are brand values that all of us can buy into. Of course, these values are well served by a larger proportion of women in leadership roles, but not if they just simply replicate a masculine way of thinking.

If the male is like water and the female like oil, then we don't need a separation here. We need an emulsion created by a vigorous and energetic leadership culture.

Problems with the playing field

Let's look at the basics of gender as applied to leadership. Some of it is physical.

Height and authority

Height is associated with authority.[5] In Malcolm Gladwell's *Blink*,[6] he suggests most powerful people are tall, which gives them an advantage in business. Gladwell found that most male CEOs were a shade under six feet tall. Most male bosses are three inches taller than other men; the average height of men in the United States is 5'9". American women are 5'4" on average. 'Most of us, in ways that we are not entirely aware of, automatically associate leadership ability with imposing physical stature', Gladwell says. 'We have a sense, in our minds, of what a leader is supposed to look like, and that stereotype is so powerful that when someone fits it, we simply become blind to other considerations.'

Confidence and loudness

Loudness is correlated with confidence[7] and men have deeper, louder voices than women.[8] This seems to matter. Training female leaders to stand tall and project their voices can help equalize these issues to level the playing field.

This does not, however, address the issue of confidence. In many instances, men's confidence is wrongly (and dangerously) correlated with confidence. We'll hear more of this later.

Are women more agreeable?

Jordan Peterson is a University of Toronto clinical psychologist. In an interview with Cathy Newman on Channel 4 in January 2018,[9] Peterson pointed out a personality trait known as *agreeableness*. Agreeable people are defined as compassionate and polite. He went on to say that agreeable people get paid less than disagreeable people for the same job and that women tend to be more agreeable. Again, much can be done to offset this with assertiveness training. This can result in more rapid promotion and more equal pay.

Is a 'hidden' patriarchy to blame?

Newman went on to suggest that the problem was a patriarchal society. This idea comes directly from antiquity. The works of Aristotle, who educated Alexander the Great, portrayed women as morally, intellectually and physically inferior to men. He saw women as the property of men. He claimed that women's role in society was to reproduce and serve men in the household. He saw male domination of women as natural and virtuous.

Feminist theory sees patriarchy as an unjust social system that enforces gender roles and is oppressive to both men and women.[10] It often includes any social, political or economic mechanism that evokes male dominance over women.

Sociologist Sylvia Walby[11] composed six overlapping structures that define patriarchy and which take different forms in different cultures and different times:

1 The state: women are unlikely to have formal power and representation.
2 The household: women are more likely to do the housework and raise the children.

3 Violence: women are more prone to being abused.

4 Paid work: women are likely to be paid less.

5 Sexuality: women's sexuality is more likely to be treated negatively.

6 Culture: women are more misrepresented in media and popular culture.

The above broadly remains the case. So, on that basis, the patriarchy lives. This is a culture, though, and as such, needs little active help to perpetuate itself. The anger with this culture is that many of its beneficiaries either turn a blind eye or do not notice or recognize it (more likely). Leaders may think a discussion in this area irrelevant, but this is more than just about gender. It's about how leaders harness all resources and understand key dynamics within the organization.

More interrupted, less listened to

Adam Grant and Sheryl Sandberg teamed up to write an opinion piece in *The New York Times* entitled 'Speaking While Female'.[12] In it, they list several studies that show how the spoken contributions of women in the workplace are consistently undervalued.

It's not just that women are interrupted more frequently than men. It's that their ideas, contributions and data are more likely to be discounted. Across environments as diverse as the television industry, politics and corporations there are similar patterns. First, men who contribute good ideas receive higher evaluations. The more men speak up, the more helpful they are perceived to be. Women's data and insights are more likely to be discounted than those of their male counterparts.

More judged on looks

In a piece entitled 'Why wearing too much makeup harms a woman's leadership chances'[13] for *The Daily Telegraph*, Science Editor

Sarah Knapton points out work by Abertay University in Scotland. Researchers asked participants to view a series of images of the same woman fresh faced, or made up as if for a night out. Computer software was used to manipulate the amount of makeup worn. They found that people judged heavily made-up women as having poorer leadership skills than those who had not used cosmetics.

The cult of the individual

Perhaps the greatest reason for the failure of leadership is far too much attention being focused on the 'leader' and too little on the 'ship', the team of people behind the leader. Could this also be reflective of a typically egocentric and male approach? The Judeo-Christian tradition places emphasis on male leadership, for example Moses, David and Jesus. It's possible we have become programmed to our model of leadership as being individual, male and infallible.

The *Führerprinzip* was another example of this leadership model. It described the basis of all political authority in the governmental structures of the German Third Reich. The idea behind it was that the order of the Führer (leader) superseded any law. All governmental policies, decisions and offices were geared towards the realization of this end. When the veneration, belief and expectation of the individual leader tend towards this sort of infallibility, is it any wonder failure is so common? It undermines the strength and collective good sense of the team.

Are women more emotionally intelligent?

One of the great problems with any sensible discussion in this area is the tendency to generalize. It's just not that simple. For instance, some measures suggest women are on average better than men at some forms of empathy. Others, that men do better than women when it comes to managing distressing emotions in themselves, at least. Any man might be as good as any woman at empathy. Every woman, as good as any man at handling upsets.

Writing in *Psychology Today* Dr Dan Goleman asked the question *Are Women More Emotionally Intelligent Than Men?*[14] Emotional intelligence has four parts: self-awareness, managing our emotions, empathy and social skill.[15] He indicated that in many tests of emotional intelligence (EI),[16] women tend to have an edge over men. In leadership roles, EI is a critical, perhaps non-negotiable, skill.

Empathy is another key skill. There are three kinds. Cognitive empathy understands how the other person sees things. Emotional empathy feels what the other person feels. Empathic concern is ready to help someone in need. Women tend to be better at emotional empathy than men, in general. This is an important leadership skill because it fosters rapport and chemistry. People who excel in emotional empathy make good counsellors, teachers and group leaders because of this ability to sense, in the moment, how others are reacting.

But why is this? Neuroscientists point to a region of the brain called the insula,[17] which senses signals from our whole body. When we're empathizing, the brain mimics what that person feels and the insula reads that pattern and tells us what that feeling is. Goleman says women differ from men where the other person is upset, or the emotions are disturbing. Women's brains tend to stay with those feelings, but men's brains do something else. They sense the feelings for a moment, then tune out of the emotions and switch to other brain areas that try to solve the problem that's creating the disturbance.

There is a great deal of neuroscience here. Some research[18] points out that while male brains are more connected within the hemispheres, female brains are more connected across them. 'On average, men connect front to back (parts of the brain) more strongly than women,' whereas 'women have stronger connections left to right', says Ragini Verma, an associate professor of radiology at the University of Pennsylvania medical school.

If the female brain is literally more joined up, could this explain why feminine thinking is considered more connected and more empathetic?[19] Dan Goleman writing in *Psychology Today* says: 'Women often complain that men are tuned out emotionally, and men that women are too emotional – it's a brain difference. Neither is better – both have advantages. The male tune-out works well when there's a need to insulate yourself against distress so you can stay calm, while others around you are falling apart – and focus on finding a solution to an urgent problem. And the female tendency to stay tuned in helps enormously to nurture and support others in emotional trying circumstances.' Goleman termed this as part of the 'tend-and-befriend' response to stress.

In another fascinating test,[20] women that were injected with testosterone became more egocentric and less attuned to the needs of the group. The hormone disrupted their ability to work together. 'Egocentricity bias is the degree to which people over-weight their own opinion. If you are more egocentric, you are more likely to think you are right', said study researcher Nicholas Wright, of University College London. 'These women were more likely to say they were right when they were on testosterone, than when they were on placebo.' In short, the testosterone made women make more selfish decisions which were less in the interests of the group.

There's another way of looking at male–female differences in emotional intelligence. Simon Baron-Cohen at Cambridge University says that there's an extreme 'female brain'[21] which is high in emotional empathy but not so good at systems analysis. By contrast, the extreme 'male brain' excels in systems thinking and is poor at emotional empathy (he does not mean that all men have the male brain, nor all women the female brain, of course; many women are skilled at systems thinking, and many men at emotional empathy).

What this points to is that a form of masculine and feminine thinking can be identified as distinct from just gender alone. This brings us back to the problem of generalization. Psychologist Ruth Malloy at the Hay Group Boston says when you only look at the stars – leaders in the top 10 per cent of business performance – gender differences in emotional intelligence abilities wash out: 'The men are as good as the women, the women as good as the men, across the board.'[22]

Do women collaborate more?

In a paper, 'Are Women More Attracted to Cooperation Than Men?',[23] Peter J Kuhn and Marie-Claire Villeval from the National Bureau of Economic Research found that women are, in fact, far more likely to collaborate than men. The two economists said it was to do with relative competence, the degree to which you think your ability matches up against that of your colleagues. In short, men tend to overestimate their abilities and downplay those of their co-workers, while women short-change their skills and defer to their peers. This theme will be echoed by other studies later, as we shall see. According to the study, women are more aware of a feeling that not everyone is getting a fair deal. Unsurprisingly, men are less sensitive to the asymmetry.

Kuhn and Villeval made the link that this approach is reflected in compensation as well. They ran an experiment allowing men and women to select teamwork versus solo work, for equal compensation. Then, they ran it again, increasing the returns from excellent teamwork by about 10 per cent. Once they did this, the cooperation gap between men and women disappeared. So, if compensation is orientated towards the team, then men will jump at the chance to work more closely with their colleagues.

Their research into the gender wage gap is also worth a look. Why, for instance, are women overrepresented in certain fields, such as the non-profit sector, and underrepresented in other fields, such as financial institutions and board positions in major companies? Women outnumber men in many caring occupations, from charitable organizations to nursing, both of which offer co-operative production with less financial reward. One reasonable question to ask about the pay gap is: How much should we blame the system and how much should we chalk this up to women's decisions?

Maybe that all sounds too theoretical? The number of Fortune 1000 companies using workgroup or team incentives for at least a fifth of their workers more than doubled between 1990 and 2002.[24]

This isn't just a story about gender wage gaps; it's a story about motivation. In manufacturing and other complex processes, teamwork is vital. It's not enough to focus on making women feel confident. It's also key to make overconfident men trust that their colleagues just might be as competent as them.

In a piece in *Forbes*, entitled 'Collaborating While Female',[25] Shani Harmon and Renee Cullinan pointed out the work of Cal Newport, a professor who has studied the habits of exceptionally productive people. In his book *Deep Work*, he makes the case for blocks of distraction-free work time (see the overload in Chapter 1). Doing so, he argues, allows the assimilation of complicated information and better results. This independent thinking time is important to effective collaboration. Independent focus on a project brought to a group for consideration brings improvement in the quality of the discussion. Most of the time people just come into a room and try to figure it out.

The alternative to deep work, he says, is interruption and jumping from task to task: going from one meeting to another, responding to e-mails as they come in, fielding social media and so on. The cost of this switching is high. When we move from one task to another, a percentage of our attention remains on the prior task. This 'attention residue' diminishes our performance on the task at hand. The more we switch between tasks, the greater the attention residue, the worse the performance.

Simply put, those who carve out 90 minutes of focused work time during the work day get more done. This is where there is another important gender divide.

Women are less likely to carve out time during the work day to focus on their top priorities because it feels selfish. Harmon and Cullinan say this is partly because women and men differ on what it means to be a good team player: 'According to research, women are more likely to agree with the statement: "Being a good team player means helping all of my colleagues with what they need to get done".' In contrast, men are more likely to agree with the statement: 'Being a good team player is knowing your position and playing it well.' While both perspectives are valid, they say, they lead to different patterns of collaboration. For men, blocking the calendar is consistent with being a great team player. For women, blocking time can feel like just the opposite.

That instinct to be available to others has a double effect. Not only are women less likely to carve out time for their own work, they're also more likely to give time away. They're also more likely to feel guilty about ignoring a request or declining a meeting in order to prioritize their own work.

Social scientist Benjamin Voyer explains why that might be: 'Guilt is an "other-focused emotion"' – an emotion that involves thinking about others, which research indicates is typically a female trait. 'Whatever the reason,' researchers say, 'the result is the same: work slips into the evenings and weekends, which may be one of the reasons why women work on average 50 minutes more a day than men.'

Introducing the LAB Brain Model

We can see the LAB Brain Model in Figure 7.1. It puts together what we already know about Western Reductionist thinking – the so-called left-brain process with its 'compare, contrast and analyse' functions – and juxtaposes it with the right-brain

FIGURE 7.1 LAB Brain Model

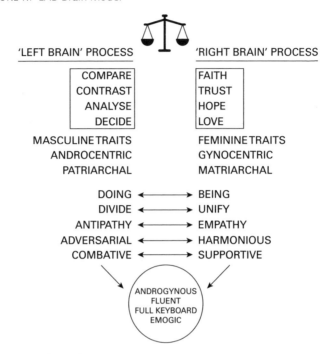

Source: LEWIS Rise Academy

process and its imaginative, divergent qualities. These processes belong to both genders.

We split these and assign gender traits to the processes, because this is where the research takes us. Attaining equality of masculine and feminine approaches is part of balanced leadership. It would be sub-optimal, however, if all board directors thought and behaved like men, irrespective of gender. A gender-biased organization is inherently inefficient. The ideal solution is a blend, where androcentricity combines with gynocentricity to create androgeneity. This is the combination of logic and emotion into the 'emogic'.

It is important to state that we do not accept that male and female ability differs due to genetics or physiology, but to socialization. One of the key variables that helps to socialize behaviour is the technology we use.

What is androcentricity?

Much of the internet-driven changes have created an *androcentricity* or overwhelmingly masculine approach. What is the evidence for this? The extent to which the technology engenders analytic and quantitative rather than qualitative thinking.

This is vested in the Top Ten Applications of the Internet,[26] which are:

- E-mail and other communications
- Research
- File downloads
- Discussion groups
- Interactive games
- Education and self-improvement
- Dating
- Electronic media
- Job-hunting
- Shopping

E-mail and other communications interrupt us. Every time this happens, we enter a left-brain process: Who is the mail from? What does it need me to do? Should I respond? The internet allows us to compare, contrast and analyse everything – ourselves, our weight, our calories, our heart rate – and it allows us to compare and contrast products and prices – again the left brain. It allows us to analyse our partners and position them against future options.

The net result is a huge uptick in data. In recent times, 'big data' has become a popular concept. The technology gives us more data to analyse. It not only allows us to compare ourselves with others but to compare ourselves today with yesterday and the year before that.

Who was the internet built by and for whom?

It's probably fair to say that men invented the internet. They developed it for the US military. They invented it in their own likeness, at least as it was in the 1970s and 1980s. The data that the internet generates are used to classify and segment and then to re-target. The internet sorts, shapes and ranks. Data are analysed, broken down and then analysed again. We think of the internet as a great leveller, a democratizer, a place that opens doors to everyone. The reality, however, is that the internet is dominated by some very specific uses.

Men are the largest consumers of pornography and sexual services. More men visit porn sites on the web than visit Amazon, Netflix and Twitter combined.[27] About a third of all web traffic is pornography.[28] One of the world's largest adult sites, Pornhub, an explicit-video-sharing site, gets 2.4 million visitors per hour. In 2015 alone, people around the globe watched 4,392,486,580 hours of its content.

Gender differences on social media

Men also dominate the conversation on comments boards across the internet, especially when they can post under a pseudonym, according to a study.[29]

Dr Fiona Martin of Sydney University took a sample of comments from 15 major websites and analysed the gender of the commenters. She categorized people as either male, female or ambiguous (Figure 7.2). On international sites, men accounted for as much as 79 per cent of the commenters, while the highest proportion of women to post on the same sites was only 20 per cent. While women were slightly more likely to comment on local news sites, reaching 35 per cent on one publication, men still appeared to dominate the conversations.

FIGURE 7.2 Gender of commenter names: international and metropolitan news services (top 100 commenters)

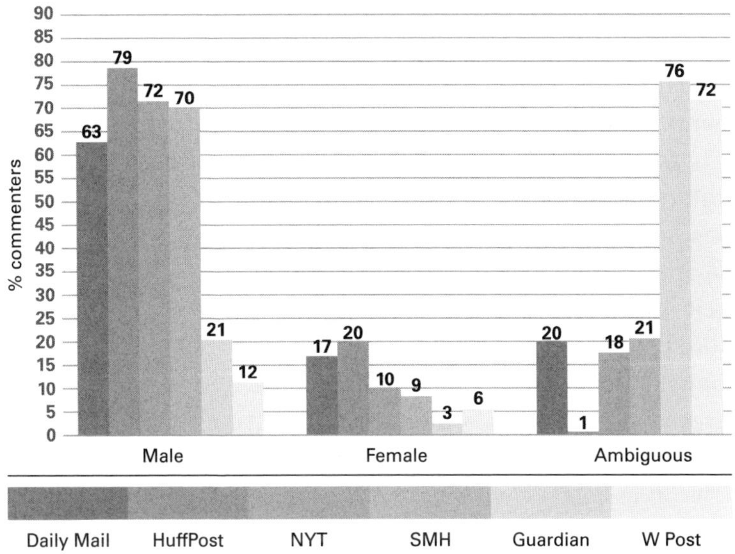

Source: Martin, F (2015) Getting my two cents worth in: access, interaction, participation and social inclusion in online news commenting, #ISOJ, 5 (1)

The findings echo work done by Emma Pierson[30] for online statistical analysis site 23andMe.com. Pierson reviewed one million comments left on the *New York Post* in 2014 and concluded that men left 75 per cent of the comments, despite only accounting for 56 per cent of the readership. Dr Martin speculated that the discrepancy could be explained by the higher rate of unpaid work that women do. 'They simply don't have as much time to spend commenting on news websites', she said. Interestingly, she suggests that online commentary is a microcosm of the everyday difficulties women face in getting their voices heard. 'It appears our experience of online conversations is reflecting our gendered experiences of the world at large', she said. 'Just like in face-to-face public conversations, like meetings or forums, women are being put off by male voices being adversarial, dismissive and sometimes abusive.'

Why does this matter to leaders? Because leaders need to communicate not just in synch with their teams, but with their demographics *and* the channels they use. If women communicate more frequently and in a less opinionated style, then men need to bear this in mind. Hearing from a leader once a year on a channel that your team doesn't use is ineffective communication.

In the United States, gender, income and education have little impact on whether or not someone uses social media. These factors, however, have a big impact on which social networks people opt to use. Facebook, Pinterest and Instagram have a strong skew towards female users. Women in the United States are more likely to use Facebook than men by about 11 percentage points, Pinterest by 29 percentage points, and Instagram by 7 percentage points, according to Pew Research Center. Twitter and LinkedIn continue to attract a mostly male audience.

In an in-depth report from BI Intelligence,[31] data from many sources were used to understand how social media demographics and preferences are still shifting. For instance, Pinterest has a large reach among women. Among US female internet users, 42 per cent reported being on Pinterest, compared to only 13 per cent of men. Instagram has become the most important and most-used social network for US teens. Thirty-two per cent of US teenagers cited it as their most important social network. LinkedIn enjoys high adoption among highly educated and high-income users. Linked In is used by 44 per cent of Americans with income of $75,000 or more. Messaging apps like Snapchat, for example, also have become more broadly popular, but skew towards the young.[32]

Overconfidence as a cause of our problems

There is something else here impinging on the gender debate. Is being overconfident part of the answer or part of the problem? Overconfident people frequently move too fast. It's worth considering here what the opposite to doubt is. In light of too much analysis, it can be reassuring to find leaders that cut through the detail confidently.

One of the factors we've witnessed in so many corporate collapses and political miscalculations, such as Brexit, has been overconfidence while at the same time being under-skilled or incompetent.

In an interview in 2014 for *The Harvard Business Review*, Professor Tomas Chamorro-Premuzic, from University College London, talked about how confidence can mask incompetence. He said that 'confident people tend to be more charismatic, extroverted, and socially skilled, which in most cultures are highly desirable features... in virtually every culture, confidence is equated with competence'. So, we automatically assume that confident people are also more skilled or talented. He points out that: 'Competent people are generally confident, but confident people are not generally competent.' He says they're good at hiding incompetence and insecurities 'mostly because they are self-deceived themselves, so they generally think that they are much better than they actually are'.

He points out that the problem with overconfidence begins with recruitment and the interview process. Assessing candidate competence is a key objective of the process, but confidence is so often the method or a path that most people take to assess it. That route leads to inaccurate evaluations of people's competence. So, for example, most people who interview really well and are assumed to be great are, in reality, just charming the interviewers during that session. He says that people need to understand that the main goal of interviewing is to discover how competent others are. Interviewers shouldn't really care about the confidence of candidates. What matters is their competence.

Premuzic adds that the problem with confidence is that it's often viewed more favourably when it's high, regardless of whether it's accurate, despite the well-documented effects that overconfidence has. This distorts the perception of danger. So, for instance, drinking, gambling, smoking, driving accidents, reckless risk-taking are often caused by having too much confidence.

Humility is perhaps a better indicator of competence because it operates as a reality check and it helps maintain awareness of weaknesses. This drives self-improvement as well. All of the evidence from psychological research suggests that humility makes leaders more likeable, even in the United States. The conclusion is that when people perceive leadership as more competent than it thinks it is, the more it likes it.

Could it be the faster we move, the more superficial our perception becomes?

The overload extracts a high price in terms of ability to concentrate on anything other than the first impression.

How many of us have ever really scrutinized the credentials of our dentist? Or do we just take a white coat, a dentist's chair and a simple recommendation as being proof enough? Imagine a world where doctors, teachers, engineers or pilots are selected on the basis of their confidence, as opposed to their actual ability? Some would say this already happens in the world of politics and we can see the results. Until we stop appointing leaders on the basis of their confidence rather than competence, we will keep having problems.

Premuzic believes this will also keep making it hard for women, who are usually both humbler and more competent than men in these domains. As far as the gender debate is concerned, he says the problem is not that women lack confidence. It's rather that men have too much of it.

He also says the criteria we use to evaluate the men are different from those we use to evaluate women. He points out that when men come across as confident or even arrogant, we assume that they are good at what they do and we call them charismatic. When women behave in the same way, 'we tend to see them as psychopathic or a threat to society or an organization.

So, society punishes manifestations of confidence in women, and rewards them in men – which only reinforces this natural difference between the genders.'

In another of his articles in *The Harvard Business Review*, entitled 'Why Do So Many Incompetent Men Become Leaders?', he pointed out three popular explanations for the clear under-representation of women in management, namely: (1) they are not capable; (2) they are not interested; (3) they are both interested and capable but unable to break the glass ceiling. Conservatives and chauvinists endorse the first; liberals and feminists the third; and those somewhere in the middle are usually drawn to the second. It's possible they all missed the big picture.

He says the main reason for the uneven management sex ratio is our inability to discern between confidence and competence. If that's the case, then it conveniently absolves men alone as the cause. That is because we (people in general) commonly misinterpret displays of confidence as a sign of competence. We are fooled into believing that men are better leaders than women. In other words, when it comes to leadership, the only advantage that men have over women is confidence, often masked as charisma or charm, which is commonly mistaken for leadership potential, and that these occur more frequently in men.

This makes sense, but what if the leadership environment has become so attuned to analytical thinking that it's become the exclusive preserve of male thinking? Could it be that men think that because they're more short-term, data-driven, they're much smarter than women? Arrogance and overconfidence are inversely related to leadership talent. Much of leadership ability is about building and maintaining high-performing teams where followers set aside their own personal agendas to work for the common interest of the group.

It's difficult to get away from some unfortunate and uncomfortable truths revealed by Premuzic's research that male thinking leads to more analytic, more short-term, tactical, arrogant, manipulative and risk-prone thinking.

An inherent bias against diversity?

The paradoxical implication is that the same psychological characteristics that enable male leaders to rise to the top of the corporate or political ladder are responsible for their downfall. In other words, what it takes to get the job done is not just different from, but also the reverse of, what it takes to do the job well. As a result, too many incompetent people are promoted to management jobs, and promoted over more competent people.

We'll hear more about this in the next chapter, but the conclusion here is scathing about leadership in general. Too many leaders, whether in politics or business, fail. The majority of nations, companies, societies and organizations can be better managed. Good leadership has always been the exception, not the norm.

So, in summary, part of the problem is that the people we elect to solve the problems look as if they know what they are doing, but so often don't. They are too busy, too analytical or too short-term. When did you last hear anyone of significant rank say they're not busy? We've developed a dangerous assumption that important people should be busy and vice versa.

It almost seems that we equate leadership with the very psychological features that make average male thinking more inept than the average female's. Premuzic asks whether we've created a system that 'rewards men for their incompetence while punishing women for their competence'?

A war on men?

Given the level of inequality and complexity, the anger can be understood. There are no simple solutions to this. Some might say men have little incentive to even recognize the problem, let alone do anything about it. This too would be a gross generalization.

Shifting prejudice to a different gender may enhance rather than eradicate it.

Organizations are just not efficient unless they are balanced. There are too many instances of board directives that have failed in the implementation phase because of 'bureaucratic resistance'. Furthermore, if groups are going to be agile enough to alter their own geometry to fit changed circumstances, then change needs to be implemented swiftly. Inefficient organizations are less likely to be able to do this.

In any case, there's little point making men the target when some of them recognize the problem and are actively engaged in tackling it. Demonizing all men is not only unjust, it's also counter-productive. There needs to be conversation. There's no doubt, though, that some men are prejudiced, involved in sexual harassment and consider all displays of feminism to be a threat.

Training for confidence

While men are sometimes overconfident and under-skilled, women have a tendency to be the opposite. How can this be countered? First, we need to recognize that confidence, low self-esteem and self-critique are linked.[33]

If this effect is valid, then it's logical to suggest that to tackle gender prejudice, one should address several variables. This would include height, loudness, assertiveness, agreeability and so on. It may well be the case that these issues are reflexive. The perceptions create an overly self-critical cycle of assessment.

Techniques for boosting confidence

When coaching professionals, it's important to point out that no one technique is suitable for everyone. Sometimes *psychological displacement* works. This is where delegates are asked to visualize and then act the role of the confident leader. This covers voice, deportment, eye-contact and so on. This is then videoed and played back against control footage to assess difference.

Another technique is known as *circle thinking*. This is where the delegate is asked to focus relentlessly on a circle around the speaker within which no critique is allowed. The white circle represents another form of psychological displacement.

In both cases, we're trying to deflect the self-critique. In the former case, critiquing an 'act' somehow makes the learning process less personal. In the latter, the displacement occupies the self-critique.

This, at least, then reduces the presence of the negative. The presence of the positive is then one of training and discipline to adopt the persona or technique until it becomes second nature.

Techniques for breaking the circle

There are many techniques that can be applied to improve meeting performance. For instance, *balanced chairing* is where meeting members take turns in speaking and time is allocated by the chair equally. It doesn't just go to the loudest or most opinionated voice. Silent brainstorms are another way of balancing gender bias in meetings. This is where a problem is set and delegates spend time in silence assessing the problem and drawing their solution. They then take it in turns to discuss.

Conclusions

Despite the opinionated debate in this area, there is room for neuroscience, clinical psychology, solid scientific research and leadership experience. As the internet disintermediates everything, we must expect it to do so for gender as well. This atomization could have profound negative effects if all we do is identify difference. The inequality is there and it's real, but it's also complex. There is no doubt that prejudice exists and sometimes it is hiding in plain view. It can be extant in basic issues such as height and loudness of voice. We know from some of the neuroscience that testosterone disrupts group working and increases egocentricity. This appears to be a key physiological difference. This also indicates that the anecdotal evidence that men are more opinionated has some scientific validation. Some will still label male leadership as hierarchical and patriarchal. Others will recognize that it is not gender alone which is desirable in achieving a balance.

We need an inclusive approach that encompasses new types of thinking. The gender debate is only part of the issue. Discrimination *is* a matter of justice, but it's a matter of efficiency, too. Modern leaders can do a great deal to redress balanced thinking through training, provided they see it as a debate about avoiding leadership failure rather than a politically correct agenda. Forcing behavioural change through coercion is only likely to create superficial inclusions that lead to long-term resentment. If we demonize and patronize, we demean our mission here. Enlightenment and education to create efficiency are better ways of improving leadership. Joining up the genders and improving our capacity to move between feminine and masculine thinking strengthen our ability to contend with the future.

Endnotes

1 McGilchrist, I (2012) *The Master and His Emissary: The divided brain and the making of the western world*, Yale University Press, New Haven, CT

2 https://www.managementtoday.co.uk/revealed-ftse-100-companies-women-dont-succeed/women-in-business/article/1431348

3 https://ourworldindata.org/what-drives-the-gender-pay-gap

4 Krouse, S (2018) BlackRock: Companies should have at least two female directors, *The Wall Street Journal*, 2 February

5 http://journals.sagepub.com/doi/full/10.1177/14747049120100314

6 Gladwell, M (2007) *Blink: The power of thinking without thinking*, Back Bay Books, Boston, MA

7 https://www.sciencedirect.com/science/article/pii/0092656673900305

8 https://www.nbcnews.com/health/mens-health/deep-masculine-voice-not-you-ladies-n569631

9 https://www.youtube.com/watch?v=aMcjxSThD54

10 https://books.google.co.uk/books?id=G28LTQltyVAC&pg=PA17#v=onepage&q&f=false

11 http://www.lancaster.ac.uk/sociology/about-us/people/sylvia-walby

12 https://www.nytimes.com/2015/01/11/opinion/sunday/speaking-while-female.html

13 https://www.telegraph.co.uk/science/2018/03/10/wearing-much-makeup-harms-womans-leadership-chances

14 https://www.psychologytoday.com/blog/the-brain-and-emotional-intelligence/201104/are-women-more-emotionally-intelligent-men

15 https://www.psychologytoday.com/basics/emotional-intelligence

16 https://www.psychologytoday.com/basics/intelligence

17 https://www.spinalcord.com/insular-cortex

18 https://www.livescience.com/41619-male-female-brains-wired-differently.html

19 http://www.sciencemag.org/news/2016/02/women-are-more-empathetic-men-yawning-study-suggests

20 https://www.livescience.com/18231-testosterone-collaborative-decisions-women.html

21 https://www.theguardian.com/education/2003/apr/17/research.highereducation

22 https://www.hrzone.com/perform/people/women-excel-at-emotional-intelligence-or-do-they

23 https://papers.ssrn.com/sol3/papers.cfm?abstract_id=2308246

24 https://www.theatlantic.com/business/archive/2013/08/why-women-prefer-working-together-and-why-men-prefer-working-alone/278888

25 https://www.forbes.com/sites/harmoncullinan/2017/10/31/collaborating-while-female/#788eafa2c02e

26 https://www.edn.com/electronics-news/4351406/Top-10-uses-of-the-Internet

27 http://www.huffingtonpost.co.uk/entry/internet-porn-stats_n_3187682

28 https://www.psychologytoday.com/blog/all-about-sex/201611/dueling-statistics-how-much-the-internet-is-porn

29 http://www.telegraph.co.uk/men/thinking-man/11544484/Why-are-most-online-commenters-male.html

30 https://qz.com/259149/how-men-dominate-online-commenting

31 http://uk.businessinsider.com/2015-social-network-demographic-trends-2015-2

32 http://uk.businessinsider.com/2015-social-network-demographic-trends-2015-2

33 https://www.livescience.com/14151-neuroscience-esteem-criticism-compassion.html

CHAPTER EIGHT

Understanding a New World

Inspiration and Inversion

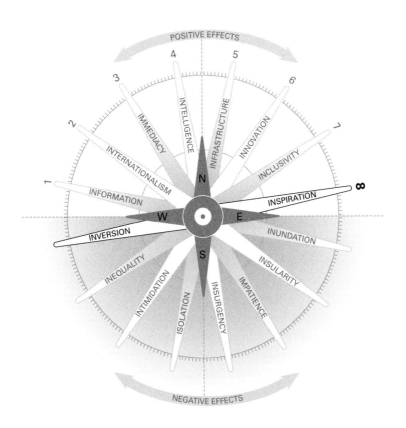

By this stage of the book, it's clear that every one of the Kythera spokes, be it economic, behavioural, geopolitical or gender, describes a significantly changed (and changing) environment. The promise of the future is exciting and inspirational. If we get it right, we're looking at an infinitely more sustainable, fairer, productive, efficient world, with greater access to education and information. A world that is healthier, better led, more optimistic and inclusive. The opportunity is compelling. The problem is that we need to tackle an inverted world to get there. For instance, despite all the indications that we're living longer, with less violence,[1] with greater wealth and better opportunities, cynicism and the opposite perception abound. Much depends on our viewpoint. If we choose to see positivity, then the Kythera tilts in our favour. If not, we remain fixated on the visible differences and iniquities that remain. Both views can be true simultaneously. It is up to us to choose.

In an atomized, rational, tangible, left-brained process world, the thing that could grant us greater happiness is what the left-brain process abhors. This is the intuitive sense of belonging, honesty, compassion, faith and trust. These are the values that unite us and that we believe in. While we can't measure them or prove them, none of us wants to live in a world without them. The left-brain process discerns the difference. The right-brain process feels the unity. The overload and the interruptions all push us more towards the left-brain process, and this has profound implications. It makes us much more attuned to spot differences and logical non-sequiturs. The balance of our lives has shifted away from unity.

Let's take the behavioural climate, for instance. There once was wide agreement about shared values. It involved patience, self-sacrifice, deferred gratification, commitment, modesty, frugality, public service, group identities, improving the condition of the poor, family integrity, marriage, children and church attendance. In the past 25 years, we've seen a massive erosion of this consensus. This is what we will investigate in this chapter.

The world is not only stranger than today's leaders believe. It is stranger than many leaders are capable of believing. This is not just a case of recognizing intergenerational value change, but of identifying enduring values around which leadership can be founded. In modern times, these notions are more complex. The challenge is to find the unifying factors in the modern team.

> **QUICK TIP** This is not just a case of leadership becoming aware that one or two vectors have changed. It needs to recognize that *the majority of the vectors* have changed.

Why does this matter for leaders? To unify, leaders must identify and develop common values to understand what is now perceived as 'good' or moral behaviour.

This is what we will cover:

- Through the looking glass
- Can we trust our leaders?
- A truly mixed reality
- Should we still work hard and save?
- Should we be patient and work together to get results?
- Is education worth it?
- Looking for a new domestic politics
- Now our friends spy on us, too
- Inversion and alignment
- Is success always rewarded?
- Is it only the bad guys who use torture?
- Does morality matter?
- Whatever happened to the future?
- A new multipolar world with walls
- Globalism is over
- Conclusions

Through the looking glass

Just about every one of our values, truths and standards has undergone a complete transformation. Our grandparents might well marvel at the technological developments of today, but they would be horrified in other ways. We have alleviated poverty, disease, famine and large-scale warfare. We have substantially reduced heart disease and cancer yet created an information culture that would bewilder them. We have also, however, presided over more debt, greater income inequality, environmental damage and more consumption than ever before. Despite more material wealth, we have rising inequality, isolation, ignorance, impatience, anger and unhappiness.

Our forebears struggled against so many of the challenges we have successfully met. For instance, food is now in such abundance that obesity, rather than starvation, is the most significant threat to Western health. To them, the rich were fat and the poor were thin. Today, that is inverted.

Our sources of truth have changed, too. We have a multiplicity of sources, but don't trust any of them. Where previously there were one or two sources that sounded like the BBC or Walter Cronkite, today that, too, has become inverted. We live with fake news and alternative facts. The news is not news. It is profitable entertainment.

In court, you still have a choice of whether to use an oath or an affirmation. The oath is: 'I swear that the evidence that I shall give, shall be the truth, the whole truth and nothing but the truth, so help me God.' The affirmation is: 'I solemnly affirm that the evidence that I shall give, shall be the truth, the whole truth and nothing but the truth.' The law has no truck with what is or isn't a fact. There are no semantics in the oath. Yet despite the oath, of all the exclusions in the Ten Commandments, Thou Shalt Not Lie is a glaring one.

The availability of facts seems somehow inversely correlated with their use. Either that, or people are choosing to wilfully ignore them because facts are a bit dull. The abundance of facts seems to devalue them. The notion that you can prove anything with statistics has taken hold. Now, what you believe is more important than what you can prove. This prompts questions. Let's look at some of the questions that are being increasingly asked.

Can we trust our leaders?

The chronic and profound failures of leadership that we've witnessed have allowed the perception of the leader to be diminished. As we explored in the Introduction, in the past 25 years the world's leadership culture has shifted on its axis. It used to be an overwhelmingly male, heterosexual, patient, predictable, real, planned, white, long-term, Western-orientated, technology-leveraged, deflationary, structured, left-brained rational, broadcast, top-down, militarily symmetric world.

Now, leadership is operating in an inverted, unreal, impatient, inflationary, selfish, spiritual, irrational, gender-fluid, polysexual, asymmetric, strategically multipolar, everywhere-facing infrastructure, bottom-up, information-soaked, multi-racial, androgynous, fluid, rapidly moving, militarily asymmetric world.

Trust in all forms of leadership is at an all-time low. It is almost impossible to find any avenue of human endeavour where there is not an example of failure. At least, if our leaders are that bad, we can get rid of them. This, though, addresses the symptom, not the cause. If a sports team keeps failing, you don't give up on the sport, you get better players. If the players are all poor, then you look at their training. That's why we need leadership that analyses and parenthesizes and thinks long- as well as short-term. We need leaders that can join the dots. We need our leaders to *be* better, not just *do* better.

A truly mixed reality

Our love of the future probably reached its zenith in the 1960s, during the era of space flight. It all seemed possible. Food in a pill. Tiny computers. Weightlessness. A man on the moon was considered the height of technological achievement. Now, it's not only the rationale of that mission that's debated. In a post-truth world, there are many questioning whether it actually happened at all.[2]

As we explored in Chapter 1, the mixed reality environment created by technology is not just about augmented reality or 3D goggles. It applies to our daily lives. Our technology diminishes our presence in the here and now. How many times have you seen families or couples out for a meal where they are all staring at their iPhones? The internet disintermediates human relationships such as parenting, and governments are belatedly beginning to intervene.[3]

Once again, we confuse communication with conversation. We live in an age where the volume of communication has evolved beyond what many believe is efficient. When communication supplants conversation, we start to get insidious and persistent issues. If you can't converse, you can't resolve emotional problems, manage people or negotiate. The more experience of conversation we have, the better at it we get. We learn this at an early stage with our families. Is it so difficult to understand the recent rise of emotional problems among young people? Could the iPhone have anything to do with it? As we saw in Chapter 3, productivity increases began to fall the same year the iPhone was launched. These events may be connected.

Having embraced science and new technology for so long, there may be signs that the public are beginning to reject it. We mentioned the Center for Humane Technology in Chapter 6. The public have also become increasingly concerned about the science in genetically modified crops, cloning, fracking, gene editing and stem cell research.

Should we still work hard and save?

As we saw in Chapter 2 about economic behaviour, what used to be 'good', savings and thrift, has been punished by low or negative interest rates. The new moral good is the exact opposite – debt and consumption. This has led everyone from college students to presidents to question the very rules of the game. Society is now at war with the economic system itself because some are working on the old morality, some on the new. This is not a hypothetical or philosophical point. Leaders are widely perceived as mountebanks, deliberating conning the public out of their money.[4]

Add a little inflation to the mix and the net result is to punish those who live within their means and who put money aside. Today's message is clear. If you want to save to ensure a life independent of welfare, the state will punish you for it, but if you're feckless and become dependent, the state will give you money. By any standards, savers are citizens whom government and central bankers want to encourage. This, often at the same time as politicians were pursuing so-called austerity measures and punishing welfare dependency by cutting pay-outs. Why should anyone be surprised if this sort of economic moral inversion on this scale triggers insurgency? It would be irrational if you weren't concerned about this.

If you can't converse, you can't resolve emotional problems, manage people or negotiate.

Should we be patient and work together to get results?

As we established in Chapter 3, impatience is also encouraged and catered for, even expected. Now those with patience are dismissed as laggards or lacking in aspiration. 'Everything comes to he who waits' has become 'Devil take the hindmost'. We can see this in rising staff-churn levels through the caring professions such as nursing, teaching, childcare and so on.[5]

We have also looked at how the average length of job tenure is declining. Former head of the US Federal Reserve Alan Greenspan said in his book *The Age of Turbulence*[6] that when he started work in the 1930s, he could not perceive of a time when the average job tenure in the United States would become so short. He grew up in an age where employees were loyal to an employer and vice versa. The recent pensions scandals have also undermined confidence in employers. Even if employers could repay loyalty, it's more likely they won't even get the chance. New forces are at work that require new thinking.

Is education worth it?

Perhaps a better question might be: 'Does education pay?' Many students have begun to question whether the cost of a university degree is worth it. The truth is more nuanced. Some degrees will pay back.[7] Others won't. McKinsey found that 42 per cent of recent graduates are in jobs that require less than a four-year college education. Worse still, 41 per cent of graduates from the nation's top colleges could not find jobs in their chosen field.[8] US college graduates aged 25 to 32, working full-time, earn about $17,500 more annually than their peers who have only a high school diploma, according to the Pew Research Center.[9] Is all this worth the average cost of $50,000 or £35,000? Thirty-seven per cent of graduates now regret going to college in the first place.[10] Some students have even sued their universities[11] because of the economic consequences of not getting the grades they wanted. Even Goldman Sachs,[12] one of the biggest graduate employers, has questioned the point of a degree. Today, vocational training is paying more than a university degree. There are shortages of welders and mechanics. They are in demand. We should start treating vocational training with less disdain.

Writer Seth Godin has pointed out in his book *Linchpin*[13] that education is currently configured for jobs that currently exist. By the time the education is complete, those jobs may have already gone away or changed.

Looking for a new domestic politics

Whether it's inequality between the genders, which we heard about in Chapter 7, or the share of income in general, income inequality has become an issue in recent years. It is estimated now that the United States' top 1 per cent of earners average $1.5 million a year and their share of average national income has risen to 22 per cent.[14] This has led to calls for greater intervention to curb the excesses of the market. Writing in *The New York Times*,[15] David Priestland said: 'The West saw a Marxist revival in the 1960s, but student radicals were ultimately more committed to individual autonomy, democracy in everyday life and cosmopolitanism than to Leninist discipline, class struggle and state power.' The rise of Momentum in the Labour Party has driven a more socialist agenda. Whether this leads on to Marxism and communism is debatable. It's more likely to lead to greater state intervention or an urge to destroy the political system itself, which is probably what we're seeing not just in the United States.

For the first time since the Second World War, Germany has a far-right party, the *Alternative fur Deutschland* (AfD), in the Reichstag. Jewish groups are already protesting that the AfD has a place on the board of the foundation for the national Holocaust memorial in Berlin.[16] Marine Le Pen's National Front party took over 30 per cent of the 2015 vote versus Emmanuel Macron.[17] In Austria, the Freedom Party[18] is now in government as well. Whether this is a return to old polarities, it's difficult to say. It looks as if voters want to experiment with something entirely new. Large numbers of US voters were genuinely split between the political extremes of Sanders or Trump, according to research.[19] What's clear is that the political system isn't working for people as it once did, so they're willing to try alternatives. In essence, though, the problems they face are more technical and cultural than political, because we can't uninvent the Boeing 747, the internet and the iPhone.

Now our friends spy on us, too

The great inversions are not just related to domestic politics. Geopolitically, the rules have been stood on their head as well. The whole purpose of diplomacy is to patiently manage relations within a context, within a system of known rules and protocols and agreements. Today, we're witnessing a breakdown of trust in the system itself. Even policymakers whose entire job it is to support and defend the system are not sure it's viable any more.

The whole purpose of diplomacy is to patiently manage relations within a context, within a system of known rules, protocols and agreements.

We see more and more blatant challenges to the system, from grass roots movements to methods being used by states that used to be considered out of bounds. For example, the film *Us versus Them*, where students at Middlebury College stop a lecturer by shouting him down and threatening violence. The young may just prevent what they see as 'the elites' from operating. Impatience erodes trust, and we're seeing this replicated at the geopolitical level, too. For example, all the major industrialized nations are now openly wiretapping each other and trying to steal secrets. What governments do, companies follow. This means that companies are often trying to steal intellectual property, covertly assisted by government agencies. This could be because everyone wants information in real-time.

As an aside, wiretapping is a thing of the past. Technology has removed the need. Now we find that any smart item that is connected to the Internet of Things is constantly broadcasting our every word and movement anyway. We were impatient to control the technology. Now the technology is controlling us.

Inversion and alignment

If it's true that the world has become inverted, then it's also true that nations that used to be opposites can become similar. Let's take East and West. We used to think that the political models of the United States and China were different, if not opposites. Maybe they are more similar now. A key leadership task is to look for these new alignments. Table 8.1 provides some other examples.

Despite many commonalities, Table 8.1 still puts the United States and China on different and potentially conflicting paths. The question is, can both the United States and China's leaders fulfil the promises they have made to their citizens simultaneously? History suggests the United States can. China does not yet have this history. It, too, is suffering from the inversion. It used to be a low-wage economy, but that is no longer true. It used to save, but that proved ill-advised. It once restricted families to one child only. That was also reversed.

Is success always rewarded?

There's a growing sense that leaders at the top of organizations are increasingly rewarded for failure[20] or over-rewarded when others are suffering. This is evidenced by the size of the pay-outs they receive when being fired. For example, in the downturn at SeaWorld after the film *Blackfish*, 311 workers lost their jobs due to cost-cutting measures. CEO Jim Atchison resigned and

TABLE 8.1 Examples of commonality between the United States and China

United States	China	Commonality
Spend on infrastructure	Spend on infrastructure (One Belt, One Road)	Both seek to create GDP and garner votes
Challenge the liberal international order by tearing it down – refusing to fund the UN, for example	Challenge the liberal international order by replacing it down with One Belt, One Road. Create new institutions such as the Asian Infrastructure Investment Bank (AIIB)	Both talk of leading the system from a position of strength
Promote the interests of domestic workers	Promote the interests of domestic workers	Obvious vote winner
Use US materials	Use Chinese materials	Obvious vote winner
Build a wall to keep troublemakers out	Build a (digital) wall to keep troublemakers out	Putting their voters first
Spend on defence	Spend on defence	Both want an economic stimulus that can be pursued without approbation
Lead from strength	Lead from strength	Obvious vote winner
Control media content by restricting or bypassing traditional media	Censor media content by restricting or bypassing international traditional media or limiting access to the internet	Message control
Reward only ideological allies	Reward only ideological allies	It's about power
Loss of civic trust (witness allegations of abuse of power such as illegal wiretapping)	Loss of civic trust (witness capital flight and rising dissent)	It's about loss of trust in the entire system, not just the policies or personalities

received a £1.7 million payoff. According to *The Washington Post*,[21] his severance pay was equal to twice his base annual salary, plus his targeted 2013 bonus. The company also confirmed that Atchison would continue as the company's vice chairman and as a consultant on international expansion.

Is it only the bad guys who use torture?

Ever since the Abu Ghraib[22] prison scandal in 2006, it's been clear that abuse and torture have been used by the Western militaries and their intelligence agencies. Despite the US Senate banning their use in 2015,[23] accusations have persisted. In January 2018, a human rights campaigner, Nils Melzer, the UN special rapporteur on torture, accused the US government of using it in Guantanamo Bay.[24] The International Committee of the Red Cross (ICRC) has consistently pointed out that the use of torture is not only illegal and immoral but also ineffective.[25] And yet, the public seem to support torture now more than ever.

> *To win hearts and minds, leadership needs to be seen to be just. Without this there can be no trust.*

Does morality matter?

Morals, like any other set of laws, are not just good for their own sake or nice to have. They can only be upheld with the consent of the majority they seek to govern. When atomized, individuality becomes the majority behaviour and thus consensus becomes harder. This partially explains the breakdown of confidence in the system of rules that has been in place over decades. Why does this matter to leaders? Simply because leaders need to motivate their teams. If they do not understand the 'rules' or even their expectations, they cannot be successful.

To understand this notion further, we can look at the works of German philosopher Immanuel Kant. His theory, developed from Enlightenment Rationalism, was that the only intrinsically good thing was intent. This would, for instance, include the duty not to lie. Today's equivalent is a demand for authenticity. Failure to align actions with image is fatal in the new world of transparency. At the heart of this notion is justice. To win hearts and minds, leadership needs to be seen to be just. Without this there can be no trust. It would seem an odd assertion that leadership needs to do good. All leaders would automatically assume that people knew that was the case. For all the reasons that we've outlined in this chapter, that assumption has been challenged. There are no shortcuts; leaders must earn trust all over again. If people don't trust their leaders, they will not trust the future either.

Whatever happened to the future?

In the 1950s and 1960s, the future looked exciting. There was ever-improving wealth, health, standards of living and social freedom. Many people became home owners and went to university for the first time. Now, in the West, children do not expect to be wealthier or freer than their parents. It is impossible for them to own property. What's more, successive governments have eroded pensions and long-term wealth. This fear of the future is reflected in popular culture. Many films set in the future are entirely dystopian. The various themes include scenarios where computers subvert human relationships (already true to some extent), they take over and force humans to their will (already true to some extent), they impoverish and destroy careers (already true for those at the bottom) and they take over as emotional partners (on its way[26]).

The opposite is true of nostalgic culture. Productions such *Dunkirk* (2017), *Darkest Hour* (2017) and *The Crown* (2016) reflect a utopian past. This was an age of grace, of unity, of pride, identity and belonging. Events such as vintage air shows and the Goodwood Revival have raised nostalgia to sell-out levels. At the latter, people dress up and browse replica stores from the 1950s and 1960s, they watch vintage car racing and Second World War aircraft fly past. We've also seen a revival of 'festivals'.[27]

When we fear the future and glamorize the past, it's a signal that we are trying to hang onto an image of reality that may already be out of date.

A new multipolar world with walls

Another element that previous generations would not recognize is strategic. Then, you knew who the enemy was. They wore a different uniform, spoke a different language, lived in a different country. Now the 'enemy' is all around. They look like us, talk like us and live among us. The world no longer has two poles, it has many. As discussed in Chapter 5, the world used to be coming closer together, with walls coming down. Now it is divided and getting more so as walls go up. What we expected to be a linear relationship with ever-greater integration and cooperation has been reversed.

Globalism is over

One view is that the public rebellion against globalism means that leaders can no longer simply assert that more trade is in everyone's best interests. The Berlin Wall came down in 1989, which was a long time ago. Leaders may still be thinking we live in a world where inflation fell or disappeared because so many new workers were willing to work for even less back then. In that world, we no longer had to spend as much money on defence because the bipolar world disappeared, leaving us with a 'peace dividend' that could divert capital away from nuclear weapons

TABLE 8.2 The LAB table of inversions

'Good' used to be...	'Good' is now...
'We the People'	'Me the People'
Communities/groups	Groups and groupthink are bad. Individuality is more admired
Thoughtful, clear, measured responses	Twitter at speed, jargon and emojis
Long-term careers	Work gigs, internships, 'experiences', fast turnover, side hustles
Simple truth	Spin, messaging, weaponized information. Fake news
Study	Hacks and shortcuts
Education	Work experience
Debate	No-platforming, anger, dictums
Restraint	Bingeing and excess
Saving	Spending
Buying	Sharing
Dress up	Dress down
Etiquette and protocol	Huddles and hang-outs
Marriage and commitment	Promiscuity and Tinder
Free speech	Censored speech: political correctness
Moral probity and decorum	Recklessness
Formal education and scholarly sources	Street. Wikipedia. YouTube. Teach yourself. Formal education declining in value
Patience	Immediacy
Anonymity, modesty	Celebrity, attention
Taxation	Tax avoidance
Conversation	Communications
Trust	Cynicism
Quality	Disposable
Innovation	Iteration

and towards more productive investments. In the old post-Berlin Wall world, it was obvious to everyone that the flow of capital and human capital across borders would benefit everyone.

In today's world, these are no longer universally shared assumptions. Yet people everywhere want to do more business, sell and buy more goods and services. Everyone is trying to figure out how to go where the growth is. Workers are no longer willing to work for ever-lower wages. Trade is becoming more global than ever as the Chinese build production facilities in the United States and Europe and the Americans invest globally. New walls are going up even as the internet tears the old ones down. The internet is paradoxical. It can close the mind while expanding trade. It can speak of the end of globalization, even as it dramatically redefines it.

When we step back and survey the landscape, it becomes ever clearer that there are many inversions of our values. We can summarize these 'inversions' as shown in Table 8.2.

Conclusions

At a superficial level, the world appears unchanged to many leaders. It has, though, undergone arguably some of the most profound technical, commercial, cultural, social, behavioural, moral and economic changes ever. This has not just changed a few things, it has changed virtually everything. It has not been a small change. It has completely upended and inverted principles, values and rules which have been unchanged for centuries. This has left our leaders speaking in tongues. It has left them disorientated and situationally bereft. The change has been so far-reaching that it has left them parroting defunct lines such as 'all the jobs are going to China', which just confirms they are out of touch. It has also made them espouse ideas that are fundamentally hypocritical or nonsensical. For instance, we want you to be independent, but we will punish you for being so.

The greatest irony of all is that the great age of inversion has had its most enduring effect on leaders themselves. Rather than being seers of events, they have become victims of events.

Endnotes

1 Pinker, S (2015) *The Better Angels of Our Nature*, Penguin, New York

2 http://www.newsweek.com/fake-apollo-moon-landing-photo-claims-show-proof-mission-was-hoax-716221

3 https://www.politicshome.com/news/uk/political-parties/conservative-party/news/93500/culture-secretary-proposes-social-media-time

4 http://www.independent.co.uk/news/world/politics/criminals-and-corrupt-politicians-steal-1trn-a-year-from-the-worlds-poorest-countries-9707104.html

5 https://www.nursingtimes.net/news/workforce/call-for-urgent-action-to-halt-rising-social-care-staff-turnover/7021589.article

6 Greenspan, A (2008) *The Age of Turbulence: Adventures in a new world*, Penguin, New York

7 https://www.economist.com/news/united-states/21600131-too-many-degrees-are-waste-money-return-higher-education-would-be-much-better

8 https://www.economist.com/news/united-states/21600131-too-many-degrees-are-waste-money-return-higher-education-would-be-much-better

9 https://www.economist.com/news/united-states/21600131-too-many-degrees-are-waste-money-return-higher-education-would-be-much-better

10 https://www.forbes.com/sites/nickmorrison/2016/08/09/if-theres-one-thing-millennials-regret-its-going-to-college/#3faa788a3536

11 http://www.telegraph.co.uk/news/2017/11/21/oxford-graduate-sues-university-1million-did-not-get-first-class

12 http://money.cnn.com/2015/12/09/news/economy/college-not-worth-it-goldman/index.html

13 Godin, G (2011) *Linchpin: Are you indispensable?* Portfolio, New York

14 https://inequality.org/facts/income-inequality

15 https://www.nytimes.com/2017/02/24/opinion/sunday/whats-left-of-communism.html

16 http://foreignpolicy.com/2018/01/15/germany-doesnt-have-a-playbook-for-a-nazi-sympathizing-parliament

17 https://www.nytimes.com/interactive/2017/05/07/world/europe/france-election-results-maps.html

18 https://www.theguardian.com/world/2017/dec/18/the-far-right-freedom-party-is-joining-austria-government-how-do-you-feel

19 https://www.cnn.com/2016/02/08/politics/new-hampshire-primary-independent-voters/index.html

20 https://www.forbes.com/sites/nathanielparishflannery/2011/10/04/paying-for-failure-the-costs-of-firing-americas-top-ceos/#5ee17a444bc7

21 https://www.washingtonpost.com/news/morning-mix/wp/2017/08/30/investors-say-seaworld-lied-about-business-downturn-after-orca-outcry-now-feds-are-investigating/?utm_term=.9fc9801df27d

22 http://www.latimes.com/nation/la-na-abu-ghraib-lawsuit-20150317-story.html

23 https://www.cnn.com/2015/06/16/politics/senate-torture-bill-cia/index.html

24 http://www.newsweek.com/torture-used-us-military-guantanamo-bay-despite-being-banned-un-says-747373

25 https://www.justsecurity.org/35816/icrc-survey-torture-glass-two-thirds-full/

26 https://venturebeat.com/2017/11/14/meet-the-robots-caring-for-japans-aging-population

27 https://www.telegraph.co.uk/travel/destinations/europe/united-kingdom/articles/Britains-best-vintage-festivals-Goodwood-Revival-and-more

CHAPTER NINE

The Global Leaders' Narrative

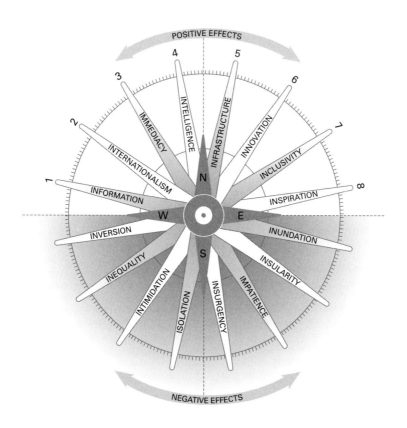

The Kythera is a tool to help leaders navigate complexity. It shows the duality of the world we live in arranged across eight 'spokes'.

The spokes used in the Kythera – information and its overload, economics and its effects, behavioural changes, geopolitics, technology, gender and the generally inverted nature of things – provide the key challenges to leadership.

The first task of all leaders is to recognize that uncertainty is the primary characteristic of the 21st century. Leadership needs to prepare for this by keeping a wide parenthesis of thinking. This is for three main reasons: it allows them flexibility; it allows the pursuit of unity; and, finally, because 'opinionated certainty' and the rigidity it engenders are a hallmark of mediocrity.

The second task is to recognize the deep paradoxes illustrated by the Kythera. The pull towards polarity is a centrifugal force constantly offsetting leadership efforts. Some days, good leadership will feel it has achieved nothing, but it has at least offset the trend. Good leadership improves on the status quo; however, sometimes, it may just maintain it.

Leadership must see the limitations of the left-brain process. We cannot analyse our way out of every problem. We need our synthetic skills to contextualize and parenthesize. We cannot consider binary outcomes any more. Only a new global leadership approach based on situation fluency will help. Leadership needs to:

- **Learn the lessons of the past**
  - Weak leadership lacks imagination, not analysis
  - Overconfidence is a problem
  - The dangers of 'big is better' thinking
  - Lessons from a general
  - Guard against short-termism, it can destroy everything
  - Control the information flows, before they control you
- **Study the present**
  - Study geopolitics and the physical world
  - Guide capitalism, don't guillotine it

- Consult conspicuously, communications are expected
- Know your team, see the gaps
- You cannot defend yourself with the facts alone
- **Prepare for the future**
  - Culture eats strategy, so lead with values
  - Lead by values
  - The 'J' word still matters more than anything
  - Failures are more visible and often due to fear
  - Use trust to kill fear, otherwise it will kill innovation
- **Commit to the leadership spirit**
  - Leadership is more than management/Leadership can always be better
  - Serve the widest community
  - Cultivate inclusivity, it breeds unity
  - No alternative but to embrace the future
  - Faith matters
  - Situational fluency
  - St Augustine of Hippo

Learn the lessons of the past

Weak imagination undermines leadership more than weak analysis

In addition to providing a guide to the future, we have catalogued leadership failures from the past in this book. They share a common denominator. Leadership fails when there is a lack of imagination. Problems happen when there is an inability or unwillingness to envisage alternative possibilities. Being as wrong as everyone else is no longer an acceptable excuse for a leader. When the financial crisis happened in 2008, the conditions for division were established. The resulting revelations about conduct destroyed lives, brands and confidence for a whole generation. It wasn't weak analysis alone that caused this. It was also a collective failure of imagination.

Overconfidence is a problem

As we established in Chapter 7, correlating competence with confidence is a prime cause of leadership failure. Our leaders often come from specialist backgrounds, with drill-down skills, steeped in heavily analysed data. The Western Reductive technique does not teach imagination. Our leaders are therefore weakened rather than strengthened by the specialisms through which they pass on their way to the top. This leads us to clues, but not necessarily conclusions, about the reasons for collective failures of leadership. The tendency to overconfidence based on quantitative data alone is a habitual problem in some, but not all, leaders. Others, of course, have too wide a perspective and too little grasp of detail. Balance is the key.

Aspirant leaders are to be encouraged because these ladder-climbers inspire and show the way. We need more of them, because what they represent is as important as what they do. They also tend to learn more on the way. There are not nearly enough leaders who have climbed all the rungs and have a catholic competence in many areas.

The dangers of 'big is better' thinking

Quantitative thinking alone ultimately leads to a fixation on numbers, for example sizes and volumes. Seldom does an organization get bigger as well as better. Making an organization better, however, does allow it to grow. Size is too often taken as an indicator of success, when, in reality, it could be seen as an indicator of poor service, lack of control and zero imagination.

Lessons from a general

There is now a growing pressure for better leadership. This is coming as much from movements such as #timesup and #metoo as it is from voters, shareholders and other stakeholders. There is a better chance that leadership will wake up to the catalogue of collective failures when they are as concentrated as they now are. We can draw lessons from past efforts to challenge leadership.

Kurt von Hammerstein-Equord was a German general famous for being an ardent opponent of Hitler and the Nazi regime. He said that he divided his leaders into four groups: 'There are clever, diligent, stupid, and lazy officers. Usually two characteristics are combined. Some are clever and diligent – their place is the General Staff. The next lot are stupid and lazy – they make up 90 per cent of every army and are suited to routine duties. Anyone who is both clever and lazy is qualified for the highest leadership duties.' He said this was because that type of leader 'possesses the intellectual clarity and the composure necessary for difficult decisions'. He finished with a warning to beware of 'anyone who is stupid and diligent', because this sort of leader 'will always cause only mischief'.[1] This approach is echoed by Warren Buffet, who chooses people based on three criteria: 'You're looking for three things, intelligence, energy, and integrity. And if they don't have the last one, don't even bother with the first two.' Today's leaders need to have the integrity to know that blindness to reality is no longer an acceptable leadership trait.[2]

> *The fixation on speed has become an obsession. It has undermined patience, planning and personal relationships.*

Guard against short-termism, it can destroy everything

The fixation on speed in all things has become an obsession. It has undermined patience, planning and personal relationships. It has also created the illusion of speed, rather than the actuality of it. Good leaders must spend time planning, thinking and patiently preparing. The imagination to foresee danger comes from quiet contemplation and conversation.

Control the information flows, before they control you

Churchill[3] said: 'First we shape our buildings. Thereafter they shape us.' The same principle applies to how we use our tools. The internet is perhaps the greatest tool mankind has ever created. It is now beginning to shape our behaviour, in many areas making us more selfish, greedy and impatient than ever. Leaders must be those who unite people in a common cause. To that end, they need to bring people together through qualitative as much as quantitative thinking. In a great digital age, big data and technology will dominate our lives like never before. We will become much more efficient. We'll be able to measure just about everything much more accurately. This left-brain process of compare, contrast, analyse will be everywhere. This, however, is a process that notices difference and comparison. It's a tool for separating one thing from another. The more we subject people to this process, the more we divide them from a common humanity. The technology storm is not helping us get a more holistic approach. The more specialized we are, the more atomized we become. We do not hear and we do not see beyond our narrow view. It's difficult to see the horizon when you're buried in data.

Study the present

Study geopolitics and the physical world

As we covered in Chapter 5, the physical world is changing. Infrastructure development is changing the very fabric of our world. This is worthy of constant study. The world is not just made up of changes occurring in cyberspace. It is kinetic as well. There are airports, canals, roads, railways and major ports being built all over the world, often in places where there has been little development. It is exciting and full of opportunities.

Guide capitalism, don't guillotine it

Many today are so angry and disappointed that they are prepared to throw out capitalism as a whole. However, perhaps the problem is not the system but the way it's been managed. It's important, though, to remember that capitalism and democracy are voluntary. Drivers stop at red lights because they agree to. When elites appear to be above the rules, it creates discontent. The system can easily fail if no-one believes they should follow the rules because those at the top won't. The anger that many clearly feel isn't just anti-capital rage. It arises from the realization that its benefits are not fairly shared and its rules are defied by those at the top. The rules that govern capitalism are based on the assumption that they serve the interests of everyone and not just those of a few.

The private sector needs to evolve its approach. Its boardrooms need to lead the way. We need to see Generally Accepted Accounting Principles (GAAP) mandate qualitative statements about the longer term, the community and welfare.

Consult conspicuously, communications are expected

It will no longer be enough to research views. Leaders will need to be seen to be consulting and they will need to actually consult. Listening (and appearing to listen) will really matter. All business is at its best when it realizes a social as well as commercial narrative. For capitalism to succeed, it needs permission, and that will only be granted when its benefits are shared. In a full employment economy, 'permission' leadership prevails. Leadership must be sensitive to how it looks and communicates. The fundamental communications equation is:

$$\text{Frequency} \times \text{duration} = \text{retention}$$

The longer and more often something is repeated, the more it is recalled. This is important when leadership has to cut through the inundation to be heard (see Chapter 1).

Know your team, see the gaps

Knowledge of the world, the subject matter and the news may help, but the leader without knowledge of *their* team is helpless. It is important to know the '1-in-10,000 skill' each person has. The more the leader knows the team, the more potential can be seen in all of them.

You cannot defend yourself with the facts alone

In most leadership groups, there's an abundance of people who defend shareholder and stakeholder value with the truth. There's someone that deals with finance and numbers (the Chief Financial Officer). There's someone dealing with the statute and precedence of the law (the General Counsel). These professionals deal with the facts. Working to the letter of the law, you may be able to prove you're not breaking any tax regulations, but that will not change the perspective if you're not operating within the spirit of the law. Offshore tax havens may be perfectly legal, but they do not look it. You may not actually be a drug cheat in sport. If, however, you're using a substance that is not normal yet not banned, but nevertheless has a beneficial effect, the perception may be of cheating. The optics matter because, as we have shown, opinions have become more important than facts.

Prepare for the future

Culture eats strategy, so lead with values

The modern leader must be aware that they can't 'do' values. They can only 'be' them. It's easier to be impatient with what someone does. This is why leaders need to have a 'to be list', as well as a 'to do list'. It is one of the hardest tasks faced by young leaders. They want to 'do' too much. This leads to inconsistency, stress and short-termism. They should not feel ashamed of doing less, first, because it allows for empowering delegation and teamwork, and second, because it means they can concentrate on what they, and they alone, can be. This is a variation of the 'management by exception' rule. Leaders need to be human beings, not human doings.

Lead by values

What are the values of the team and the organization? What should they be? The values will always tell you what the team is capable of (for good or bad). Is it dedicated, committed, honest, diligent, imaginative and energetic? What values does the team admire? Has anyone ever asked? Values matter because they can unify teams at a wider level irrespective of their individual differences.

The 'J' word still matters more than anything

However we define 'judgement', it is still the most highly sought-after leadership skill. It remains both a science and an art combined. Situational fluency is important to it and so is timing. It involves judging the mood and sensing the environment. It's almost impossible to teach or even to define, but it remains the quality that separates the leadership candidates.

On 29 July 2006, at a meeting of The World Future Society, Dr Bruce Lloyd, Professor of Strategic Management at London South Bank University, presented a paper called *Wisdom & Leadership: Linking the Past, Present & Future*.[4] It is one of the best papers ever written on leadership thinking. He pointed out that:

> Wisdom is the way we incorporate our values into our decision-making process and it is our values that determine the way we define that critical word 'quality'. The word 'quality' can also be seen as another way of distinguishing process from change.

Not all change is progress and it is our values that ultimately determine our priorities. It is these priorities that then become the criteria we use to distinguish between change and progress.

Failures are more visible and often due to fear

The numerous and visible examples of failure should damn all leadership. There are great leaders out there and the LAB met many of them. Of course, it's in the nature of things that no-one notices good leadership, because disasters simply don't happen. For this reason, good leadership needs to celebrate the routine, the reliable and the consistent as well as the extraordinarily good.

Change accelerates as it moves towards leaders. When people are fearful, knowledge or planning coming from leadership can be empowering. Weak leadership, though, is often exposed because it fails to evolve new ways of thinking. This causes it to be paralysed in the face of change and the resulting fear is contagious. Much of navigating a changing world has to do with managing fear – fear of the unknown, fear of failure and fear of embarrassment. This does not always manifest as fear. Most often it appears as intransigence or inertia. Neuroscientists believe that fear makes people behave less intelligently and makes them less likely to move from their comfort zone. This reaction is known as the 'amygdala hijack'. This was a term coined by Daniel Goleman in his book *Emotional Intelligence: Why it can matter more than IQ*.[5] Where there is a fight, flight or freeze situation, the rational brain is effectively overruled. When the amygdala perceives a threat, it can cause an irrational and destructive reaction. This is characterized by three signs: strong emotional reaction, sudden onset and post-episode realization, if the reaction was inappropriate.

> *Much of navigating a changing world has to do with managing fear – fear of the unknown, fear of failure and fear of embarrassment.*

Use trust to kill fear, otherwise it will kill innovation

Innovation can be a delicate flower. It can be killed at the point of conception. Ideas will only be advanced if it is felt that they won't be judged harshly. It is difficult for some to come forward with ideas. Leaders must create a level playing field to allow as many ideas as possible to come forward. Trust must be built over time. This means repeatedly applying 'Safe Enough to Try' rules so that risk can be encouraged without killing creativity.

Understand how skills and values have changed

If there's one great strategic take-away from this book, it's that leadership skills have changed fundamentally over the past 25 years. Table 9.1 is a distillation of key leadership skill changes that LAB delegates felt were important themes.

In the future, changes clearly show the scale of the transformation. Leadership which was once rigid, fixed, firm, traditional, legacy, slow and judgemental, in the future will demonstrate flexibility, agility, imagination, values and open-mindedness.

Commit to the leadership spirit

Leadership is not just management

H G Wells said: 'Human history becomes more and more a race between education and catastrophe.'[6] The more change there is, the more important our learning and leadership become. That's the only way we have any chance of being able to equate change with progress. So, if we want to have a better future, the first and most important thing that we must do is improve the quality and effectiveness of the learning.

The world has excellent economics, business, management and military schools. Leaders also learn on the job, as do politicians.

TABLE 9.1 Changes in key leadership skills

20th-century leaders	21st-century leaders
Operated to the letter of the law	Operate to the spirit of the law
Won at any price	Win fairly
Managed in the interests of a few	Manage in the interests of the many
Applied more logic	Apply more imagination
Maximized strategy	Maximize culture
Created an androcentric culture	Create androgynous cultures
Planned for either/or	Plan for both/many scenarios
Supported 'the system'	Smash or adapt 'the system'
Made binary decisions	Allow quantum 'super-position'
Used black and white	Use the full palette/rainbow
Used labels and certainty	Plan for uncertainty and ambiguity
Predicted	Prepare
Researched science and facts	Use opinions and pose questions
Concentrated more on doing and objectives	Concentrate more on being/values
Understood, expected, knew	Expect it to be stranger than they think
Expected it to be predictable	Expect unimaginably good or bad
Used business books	Use theology and philosophy books
Valued dynamism and immediacy	Value patience and listening
Prioritized youth education	Prioritize lifetime education
Stopped/detected/prevented failure	Embrace/understand/allow failure
Wanted big and bigger	Want better
Owned assets	Share assets
Operated rigid resistance	Be fully flexible

TABLE 9.1 (*Continued*)

20th-century leaders	21st-century leaders
Coped with events	Have a process to anticipate change
Wielded authority	Empathize
Saw work as work	See work as play
Managed adult behaviour	Manage infantile behaviour
Used judgement and intolerance	Use love and empathy
Exercised control	Ask for permission
Centralized	Distribute
Learnt the lessons of history	Embrace the future
Were 'waterboarded' busy leaders (see Chapter 1)	Are open and available
Were serious	Are playful
Saw the board as compliance	See the board as a justice forum
Saw the board as a congregation/club	See the board as a conscience

Strangely, there is still one job that requires no formal training, that of political leader. That should change. The central problem for the institutions as a point of provenance for leaders is that they were shaped by Western Reductive methods. They overwhelmingly teach how to analyse. Leaders end up in generalist roles, but they get there by being a specialist. Orchestra conductors are generally not expert soloists, but they know how to inspire performance.

Leadership is not perfect, but it can be better

We must be realistic about leaders. It's OK for them to take risks. In fact, all progress depends on it. We can be too quick to punish them as individuals for innocent failure. The unstable toddler gets up partly by instinct but partly through encouragement and love. What is repeated failure, though, except the parent of success? As Kipling says in *Tommy*:[7] 'An' if sometimes our conduck isn't all your fancy paints, Why, single men in barricks don't grow into plaster saints.' Leaders of organizations will never be the acme of behaviour. They should not be held up as paragons of all virtue. It's the leadership team that matters. They can be trained to work together. We can teach them to be more patient and think longer-term. We can reward stability, consistency and teamwork.

Serve the widest community

For many, the future is frightening. Without change, we face the dark side of the Kythera. With increasing levels of income inequality, we could head backwards to division, violence, war or a new type of feudalism where beneficiaries ring themselves first in gold and then in steel. The place for leaders is not behind bars in any context. The community is the provenance of the leaders, whether they recognize it or not. Leadership is not just something leaders do at work. Their leadership of social causes will also highlight their moral leadership. They must emanate light, faith, positivity and hope and be rooted in the people they serve. There will be much at stake and very high risks. The higher the rank, the higher the risk and the higher the trust we require from them.

If leaders want to demonstrate their contribution to the community, then it needs to be done on a genuine and sustainable basis.[8] Responsible Business Conduct (RBC) is replacing Corporate Social Responsibility (CSR). The problem with the old CSR model is that it is often associated with voluntary philanthropy and as an add-on external to core business operations. There is a discretionary element of this which is unlikely to be enduring. No amount of discretionary donation to any charity would change the perception of any of the wrongdoers listed in this book.

Cultivate inclusive thinking, it breeds unity

All teams need a diversity of thinking, not just a diversity of people. We must guard against simplistic solutions that swap one prejudice for another. If we condemn leaders for being 'pale, male and stale', then we swap one skin, gender and age prejudice for another. Masculine skills do not reside solely in men, nor feminine skills in women. We need to be thinking less about defining people by skin colour and gender and more about the values and skills diversity brings. If we want more female thinking in leadership, then we need to make our cause more than just about a single gender. It's about balance and shared goals such as modernity, aspiration and representation. All genders can focus on these objectives. It is not about men or their shortcomings. If one gender wins at the expense of another, then everyone loses irrespective of who's victorious.

Inclusivity is all about democracy. Free markets and democracy walk hand in hand. Democracy, at its heart, is about sharing – sharing resources, sharing wisdom and sharing hope for the future. Democracy harnesses resources to make more resources. It does this because it harnesses the individual. The more democracies, the more the resources we can share. At the heart of this is a belief that the more we give, the more we receive. This is the essence of leadership.

We cannot be blind to the differences, but let us also direct attention to our common interests and to the means by which those differences can be resolved – through leadership. We cannot end our differences, nor should we. Democracy and diversity should be synonymous. Of course, leadership is not a democracy, but it's better when it is. Democracy is not just an idea that we stick to occasionally when it suits us. Brexit, for instance, might not be to everyone's taste, but we believe in democracy enough to put those with whom we disagree in power. This is democracy in action. Democracy is something that is shown. Not something that is told.

Some lament how divided the democracies are. They point out that never before have there been such sharp divisions in opinions. They say this as if it were something to be apologized for. As if, somehow, division were a weakness. There are many parts of the world, however, where there is no division or difference. This is in no way a demonstration of strength. Quite the contrary in fact. If an idea isn't strong enough to withstand the opinions of others, then it is no sort of idea at all. Ideas are made stronger by disagreement, not vice versa.

So, let this be an abiding thought. When democracy is challenged by those who disagree with it, let that challenge make it stronger. Whether it be Brexit or domestic politics or our new approach to humanitarian aid. Because through it, we demonstrate our commitment to share democracy and our willingness to share the future. When we feed democracy, we feed inclusivity, we feed the future and we feed leadership.

No alternative but to embrace the future

There is no way home to some Ambrosian land where things were better. To hear some, you'd think the whole 21st century was the wrong exit from the motorway, where they just want to find a way back to the 1950s. When faced with the opportunities, it is a chance for each of us to return to our youth and embrace it with simple mindfulness and joy. We can gorge on nostalgia by the kilo, but we're better served by a child's appetite for the future. We cannot uninvent the modern world – unplug the internet, ground all the 747s, deny individualism. A transcendent quality of Marxism was its reliance on group identities. There can be no return to that. Jung recognized that the only way to reach individual potential was through what he called Individuation.[9] The internet offers this potential if our leaders are able to meet the challenge.

Faith matters

How did we end up here? We still rely upon the same leadership institutions (often run by alumni) educating on and issuing the same leadership credentials. We have met a crisis in Western Reductionist thinking with yet more of the same. It's almost as if we thought we could cure obesity with yet more food. These institutions do not teach divinity. They teach leadership as they know it. They are not pastoral, nor ecumenical, much to their detriment. Leadership is as much about faith as it is about finance. The institutions know the importance of this. Leaders should be aware of the spiritual, emotional and physical welfare of their teams. They and their teams would be the better for it.

The importance of situational fluency

The world has changed so far, so fast, as to completely disorientate the unwary. There have been repeated failures, creating perhaps the worst crisis in leadership since the world wars. We catalogued these in Chapter 8. There are many reasons for this. Structures became big and unwieldy, encouraging a lack of personal responsibility, even a dereliction of diligence. There was an over-reliance on Western Reductionism and left-brain thinking, overconfidence (and under-skilled people at the top) and an abundance of resource brought by technology in information. Above everything, leaders lacked a situational fluency to be able to see how events might move in several dimensions.

St Augustine of Hippo

Where will we find this new leadership spirit? This book is about the spirit of leadership, so it's fitting to close it with the words of St Augustine of Hippo: 'Don't you believe that there is in man a deep so profound as to be hidden even to him in whom it is?'[10] Humanity's future is a darkened path. Leadership's job is to be

249

the beacon that illuminates our way. Only a new approach can ensure that light shines brighter than ever before. Leaders will have to open their hearts, as well as their minds, to find it. When they do, all humanity will follow.

Endnotes

1 Enzensberger, H M (2009) *The Silences of Hammerstein* (trans M Chalmers), Seagull Books, New York, p 87

2 https://www.fs.blog/2013/05/warren-buffett-the-three-things-i-look-for-in-a-person

3 https://www.standard.co.uk/comment/comment/rohan-silva-take-a-lesson-from-churchill-in-rebuilding-new-housing-estates-a3153271.html

4 http://www.wisdompage.com/blloyd02.html

5 Goleman, D (1996) *Emotional Intelligence: Why it can matter more than IQ*, Bloomsbury, London

6 Wells, H G (2017) *The Outline of History*, CreateSpace Independent Publishing Platform, https://www.createspace.com/diy

7 http://www.kiplingsociety.co.uk/poems_tommy.htm

8 https://medium.com/@OECD/2016-corporate-social-responsibility-is-dead-what-s-next-60d22fee8bad

9 http://jungiancenter.org/components-of-individuation-1-what-is-individuation

10 http://awakesociety.com/philosophy-quotes

Index

Note: page numbers in *italic* indicate figures or tables.

TOM GOODWIN

DIGITAL DARWINISM

SURVIVAL OF
THE FITTEST
IN THE AGE OF
BUSINESS
DISRUPTION

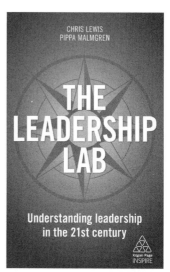

CHRIS LEWIS
PIPPA MALMGREN

THE LEADERSHIP LAB

Understanding leadership
in the 21st century

HUMANITY WORKS

MERGING TECHNOLOGIES
AND PEOPLE FOR
THE WORKFORCE
OF THE FUTURE

ALEXANDRA LEVIT

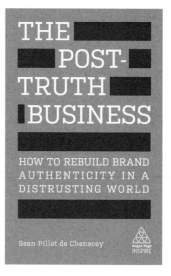

THE POST-TRUTH BUSINESS

HOW TO REBUILD BRAND
AUTHENTICITY IN A
DISTRUSTING WORLD

Sean Pillot de Chenecey